GIDEON'S TRUMPET

GIDEON'S TRUMPET

BY

Anthony Lewis

 VINTAGE BOOKS

A DIVISION OF RANDOM HOUSE

New York

VINTAGE EDITION, *February, 1966*

VINTAGE BOOKS

are published by Alfred A. Knopf, Inc.
and Random House, Inc.

Much of the material in this book first appeared in The New Yorker, *in a somewhat different form.*

Manufactured in the United States of America

To my parents

But the Spirit of the Lord came upon Gideon, and he blew a trumpet. . . .

JUDGES VI, 34.

GIDEON'S TRUMPET

1

In the morning mail of January 8, 1962, the Supreme Court of the United States received a large envelope from Clarence Earl Gideon, prisoner No. 003826, Florida State Prison, P.O. Box 221, Raiford, Florida. Like all correspondence addressed to the Court generally rather than to any particular justice or Court employee, it went to a room at the top of the great marble steps so familiar to Washington tourists. There a secretary opened the envelope. As the return address had indicated, it was another petition by a prisoner without funds asking the Supreme Court to get him out of jail—another, in the secretary's eyes, because pleas from prisoners were so familiar a part of her work. She walked into the next room and put the envelope on the desk of an assistant clerk of the Supreme Court, Michael Rodak, Jr.

Mr. Rodak, among other duties, concerns himself with what the Supreme Court calls its Miscellaneous Docket. This is made up mostly of cases brought by persons who are too poor to have their court papers printed or to pay the usual fee of one hundred dollars for docketing a case in the Supreme Court—bringing it there. A federal statute permits persons to proceed in any federal court *in forma pauperis*, in the manner of a pauper, without following the usual forms or paying the regular costs. The only requirement in the statute is that the litigant "make affidavit that he is unable to pay such costs or give security therefor."

The Supreme Court's own rules show special concern for *in forma pauperis* cases. Rule 53 allows an impoverished person to file just one copy of a petition, instead of the forty ordinarily required, and states that the Court will make "due allowance" for technical errors so long as there is substantial compliance. In practice, the men in the Clerk's Office—a half dozen career employees, who effectively handle the Court's relations with the outside world—stretch even the rule of substantial compliance. Rule 53 also waives the general requirement that documents submitted to the Supreme Court be printed. It says that *in forma pauperis* applications should be typewritten "whenever possible," but in fact handwritten papers are accepted.

Gideon's were written in pencil. They were done in carefully formed printing, like a schoolboy's, on lined sheets evidently provided by the Florida prison. Printed at the top of each sheet, under the heading Correspondence Regulations, was a set of rules ("Only 2 letters each week . . . written on one side only . . . letters must be written in English . . .") and the warning: MAIL WILL NOT BE DELIVERED WHICH DOES NOT CONFORM TO THESE RULES. Gideon's punctuation and spelling were full of surprises, but there was also a good deal of practiced, if archaic, legal jargon, such as "Comes now the petitioner. . . ." It seemed likely to Rodak that Gideon had a copy of the Supreme Court Rules.

The first of the documents in the envelope was a two-page affair headed "Motion for leave to proceed in forma pauperis" and including the notarized affidavit that the statute requires. A quick check indicated to Rodak that this prisoner had substantially complied with the rules. He appeared, for example, to have met the requirement that criminal cases be brought to the Supreme Court within ninety days of the lower court decision. Gideon had applied to the Florida Supreme Court for a writ of habeas corpus—an order freeing him on the ground that he was illegally imprisoned. He enclosed a copy of that application and of a brief order of the Florida court denying it. The Florida ruling against him, which he wanted the Supreme Court of the United States to review, was dated October 30, 1961, less than ninety days before.

There was very little in what he had sent to the Court to portray Clarence Earl Gideon the man. His age, his color, his criminal record if any—not even these basic facts appeared, much less any details for a more complete portrait. Because the case came from the South, one's assumption might have been that he was a Negro. He was not.

Gideon was a fifty-one-year-old white man who had been in and out of prisons much of his life. He had served time for four previous felonies, and he bore the physical marks of a destitute life: a wrinkled, prematurely aged face, a voice and hands that trembled, a frail body, white hair. He had never been a professional criminal or a man of violence; he just could not seem to settle down to work, and so he had made his way by gambling and occasional thefts. Those who had known him, even the men who had arrested him and those who were now his jailers, considered Gideon a perfectly harmless human being, rather likeable, but one tossed aside by life. Anyone meeting him for the first time would be likely to regard him as the most wretched of men.

And yet a flame still burned in Clarence Earl Gideon. He had not given up caring about life or freedom; he had not lost his sense of injustice. Right now he had a passionate—some thought almost irrational—feeling of having been wronged by the State of Florida, and he had the determination to try to do something about it. Although the Clerk's Office could not be expected to remember him, this was in fact his second petition to the Supreme Court. The first had been returned for failure to include a pauper's affidavit, and the Clerk's Office had enclosed a copy of the rules and a sample affidavit to help him do better next time. Gideon persevered.

Assistant Clerk Rodak, knowing and caring nothing for any of this, stamped Gideon's papers and gave them a number—890 Miscellaneous, meaning that the case was the 890th entered on the Miscellaneous Docket in the October Term, 1961. (Supreme Court terms, which usually run from October into June, are formally designated by the month in which they begin.) On a green file card a secretary typed the number and the title of the case: Clarence Earl Gideon, petitioner, versus H. G. Cochran, Jr., Director, Division of Corrections, State of Florida, respondent. Then the papers were put into a large red folder and tied with a string. (Red is the color for Miscellaneous cases; regular prepaid cases, on what is called the Appellate Docket, go into blue folders.) The Gideon folder was dispatched to the file room, one floor down, by an electric dumbwaiter.

Sometimes Rodak or his colleague in the Clerk's Office, Edward Schade, looking over the confused and often unintelligible prisoners' petitions that come before them, will spot one with an impressive legal claim. Their view has nothing whatever to do with the action the Supreme Court may take, since only the nine justices act for the Court and they do not discuss the merits of cases with the employees in the Clerk's Office. Still, just in the office, it enlivens things to say once in a while: "Here's one that I'll bet will be granted."

No one said that about *Gideon v. Cochran,* No. 890 Miscellaneous, October Term, 1961. In the Clerk's Office it had no ring of history to it. It was just one of nine *in forma pauperis* cases that arrived in the mail on January 8, 1962. Four others were, like Gideon's, criminal cases from the state courts—from Iowa, Washington, New York and Illinois. Two were appeals from federal convictions. One was a civil case, a claim by an unhappy and unaffluent author that someone had plagiarized his copyrighted play. The last was so confused that the Clerk's Office was unable to put it in any category at all.

Gideon's main submission was a five-page document entitled "Petition for a Writ of Certiorari Directed to the Supreme Court State of Florida." A writ of certiorari is a formal device to bring a case up to the Supreme Court from a lower court. In plain terms Gideon was asking the Supreme Court to hear his case.

What was his case? Gideon said he was serving a five-year term for "the crime of breaking and entering with the intent to commit a misdemeanor, to wit, petty larceny." He had been convicted of breaking into the Bay Harbor Poolroom in Panama City, Florida. Gideon said his conviction violated the due-process clause of the Fourteenth Amendment to the Constitution, which provides that "No state shall . . . deprive any person of life, liberty, or property, without due process of law." In what way had Gideon's trial or conviction assertedly lacked "due process of law"? For two of the petition's five pages it was impossible to tell. Then came this pregnant statement:

"When at the time of the petitioners trial he ask the lower court for the aid of counsel, the court refused this aid. Petitioner told the court that this Court made decision to the effect that all citizens tried for a felony crime should have aid of counsel. The lower court ignored this plea."

Five more times in the succeeding pages of his penciled petition Gideon spoke of the right to counsel. To try a poor man for a felony without giving him a lawyer, he said, was to deprive him of due process of law. There was only one trouble with the argument, and it was a problem Gideon did not mention. Just twenty years before, in the case of *Betts v. Brady*, the Supreme Court had rejected the contention that the due-process clause of the Fourteenth Amendment provided a flat guarantee of counsel in state criminal trials.

Betts v. Brady was a decision that surprised many persons when made and that had been a subject of dispute ever since. For a majority of six to three, Justice Owen J. Roberts said the Fourteenth Amendment provided no universal assurance of a lawyer's help in a state criminal trial. A lawyer was constitutionally required only if to be tried without one amounted to "a denial of fundamental fairness." The crucial passage in the opinion read:

"Asserted denial [of due process of law] is to be tested by an appraisal of the totality of facts in a given case. That which may, in one setting, constitute a denial of fundamental fairness, shocking to the universal sense of justice, may, in other circumstances, and in the light of other considerations, fall short of such denial. In the application of such a concept there is always the danger of falling into the habit of formulating the guarantee into a set of hard and fast rules the application of which in a given case may be to ignore the qualifying factors. . . ."

Later cases had refined the rule of *Betts v. Brady*. To prove that he was denied "fundamental fairness" because he had no counsel, the poor man had to show that he was the victim of what the Court called "special circumstances." Those might be his own illiteracy, ignorance, youth, or mental illness, the complexity of the charge against him or the conduct of the prosecutor or judge at the trial.

But Gideon did not claim any "special circumstances." His petition made not the slightest attempt to come within the sophisticated rule of *Betts v. Brady*. Indeed, there was nothing to indicate he had ever heard of the case or its principle. From the day he was tried Gideon had had one idea: That under the Constitution of the United States he, a poor man, was flatly entitled to have a lawyer provided to help in his defense.

Gideon was tried on August 4, 1961, in the Circuit Court of the Fourteenth Judicial Circuit of Florida, in and for Bay County, before Judge Robert L. McCrary, Jr. The trial transcript begins as follows:

The Court: The next case on the docket is the case of the State of Florida, Plaintiff, versus Clarence Earl Gideon, Defendant. What says the State, are you ready to go to trial in this case?

Mr. Harris (William E. Harris, Assistant State Attorney): The State is ready, your Honor.

The Court: What says the Defendant? Are you ready to go to trial?

The Defendant: I am not ready, your Honor.

The Court: Did you plead not guilty to this charge by reason of insanity?

The Defendant: No sir.

The Court: Why aren't you ready?

The Defendant: I have no counsel.

The Court: Why do you not have counsel? Did you not know that your case was set for trial today?

The Defendant: Yes sir, I knew that it was set for trial today.

The Court: Why, then, did you not secure counsel and be prepared to go to trial?

The Defendant answered the Court's question, but spoke in such low tones that it was not audible.

The Court: Come closer up, Mr. Gideon, I can't understand you, I don't know what you said, and the Reporter didn't understand you either.

At this point the Defendant arose from his chair where he was seated at the Counsel Table and walked up and stood directly in front of the Bench, facing his Honor, Judge McCrary.

The Court: Now tell us what you said again, so we can under-
· stand you, please.

The Defendant: Your Honor, I said: I request this Court to appoint counsel to represent me in this trial.

The Court: Mr. Gideon, I am sorry, but I cannot appoint counsel to represent you in this case. Under the laws of the State of
Florida, the only time the court can appoint counsel to represent a Defendant is when that person is charged with a capital
offense. I am sorry, but I will have to deny your request to appoint counsel to defend you in this case.

The Defendant: The United States Supreme Court says I am entitled to be represented by counsel.

The Court: Let the record show that the defendant has asked
the court to appoint counsel to represent him in this trial
and the court denied the request and informed the defendant
that the only time the court could appoint counsel to represent a defendant was in cases where the defendant was charged
with a capital offense. The defendant stated to the court that
the United States Supreme Court said he was entitled to it.

Gideon was wrong, of course. The United States Supreme Court had not said he was entitled to counsel; in
Betts v. Brady and succeeding cases it had said quite the opposite. But that did not necessarily make Gideon's petition
futile, for the Supreme Court never speaks with absolute
finality when it interprets the Constitution. From time to
time—with due solemnity, and after much searching of conscience—the Court has overruled its own decisions. Although he did not know it, Clarence Earl Gideon was calling for one of those great occasions in legal history. He was
asking the Supreme Court to change its mind.

2

The Supreme Court of the United States is different from all other courts, past and present. It decides fundamental social and political questions that would never be put to judges in other countries—the boundaries between church and state, the relations between the white and Negro races, the powers of the national legislature and executive. One could easily forget that it is a court at all. Its public image seems sometimes to be less that of a court than of an extraordinarily powerful demigod sitting on a remote throne and letting loose constitutional thunderbolts whenever it sees a wrong crying for correction.

But the Supreme Court is not a demigod, nor even a roving inspector general with a conscience. It is a court, and for all its power it must operate in significant respects as courts have always operated. It cannot, like a legislature or governor or President, initiate measures to cure the ills it perceives. It is, as Justice Robert H. Jackson said, "a substantially passive instrument, to be moved only by the initiative of litigants." In short, the Court must sit and wait for issues to be presented to it in lawsuits.

And not every issue, nor every lawsuit, can come to the Supreme Court of the United States. Its jurisdiction—the reach of the Court's power—is limited by the Constitution itself, by statutes and by the Court's own precedents. The first question in the case of *Gideon v. Cochran*, as in any case brought to the Supreme Court, was whether it was within the Court's jurisdiction.

The Constitution defines and limits "the judicial Power of the United States" in Article III. Taking only the most important clauses, the article provides that the jurisdiction of federal courts may extend (subject in most instances to the wish of Congress) to "all Cases, in Law and Equity, arising under this Constitution, the Laws of the United States, and Treaties made . . . ; to all Cases of Admiralty and maritime Jurisdiction; . . . to Controversies between two or more States; . . . [and] between Citizens of different States. . . ." Volumes have been written on the meaning of those brief phrases, and great cases litigated over them. When, for instance, can a legal dispute be said to "arise under" the Constitution? But such intricate questions may be put aside for some generalities.

An Englishman or a Frenchman lives under one national law; not so the American. Our Constitution created a system of dual governments, state and federal, each with its own laws. To take a simple example: A New Yorker must fill out an income-tax return whose intricacies are written by Congressmen in Washington; he also has to fill out an annoyingly different New York State return drafted by legislators in Albany. This is the kind of civil statute that concerns most citizens. On the criminal side, take the case of a car thief. He breaks the law of New York when he drives away a Chrysler parked on East Eighty-seventh Street, Manhattan, with the key conveniently left in the ignition; if he drives across the George Washington Bridge to New Jersey, he also violates a federal law against interstate transportation of stolen vehicles.

Most of the law under which an American lives is the law of his state. His marriage, his property, his will are all governed by state law. If he gets into a lawsuit about a business contract or a real estate deal or an automobile accident, the result will ordinarily be determined by state law—law laid down in state and local statutes and by the decisions of state courts.

Cases of this kind, which are brought by the hundreds of thousands in the United States every year, are almost all tried by state courts. They can get into the federal courts only in one circumstance—if they are suits between citizens of different states. This diversity-of-citizenship jurisdiction of the federal courts, as it is called, was included in Article III of the Constitution to protect out-of-state litigants from prejudice in the local courts: The Vermonter involved in a lawsuit in South Carolina could hope for more impartial justice from a federal judge. But in diversity-of-citizenship cases federal courts must apply state statutes and state decisions; if state courts have held that a certain kind of oral contract is binding, the federal judge hearing a diversity case on that issue must follow the same rule, no matter how wrong-headed it may seem to him. The Supreme Court so held in 1938, brusquely overruling a hundred-year-old precedent that allowed federal courts to ignore state-court decisions in diversity cases.

On the pervasive issues of state law the Supreme Court has absolutely no power to revise the decisions of state courts. When the Supreme Judicial Court of Massachusetts rules that an automobile driver was negligent, he has no recourse on that issue in the Supreme Court of the United States. The same is true of most rulings in most criminal cases. A state court's decision of a claim that certain evidence was inadmissible as hearsay is not reviewable in the Supreme Court. Thus the Supreme Court never has anything to do with the vast majority of cases decided every year by courts across the country. Of the more than 10,000,000 cases tried in American courts every year, no more than 300,000 are appealed at all, and only 2,500 or so are taken to the Supreme Court.

The decisions which the Supreme Court can and does re-examine are those involving questions of *federal* law. The question might be the meaning of a Congressional statute—whether, for example, the Taft-Hartley Law permits a union to picket in a certain way. It might be a question of the right of an injured seaman or railroad worker to recover damages under federal statutes that protect these occupations because they are in maritime and interstate commerce. It might be a treaty question: Does an agreement with Canada to protect a species of migratory birds override a state game law declaring open season on them? Or, not least, it might be a question arising under the Constitution—whether, for example, a man had been convicted of crime in a trial so unfair that it could not be called "due process of law." That was Gideon's case.

The Gideon case illuminates a curious and vital aspect of the American legal system. This is that many issues of federal law arise in the state courts. If all questions of federal law were confined to federal courts, life would be simpler for law students and judges. But it is easy to see that they cannot be so confined. When a state judge is asked by a struck company to enjoin the union's picketing, the union lawyer will doubtless argue that federal law—the Taft-

Hartley Act—forbids a state-court injunction; then the judge has to become for the moment an expert on federal legislation. When Clarence Earl Gideon stood up and said that the Constitution entitled him to a lawyer, the trial judge in Panama City and then the Supreme Court of Florida had to pass on his federal claim.

When state courts decide issues of federal law, the Supreme Court has power to review their decisions. But that power was not always taken for granted. It was, in fact, one of the first great issues of federal-state conflict in this country. Some states and their courts, arguing from what today would be called a states'-rights position, bitterly resisted such review by the Supreme Court as an intrusion on their independence.

The Constitution made clear that federal law, within its sphere, was superior to state law and had to be applied by state courts. Article VI provided: "This Constitution, and the Laws of the United States which shall be made in Pursuance thereof; and all Treaties made . . . shall be the supreme Law of the Land; and the Judges in every State shall be bound thereby, any Thing in the Constitution or Laws of any State to the Contrary notwithstanding." The states'-rights argument was that the highest court of each state should be relied upon to interpret and apply the federal Constitution, laws and treaties, free of any supervision by national authority. The First Congress thought otherwise; one of the very first statutes it enacted, the Judiciary Act of 1789, explicitly gave the Supreme Court of the United States (which did not yet exist) jurisdiction to review state-court decisions on federal questions. But still there was resistance.

The issue came to a head in 1816, in the great case of *Martin v. Hunter's Lessee*. The dispute was basically about the ownership of lands in Virginia, but it turned on whether title was determined by an old Virginia statute or by the Jay

Treaty of 1794 between the United States and Britain. The Virginia court said the state statute ruled. The Supreme Court reversed that judgment, saying the treaty must prevail. The Virginia court then simply refused to comply. Under the bitter leadership of its presiding judge—Spencer Roane, a friend of Jefferson and like him an implacable enemy of their fellow Virginian, John Marshall, the great Chief Justice of the United States—the Virginia Court of Appeals unanimously resolved "that the appellate power of the Supreme Court of the United States does not extend to this court. . . ."

When that resistant decision was taken to the Supreme Court, Chief Justice Marshall did not sit; he had a claim to some of the lands in dispute. The opinion of the Court was written by Justice Joseph Story, first in a line of Massachusetts scholars (he continued to lecture at Harvard while a justice) to serve on the Supreme Court, who was just thirty-two years old when appointed in 1811. Justice Story, for a unanimous bench, reaffirmed the constitutionality of the Supreme Court's jurisdiction over state-court decisions on issues of federal law. His opinion dipped deep into governmental philosophy to answer the states'-rights argument.

"A motive perfectly compatible with the most sincere respect for state tribunals," Justice Story wrote, "might induce the grant of appellate power over their decisions. That motive is the importance, and even necessity, of *uniformity* of decisions throughout the whole United States, upon all subjects within the purview of the Constitution.

"Judges of equal learning and integrity, in different states, might differently interpret a statute, or a treaty of the United States, or even the Constitution itself; if there were no revising authority to control these jarring and discordant judgments, and harmonize them into uniformity, the laws, the treaties and the Constitution of the United States would be different in different states and might, perhaps, never have precisely the same construction, obligation or efficacy in any two states.

"The public mischiefs that would attend such a state of things would be truly deplorable; and it cannot be believed that they would have escaped the enlightened convention which formed the Constitution. What, indeed, might then have been only prophecy, has now become fact; and the appellate jurisdiction must continue to be the only adequate remedy for such evils. . . ."

It is no exaggeration to call the decision in *Martin v. Hunter's Lessee* an essential ingredient in the survival of the United States as a nation. For what was still to a large extent prophecy when Justice Story wrote in 1816 has since become fact many times: The states and their courts have interpreted the federal Constitution and laws in different ways, jarring and discordant, and it has required the Supreme Court of the United States to harmonize the decisions into uniformity. Again and again there have arisen those who would challenge the Court's power to interpret and apply to every state and every section "the supreme Law of the Land"; for examples one need look no farther back than Oxford, Mississippi, and Little Rock, Arkansas. Without that unifying judicial power it is doubtful that a great federal union could have been created on this continent, and preserved.

All this discussion is by way of indicating that so abstract-seeming a question as the jurisdiction of the Supreme Court may involve great issues of policy and power in the real world. For the purposes of Gideon's case, history had settled the question. There were still many evidences of resentment, on the part of state judges and other officials, of Supreme Court review, especially in criminal cases such as Gideon's. But the case was unquestionably within one of the constitutional categories of Supreme Court jurisdiction. The Court had power under the Constitution to review the Florida judgments that kept Gideon in prison.

But that was only the first of many obstacles that Gideon had to overcome. Over the years other limits on the Court's jurisdiction have been developed, by Congress and the Court itself, with the aim in part of minimizing state objections to Supreme Court scrutiny.

One statute provides that the only state-court decisions reviewable in the Supreme Court are "final judgments or decrees rendered by the highest court of a State in which a decision could be had." The purpose behind this requirement is evident. Proper respect for the judicial system of a state demands that it be allowed to complete its processing of a case before the federal Supreme Court steps in; intervention from Washington is not justified to correct some preliminary ruling, or one that may still be reversed by higher state courts. It should be noted that the "highest court" rule does not prevent the Supreme Court from reaching down to the bottom rung of a state judicial ladder when that is the highest level at which a decision "could be had." In 1960 the Court reviewed a judgment of the Police Court of Louisville, Kentucky, imposing two ten-dollar fines on one Sam Thompson. "Shuffling Sam," as the newspapers called him, had been convicted of loitering and disorderly conduct after the police found him shuffling in a café. Under Kentucky law, fines under twenty dollars could not be appealed to any state court, so Sam Thompson's lawyer went directly to the Supreme Court of the United States. There the convictions were found unconstitutional—in violation of the Fourteenth Amendment's due-process guarantee—because there was absolutely no evidence to support them.

A person with a federal claim on which he may eventually want the Supreme Court to pass must raise that claim at the earliest possible moment in a state court proceeding. The Supreme Court, again in deference to the states, will not consider federal issues injected into a lawsuit as an afterthought or as a desperate measure by someone defeated on the battlefield of state law. But if a state appellate court agrees to hear, and actually decides, a federal claim raised late, then the state has in effect waived any objection to tardiness and the rule does not apply.

Finally, among these requirements designed to pay proper respect to state judicial systems, there is the rule that the person with a federal claim must follow procedures generally applicable in the state courts. If he filed his state appeal two weeks after the deadline and the state supreme court threw his case out for that reason, it does not matter how compelling his basic argument on federal law may be; the Supreme Court will not hear it. Once more there is a logical exception to the rule: If a state court applies its procedural requirements in a way that discriminates against parties claiming federal rights, an alleged procedural flaw will not be permitted to bar review in the Supreme Court. The Alabama Supreme Court dismissed an appeal by the National Association for the Advancement of Colored People on the ground that the N.A.A.C.P. had used the wrong form of writ. But the United States Supreme Court found that the Alabama judges had never applied such a rule before and had evidently devised it just for the N.A.A.C.P.; the Court put aside the Alabama findings and took jurisdiction of the case. State courts, said Justice Holmes in 1924, may not in their procedural rulings set "springes" for federal rights.

When someone asserts that an action of government, state or federal, violates the Constitution, he faces further barriers to Supreme Court review. These have been erected over the years by the Court itself, out of a recognition that it is a grave step to invoke the Constitution against government officials—one not to be taken lightly—and that the Court has occasionally got itself into deep difficulty by venturing too hastily into constitutional decisions. Chief Justice Taney's opinion in the Dred Scott case, holding that Congress had no power to prohibit slavery in new territories, brought the severest criticism on the Court and hurt its reputation for years; Chief Justice Hughes called it a "self-inflicted wound" because the issue need not have been decided at all.

"The most important thing we do is not doing," Justice Louis D. Brandeis used to say, expressing his almost Puritan resistance to the temptation of making great constitutional decisions. It is to avoid premature or unnecessary invocation of the Constitution that the Court has developed rules of self-control—"for its own governance," Justice Brandeis said, adding that under these precepts the Court had "avoided passing upon a large part of all the constitutional questions pressed upon it for decision."

One concept, found in the law generally but applied with special care by the Supreme Court in constitutional cases, is "standing." This means that the party complaining of some action in a lawsuit must show that he was personally injured or affected by it. If Tom assaults Dick, Harry has no standing to sue Tom for damages. A well-meaning citizen in Panama City, Florida, charged with no crime himself, could not bring a suit to make the state appoint counsel for Clarence Earl Gideon. A noted decision on standing arose from Connecticut's birth-control law, making it a crime to use contraceptives. The Supreme Court threw out a Connecticut doctor's claim that the law deprived his patients of their constitutional rights, holding that the doctor had no standing to assert the patients' rights. Years later some Connecticut women in medical need of contraceptives themselves sued, but then a divided Supreme Court invoked another doctrine to dismiss the case. The women had sued to have the law declared unconstitutional rather than waiting to be subjected to a criminal prosecution for using contraceptives. In those circumstances, the Court said, there was no sign that Connecticut would actually enforce the archaic birth-control law and the Court should not decide so new and delicate a constitutional question.

If there is any other way to resolve a case, the Court makes it a practice to avoid constitutional issues, no matter how strongly pressed. At the height of the Federal Government's loyalty-security program, the dismissal of those who were alleged to be security risks on the basis of secret charges by unnamed informants was attacked as unconstitutional in the Supreme Court. Both the Government and lawyers for the dismissed employee who had brought the case urged the Court to decide the basic constitutional issue; but a majority of the justices declined to do so, finding instead that the dismissal was invalid because Government officials had violated their own regulations. Ten years later the constitutionality of security dismissals on undisclosed charges has still not been settled, and it may never be. The rule, in Brandeis's language, is that the Court will not "anticipate a question of constitutional law in advance of the necessity of deciding it."

The Court has made it a practice not to give advisory opinions, even to Presidents. (Washington sought one and was turned down by the justices.) Nor will the Court ordinarily decide "feigned cases," got up by friends just to obtain an interpretation of the Constitution. Ours is an adversary system of justice, and its assumption is that the truth is best brought out in a genuine lawsuit between genuinely opposing parties. Brandeis said: "The Court will not pass upon the constitutionality of legislation in a friendly, nonadversary proceeding, declining because to decide such questions is legitimate only in the last resort, and as a necessity in the determination of real, earnest and vital controversy between individuals."

Gideon's case appeared to meet all these requirements. He had certainly raised his federal claim, that the Constitution entitled him to a lawyer, at the earliest possible moment—when his case was called for trial. He had not appealed his conviction, and in some states that would have been a fatal procedural error. But in Florida a prisoner may challenge the constitutionality of his conviction by petitioning the state supreme court to issue a writ of habeas corpus. Gideon had done just that, stating his constitutional claim for counsel again in the petition, and the Florida Supreme Court had presumably passed on and rejected the claim when it summarily denied his petition. Its judgment was final, and therefore ripe for review in the United States Supreme Court. Since this was a criminal case, such problems as standing did not arise; a man who has been sent to jail in a manner he terms illegal certainly has been injured, and his case is not feigned or advisory or premature.

The claim that Gideon presented to the Supreme Court was, in sum, one that the Court *could* hear. Whether the Court *would* hear it was another and very different question.

If the Court were required to hear every case that a nation of one hundred and eighty million litigious people could contrive to bring within its jurisdiction, the judicial process would quickly break down. Chief Justice Charles Evans Hughes explained in 1937:

"No single court of last resort, whatever the number of judges, could dispose of all the cases which arise in this vast country and which litigants would seek to bring up if the right of appeal were unrestricted."

Hughes wrote this in a letter to Senator Burton K. Wheeler that was instrumental in defeating President Franklin Roosevelt's plan to pack the Court. The President wanted to add a justice for each member of the Court over seventy years old—six at the time. Everyone knew his real reason was that he disapproved of the judicial philosophy of the 1937 Court, but he gave the explanation that the older judges needed help to turn out their work. In addition to showing that the Court was well up on its work, the Hughes letter devastated the argument that more judges would, as he put it, "promote the efficiency of the Court." To the contrary, he noted, "there would be more judges to hear, more judges to confer, more judges to discuss, more judges to be convinced and to decide." (Writing of the same problem of collective judging exactly a hundred years earlier, when there were eight Supreme Court justices, Justice Story said: "I verily believe, if there were twelve judges, we should do no business at all, or at least very little.") An efficiency expert would doubtless recommend that the Court sit in panels of three instead of all nine in every case. Dealing with that idea, Hughes remarked that the Constitution speaks of "one supreme Court" and concluded—some thought he was giving an advisory opinion—that "the Constitution does not appear to authorize two or more Supreme Courts or two or more parts of a Supreme Court functioning as separate courts." In any case, whether constitutionally permissible or not, it seems most unlikely that the country would tolerate having the decisions of so final and powerful a judicial body depend on which three justices happened to sit in each case.

And so, to let our one Supreme Court perform its great functions, a method had to be devised to reduce the burden of incoming cases. The problem became acute in the early years of this century, when the Court found itself falling farther and farther behind in its docket. The justices were being buried in trivia, and important cases were being reached years after they were filed. The Court itself, through a committee of justices, drafted a legislative solution, and Congress enacted it into law as the Judges' Bill of 1925. The solution was simply to make the Court's jurisdiction to a large extent discretionary, with the justices free to choose which cases they would hear among those admittedly within their judicial reach. For the litigant, a new phase was added to the process of obtaining a Supreme Court decision on his case: He first had to persuade the Court to hear the case at all.

Since 1925 one of the most important duties of the Supreme Court has been to decide whether it will decide. The technical device used is a petition for a writ of certiorari. This formidable-sounding beast is descended etymologically from the Latin *certiorari volumus*, "we wish to be informed" —an old writ used to bring the certified record of a case up from a lower court for immediate scrutiny by a reviewing bench. The writ is not so mysterious as its name. In applying for one, the litigant is simply asking the Supreme Court to hear his case. When the Court grants the writ, there are no great formalities that follow; both sides are simply notified by the Court's published orders and by brief letters from the Clerk that the justices are going to review the decision of the lower court.

The principle underlying the grant of this great discretion to the Supreme Court—the power to select cases for decision—has been expounded by three Chief Justices. William Howard Taft, testifying before Congress on what became the 1925 Act, said:

"No litigant is entitled to more than two chances, namely, to the original trial and to a review, and the intermediate courts of review are provided for that purpose. When a case goes beyond that, it is not primarily to preserve the rights of the litigants. The Supreme Court's function is for the purpose of expounding and stabilizing principles of law for the benefit of the people of the country, passing upon constitutional questions and other important questions of law for the public benefit."

Hughes put the same thought more succinctly in his letter

to Senator Wheeler: "Review by the Supreme Court," he said, "is in the interest of the law, its appropriate exposition and enforcement, not in the mere interest of the litigants." And in 1949 Chief Justice Fred M. Vinson, addressing the American Bar Association, told the lawyers: "To remain effective, the Supreme Court must continue to decide only those cases which present questions whose resolution will have immediate importance far beyond the particular facts and parties involved. Those of you whose petitions for certiorari are granted by the Supreme Court will know, therefore, that you . . . represent not only your clients, but tremendously important principles, upon which are based the plans, hopes and aspirations of a great many people throughout the country."

Cases come to the Supreme Court of the United States from a variety of sources: From the judicial systems of the fifty states; from the eleven United States Courts of Appeals, the intermediate federal appellate courts, each in a circuit covering a section of the country; from specialized federal tribunals, like the Court of Claims and the Court of Customs and Patent Appeals, and in unusual instances from the eighty-nine federal trial courts, the district courts.

More than ninety percent of the cases filed in the Supreme Court are brought by petitions for certiorari. There is still a limited class of matters that one has an absolute right to appeal to the Supreme Court of the United States. For example, a district-court decision on an antitrust suit brought by the Government is reviewable not in the Court of Appeals but only on direct appeal to the Supreme Court. In theory, the Supreme Court may not simply refuse to consider cases brought by appeal. In practice, the Court has developed ways to dispose of most of them summarily, without hearing argument or giving them extended consideration. Many appeals are dismissed "for want of a substantial federal question," or for other reasons showing that the

Court considered the issue trivial or the lower court's decision plainly correct. In short, the Court has virtually complete freedom to select the approximately one hundred and fifty cases to which it will give a full hearing each term, out of more than twenty-five hundred filed.

What are the rules of this winnowing process? How does a petition for certiorari qualify? In granting or denying petitions the justices ordinarily give no reasons at all; if they had to, much of the burden-relieving purpose of the discretionary certiorari jurisdiction would be defeated. Number 19 of the Supreme Court's rules does give some examples of persuasive reasons for granting petitions: "Where a state court has decided a federal question of substance . . . in a way probably not in accord with applicable decisions of this court. Where a [federal] court of appeals has rendered a decision in conflict with the decision of another court of appeals on the same matter. . . ." But Rule 19 warns that its examples are not controlling, and it says: "A review on writ of certiorari is not a matter of right, but of sound judicial discretion, and will be granted only where there are special and important reasons therefor."

The reasons for denying a petition for certiorari may have little or nothing to do with the merits of the legal claim it argues. That is why various justices have tried to educate the public to the fact that denial of a petition does not constitute approval of the lower-court decision that the petitioner wanted reviewed. (The educational process has not been much of a success; when the Court denies a certiorari petition in an agitated case, such as that of Mississippi's Governor Barnett, too many newspaper headlines still read: "Supreme Court Upholds Order Against Barnett.") All the denial means, in fact, is that the Court did not want to hear the case. That could be so even though the justices thought the lower-court opinion wrong—if, for example, the record of the case was so confused or inadequate that it did not seem an appropriate vehicle for resolution of the legal issue. Or, most significantly, considerations of timing could be involved. The law of the Constitution, like all law, develops slowly, and there are great currents of change that can be felt. The Court may believe it unwise to tackle a new question too soon, before the lower courts have had a chance to consider it and throw light on the problem. Or a claim, however sincerely pressed, may be out of time, out of the current of the law, as are the occasional petitions these days from southern officials in effect seeking to reverse the momentum of desegregation. Or, finally, some of the justices may feel strongly that a judgment should be reversed but despair of obtaining a majority; they might then prefer denying certiorari to taking the case and having the Supreme Court's imprimatur put on the outcome they so dislike. If certiorari is denied, there is always the chance that when the issue comes along another time, minds or even the membership of the Court will have changed. Such factors explain the comment of Justice William J. Brennan, Jr.: "Very often I have voted to deny an application when I thought that the [lower] court's result was very wrong."

Clarence Earl Gideon's petition for certiorari inevitably involved, for all the members of the Court, the most delicate factors of timing and strategy. The issue he presented —the right to counsel—was undeniably of first-rank importance, and it was an issue with which all of the justices were thoroughly familiar. Year after year since 1942 the Court had struggled to apply the rule of *Betts v. Brady:* that only in special circumstances were impoverished criminal defendants entitled to free counsel; few legal problems could have been so continuously on the justices' minds and consciences. And *Betts v. Brady* was not, like the School Segregation decision, a precedent to which the Court was so firmly committed that a plea for reconsideration was an obvious waste of time. Professional comment on the Betts case, in the law reviews, had always been critical and was growing stronger, and within the Supreme Court several justices had urged its overruling. On the other hand, a majority might well draw back from so large a step, especially if a new rule requiring counsel in all criminal cases were to be applied to men already in prison; in an earlier counsel case Justice Felix Frankfurter had warned that "such an abrupt innovation as recognition of the constitutional claim here . . . would furnish opportunities hitherto uncontemplated for opening wide the prison doors of the land." Was it wise for the Court to change its mind so drastically after two decades? Was a majority now prepared to do so? Was this the appropriate case? These were some of the questions inherent in No. 890 Miscellaneous, *Gideon v. Cochran,* as it began its course through the process established in the Supreme Court for consideration of petitions for certiorari.

3

Justice Brandeis is credited with the comment that "however much one could criticize the Supreme Court of the United States, it endured and deserved its place in our political structure because it did its own work." That is no small claim in the city of Washington, where few high officials write their own speeches or even their own letters. Alone among the great institutions in Washington the Court seems to have escaped Parkinson's Law—the thesis that the number of employees in any office continually increases and the work expands to occupy the new hands. The work at the Supreme Court is still done by nine men, assisted by eighteen young law clerks. Nothing is delegated to committees or task forces.

Indeed, what the Court turns out is not an institutional product in the sense that the work of Executive Departments is. In the Justice Department, for example, a legislative proposal would be drafted in rough by junior lawyers, worked over by more experienced hands, scrutinized by section chiefs, approved by one or more assistant attorneys general and the deputy attorney general, and finally put before the Attorney General for his approval. It is a hierarchical system, necessarily and appropriately.

At the Supreme Court there is no hierarchy. Even the Chief Justice is only, as has been said, "first among equals." He has symbolic and administrative pre-eminence, for example presiding over the sessions of the Court and over the Judicial Conference of the United States, which includes representatives of all the federal courts. But in the business of the Supreme Court his influence depends entirely on his moral and intellectual power to persuade. Each justice has one vote, and it is in the keeping of his own mind and conscience. Each works largely on his own, with his law clerks when he chooses, and the result is that there really are nine separate law offices—different in work habits as well as in philosophy. Justice Jackson said: "The fact is that the Court functions less as one deliberative body than as nine, each justice working largely in isolation except as he chooses to seek consultation with others. These working methods tend to cultivate a highly individualistic rather than a group viewpoint."

Each justice is responsible for every case that comes before the Supreme Court. There is no division of labor among committees or panels. This is a fact that has long escaped public understanding. Even some lawyers seem to think the petitions for certiorari are divided up among the justices. Chief Justice Hughes complained of this misconception as long ago as 1934: "I find that some think that applications for certiorari are distributed among the justices

ratably, that is, one-ninth to each justice. . . . Now the
fact is that all matters calling for action by the Court in the
disposition of cases are dealt with by all the members of the
Court. . . . All the Justices pass upon all the applications
for certiorari."

As a mechanical matter, petitions for certiorari in the
ordinary case are handled as follows. The party seeking review is required to file forty printed copies of its petition.
(The Court's rules are most particular about printing: All
printed documents filed in the Court must be 6⅛ inches by
9¼ in size, with type no smaller than 11-point, "adequately
leaded," and the paper "opaque and unglazed.") The other
side has thirty days to file a brief in opposition to the grant
of review. To prevent the justices from forming any views
on a case before both sides are available, the practice is to
have the Clerk's Office hold each petition for thirty days
and then distribute it together with the brief in opposition
if one has been received. One copy goes to each of the nine
offices. There individual practices set in.

Most justices, but not all, have their law clerks look over
each petition (and the opposing response) and prepare a
brief memorandum summarizing the issues. This fact led to
an inflated view of the law clerk's role. Justice Jackson
joked about it, saying he detected a suspicion at the Bar that
"the law clerks constitute a kind of junior court which
decides the fate of certiorari petitions." More recently Justice Tom C. Clark remarked that he had been "asked by
prominent lawyers, who should know better, to please speak
to my law clerks about their petitions."

The law clerks to the individual justices are not to be
confused with the permanent employees in the office of the
Clerk of the Supreme Court. The former assist a justice for
a year or two, working for him personally—not for the
Court as a whole. They are bright young men who are at
most a few years out of law school, where they stood near

the top of the class and probably were on the law review. Almost all federal and many state judges now have law clerks, and the competition is intense for the honor of a clerkship, especially in the Supreme Court. There each justice selects his clerks by his own method, one delegating the job to a professor at his old law school, another to a committee, others making the choice themselves after interviewing applicants. Many Supreme Court law clerks have gone into teaching, and they are among the country's most ·respected legal scholars. Others have become prominent in public office (Secretary of State Dean Acheson was clerk to Brandeis), in business (the late Irving S. Olds of United States Steel clerked for Holmes), and on the bench (Justice Byron R. White was clerk to Chief Justice Vinson).

Some of today's right-wing critics of the Supreme Court have picked on the law clerks as a convenient target, attributing to them Svengali-like powers over the justices. The truth is less interesting. Law clerks assist in research and may write drafts of material for the justice. They also perform the function of keeping him in touch with current trends of legal scholarship, especially the often critical views of the law schools about the Supreme Court. That is an important role in a Court which could so easily get isolated in its ivory tower. But the law clerks do not judge. They can only suggest. As a practical matter, a young man who is there only briefly is unlikely to make any significant change in the actual votes cast on cases by a judge who has been considering these problems for years.

The procedure for handling certorari petitions, as described so far, is that used for the printed petitions on the regular appellate docket. *Gideon v. Cochran* was, of course, an *in forma pauperis* petition, and the Court has had to devise special methods of handling such cases because of the special difficulties they present.

The paupers' petitions, Justice Frankfurter once wrote,

are often "almost unintelligible and certainly do not present a clear statement of issues necessary for our understanding." Their meager content can be contrasted with the information that the man of means is required to supply when he files a petition for certiorari. The rules require him to show the jurisdictional basis for Supreme Court review, including the time when he raised his federal questions. He must print the text of the lower court's opinions in the case, and he must supply at least one typewritten copy of the transcript of the trial-court proceedings. Prisoners rarely supply any of this material in their *in forma pauperis* petitions. The result is that there is often great difficulty even figuring out what happened to the prisoner—what the case is all about. Lower-court opinions would be informative, but in the prisoners' case the lower courts rarely bother to write any. That was true with Gideon. The Florida Supreme Court had turned him down in a stereotype order making no reference to the facts of his case. All it said was: "The above-named petitioner has filed a petition for writ of habeas corpus in the above cause, and upon consideration thereof, it is ordered that said petition be and the same is hereby denied." Not very helpful to a justice in Washington trying to find out what was decided in Florida.

The burden of the paupers' cases has been steadily growing heavier in the Supreme Court. In recent years their number has increased much more sharply than the volume of business on the regular docket. Twenty-five years ago fewer than one hundred *in forma pauperis* cases were filed each term. The number passed one thousand in the 1949 term and for the first time exceeded the volume of prepaid appellate cases. Now there are about fifteen hundred each term. The Court itself has taken a broad view of the statute allowing poor persons to file without formalities. It said in 1948 that one need not be "absolutely destitute" to qualify. In that case Justice Hugo L. Black wrote: "We think an affidavit is sufficient which states that one cannot because of poverty pay or give security for the costs and still be able to provide himself and dependents with the necessities of life." Otherwise an impoverished man would have to choose between his family and his cause—perhaps abandoning "what may be a meritorious claim in order to spare himself complete destitution." As a practical matter the Court seldom second-guesses a man's own declaration of poverty in an *in forma pauperis* affidavit.

Few of the paupers' petitions turn out to be worth the Supreme Court's time. Only about 3 percent are granted, as compared with approximately 13 percent of the petitions for certiorari on the regular docket. The prisoners' claims, Justice William O. Douglas has said, "are often fantastic, surpassing credulity. They are for the most part frivolous." (One recent petitioner said he was a descendant of the Spanish Grandee of Southern California and thus owned all the land.)

Given the difficulty of processing all these applications, it would be understandable if the Court did not try very hard to find the occasional needle in the haystack. But as Justice Walter V. Schaefer of the Illinois Supreme Court once said of a comparable problem, "It is not a needle we are looking for in these stacks of paper, but the rights of a human being." And so the Supreme Court has devised a careful procedure for sifting the frequently incomprehensible documents that pour in from the country's prisons. Justice Douglas has said he is confident that this procedure "dispenses justice at a level long neglected in the nation."

The Gideon case was handled in the usual way for *in forma pauperis* cases. Gideon's handwritten papers were held for thirty days, in their red envelope, to allow time for a reply by the Florida authorities. They knew of his petition because he had been required by the rules to mail a copy to the named respondent, H. G. Cochran, Jr., head of the

Florida prison system. But the states rarely answer prisoners' petitions, and there was no response to Gideon's during the thirty days. When that time was up, on February 8, 1962, the papers were sent to the office of Chief Justice Earl Warren.

The Chief Justice's three law clerks have the special duty of scrutinizing the *in forma pauperis* applications. (He has three instead of the two clerks allotted to other justices so that this arduous job can be done.) One of the clerks prepares a typewritten memorandum on each case, stating what the claim appears to be and any relevant legal framework. The memorandum is then circulated among the nine justices. If the claim seems to be a serious one, and in all cases of prisoners under death sentence, the original red envelope containing the application is attached to the law clerk's memorandum when it is circulated; in any case a justice can call for the file. If a case raises a question that the law clerk examining the file thinks may interest the Court, he may suggest to the Chief Justice even before the papers are circulated that the state authorities be asked to file a response. The hope is that a response may clarify the legal issues, fill in the factual background and bring out any obstacles to the Court's taking jurisdiction of the case.

That is what was done in Gideon's case. The Chief Justice's office instructed the Clerk's Office, which sends all such communications, to call for a response. On March 8, 1962, Michael Rodak, Jr., the assistant clerk who had originally handled Gideon's petition, sent this letter to the attorney general of Florida, Richard W. Ervin:

RE: GIDEON v. COCHRAN

No. 890 Misc., October Term, 1961

Dear Sir:

On January 8, 1962, Clarence Earl Gideon, an inmate of the Florida State Prison, at Raiford, filed a petition for writ of certiorari in this Court to review the order of the Supreme Court of Florida, dated October 30, 1961, in the above-entitled case. Our records indicate that you have been served with a copy of the petition.

The Court has directed this office to request that you file a response to the petition. One typewritten copy of your response, together with proof of service thereof, should reach this office on or before April 7, 1962.

> John F. Davis, Clerk
> by *Michael Rodak, Jr.*
> Assistant

On April 9th the Court received a brief in opposition signed by Attorney General Ervin and one of his assistants, Bruce R. Jacob. It was thirteen typewritten pages, and it sounded one theme: Gideon had not been entitled to trial counsel under the rule of the 1942 decision in *Betts v. Brady*, that the Constitution guaranteed free counsel to indigent defendants in state criminal cases only when "special circumstances" showed that a fair trial would otherwise be impossible. The brief reviewed the cases since *Betts v. Brady* and then rested on the indisputable fact that Gideon had never even claimed to be the victim of any special disabilities which would bring him within the rule of that case.

"Petitioner Gideon," the brief said, "has made no affirmative showing of any exceptional circumstances which would entitle him to counsel under the Fourteenth Amendment. . . . There has been presented no evidence of petitioner's maturity or capacity of comprehension. Petitioner merely alleges that he was without funds, that he pleaded not guilty and that he requested court-appointed counsel, while being tried on a non-capital charge. The petition contains no allegations as to petitioner's age, experience, mental capacity, familiarity or unfamiliarity with court procedure, or as to the complexity of the legal issues presented by the charge.

[All these were factors that had been held to produce special circumstances under the *Betts* rule.] Petitioner has made no showing of unfairness or of a lack of fundamental justice in the trial proceedings. In fact, his petition is notable for its lack of material allegations such as would entitle him to counsel under the Fourteenth Amendment. Since there have been no allegations as to exceptional circumstances, the presumption must be indulged that the trial proceedings were fair and just."

The one thing notable about the response, to an outside observer, was its assumption that the rule of *Betts v. Brady* was inviolate. The possibility that the Court might be prepared to overrule it was never considered.

The response ended with a certification by Assistant Attorney General Jacob that he had mailed a copy "to Mr. Clarence Earl Gideon, In Proper Person, Box 221, Raiford, Fla." On April 21st the Court received a reply brief from Gideon. It was four pages long, again written in pencil, and it began with a modest disclaimer.

"Petitioner cannot make any pretense at being able to answer the learned Attorney General of Florida," Gideon wrote, "because the petitioner is not attorney or versed in law nor does not have the law books to copy down the decisions of this Court. But the Petitioner knows there is many of them."

The reply brief stuck resolutely to the simple proposition Gideon had argued from the beginning.

"The respondent claims," it said, "that a citizen can get a equal and fair trial without legal counsel. . . . Petitioner will attempt to show this Court that a citizen of the state of Florida cannot get a just and fair trial without the aid of counsel. . . . If the petitioner would of had attorney there would not of been allowed such things as hearsay, perjury or Bill of attainer against him. . . . It makes no difference how old I am or what color I am or what church I belong too if any. The question is I did not get a fair trial. The question is very simple. I requested the court to appoint me attorney and the court refused. . . ."

The reply was, in fact, telling in its simplicity. "It makes no difference how old I am or what color I am or what church I belong too if any." Intended or not, that sentence was an effective parody of the sophisticated reasoning that in past years had determined—under the "special circumstances" approach—whether a man should have had a free lawyer at his trial.

By the time the Florida response and Gideon's reply had come in, the Court was in its busiest period. Every spring the justices struggle to overcome procrastination, to compromise their differences, to finish up opinions on all the argued cases so that they can end the term in June, as scheduled, and go off to lie in the sun or make speeches at lawyers' meetings, as the spirit moves them. In the office of the Chief Justice the *in forma pauperis* petitions may not have top priority. But the Gideon papers were again examined and summarized by a law clerk, and now his memorandum—with the full file attached—was circulated to the other eight justices.

During the last week in May the Chief Deputy Clerk of the Court, Edmund P. Cullinan, was informed that the case of *Gideon v. Cochran* was ready for discussion at the formal conference of the Court. It was then Cullinan's duty to include the case on the next conference list—a mimeograph, distributed to the justices, that shows all the items ready for the next conference. Cullinan put *Gideon v. Cochran* on the list for the conference of Friday, June 1st.

The nine justices meet in a formal conference every Friday during or preceding a week in which cases are argued or opinions announced—about three Fridays out of four during the October-to-June term. The conference room is an oak-paneled chamber adjoining the Chief Justice's office in the rear of the Court building. Book shelves lining the walls are filled with law reports, and there is a long massive table in the center of the room. A single portrait, of Chief Justice John Marshall, looks down at the justices seated around the table.

The conference has a record for secrecy probably unrivaled in official Washington. So far as is known, no one not a justice of the Supreme Court has ever been allowed into the conference room during one of the sessions. No secretaries, no law clerks, no librarians, no messengers. If a message arrives, the junior justice—the one most recently appointed—goes to the door to get it. The purpose of this absolute secrecy is twofold. It ensures against premature disclosure of the Court's decisions, and it protects the privacy of the justices' discussion. The latter may be the more important reason. Genuine intellectual exchange among men of strong views is not always easy at best; it would be the more difficult if each justice had to fear public recriminations about some argument he advanced in the heat of debate. The justices must be free to argue to the hilt, without fear of reading in some popular journal that "Justice X wanted another Munich."

Members of the Court have disclosed, however, the general way the conference is conducted. It begins at ten A.M. and usually runs on until late in the afternoon. At the start each justice, when he enters the room, shakes hands with all the others there (thirty-six handshakes altogether). The custom, dating back generations, is evidently designed to begin the meeting at a friendly level, no matter how heated the intellectual differences may be. The conference takes up, first, the applications for review—a few appeals, many more petitions for certiorari. Those on the Appellate Docket, the regular paid cases, are considered first, then the paupers' applications on the Miscellaneous Docket. (If any of these are granted, they are then transferred to the Appellate Docket.) After this the justices consider, and vote on, all the cases argued during the preceding Monday through Thursday. These are tentative votes, which may be and quite often are changed as the opinion is written and the problem thought through more deeply. There may be further discussion at later conferences before the opinion is finally handed down.

Because so many men are involved, with the resulting risk of chaos, the discussion follows a quite formal procedure. The Chief Justice begins the consideration of each case by stating the issue and his views. The senior associate, now Justice Black, speaks next, and so on down the line. As presiding officer the Chief Justice shapes the character of the conference, not only by the way he first formulates the issues but by deciding, for example, how long to let debate continue before calling for a vote. Chief Justice Hughes was regarded by some as the greatest master of the conference. "To see him preside," wrote Justice Frankfurter, "was like witnessing Toscanini lead an orchestra." But during the Hughes years Justice Harlan F. Stone complained that the Chief was too firm, too controlling. Then Stone became Chief Justice, and his colleagues protested that the conferences dragged because he was not firm enough.

At the typical conference these days the justices pass on nearly one hundred matters, a formidable number. A little arithmetic will quickly indicate how impossible a burden that would impose if every justice were to talk on every case. Ten years ago, when the docket was significantly shorter than today's, Justice Jackson figured that the average conference list would permit "five minutes of deliberation per item, or about thirty-three seconds of discussion per item by each of the nine justices. . . . All that saves the Court from being hopelessly bogged down," Jackson added, "is that many of these items are so frivolous on mere inspection that no one finds them worthy of discussion, and they are disposed of by unanimous consent." Each justice, before the weekly conference, sends to the Chief's Office a list of cases he considers not worthy of discussion; the cases on which all nine are agreed are thereupon passed over at the conference.

Voting in the conference is in inverse order to discussion: the junior justice first. It takes only four votes to grant certiorari or to put an appeal down for oral argument. The theory of having less than a majority grant review is that a case deemed important by as many as four justices is at least worthy of the Court's consideration; the majority is always free to work its will later, on the merits of the issue presented. (Justice Frankfurter argued that a majority of five should be free, indeed, to dismiss the writ of certiorari as "improvidently granted," but this view was rejected as inconsistent with the integrity of the so-called Rule of Four for granting review.) Even when there are fewer than four justices who personally want to take on a case, the necessary four votes may well be obtained by judicial log-rolling. (You vote for my case and I'll vote for yours.) The outside world does not know how the Court reaches the decision to grant or deny review of a case—or how it reaches any decision at conference, although some of these secrets have been disclosed by the publication of justices' papers. Most thoughtful persons have concluded that there should be no such publication at least until all participants in the events described have left the Court, lest freedom of discussion at conference be inhibited by the fear of premature disclosure. One member of the present Court was so distressed by the gossip retailed in one judicial biography that he ordered all his own papers burned—to prevent their misuse in the event of his death.

At the conference of June 1, 1962, the Court had before

it two jurisdictional statements asking the Court to hear appeals, twenty-six petitions for certiorari on the Appellate Docket, ten paupers' applications on the Miscellaneous Docket and three petitions for rehearing. (The last are almost never granted.) There were some important cases among these. One was a challenge to the constitutionality of New York's legislative districts; the justices decided to send this back to a federal court in New York for reconsideration in light of their recent decision, in a Tennessee case, that federal courts could scrutinize state legislative apportionments. Another case arose from the Freedom Rides. Six Negroes had been convicted of breach of the peace for their effort to desegregate a Shreveport, Louisiana, bus terminal. The Court, having read the printed petition and response in this case, decided to grant the petition for review and then summarily to reverse the convictions for lack of any supporting evidence except the constitutionally impermissible fact that they had violated the custom of segregation. The Kohler Company of Wisconsin was asking the Court to review the finding of the National Labor Relations Board that it had committed unfair labor practices in the bitter dispute, dating back to 1954, with the United Automobile Workers. The justices also considered some of the cases that had been argued earlier in the term and that now were ready for disposition. They discussed some draft opinions. They decided to put down for re-argument next fall the great dispute between Arizona and California over the water of the Colorado River. And, finally, they passed on the handwritten petition for certiorari filed by Clarence Earl Gideon, prisoner No. 003826, Florida State Penitentiary, Raiford, Florida.

The results of the deliberations at this conference were made known to the world shortly after ten A.M. the following Monday, June 4th, when a clerk posted on a bulletin

board the mimeographed list of the Supreme Court's orders
for that day. One order read:

890 Misc. GIDEON v. COCHRAN

The motion for leave to proceed *in forma pauperis* and
the petition for writ of certiorari are granted. The case is
transferred to the appellate docket. In addition to other
questions presented by this case, counsel are requested to
discuss the following in their briefs and oral argument:

"Should this Court's holding in *Betts v. Brady*, 316 U.S.
455, be reconsidered?"

4

In the Circuit Court of Bay County, Florida, Clarence Earl Gideon had been unable to obtain counsel, but there was no doubt that he could have a lawyer in the Supreme Court of the United States now that it had agreed to hear his case. It is the unvarying practice of the Court to appoint a lawyer for any impoverished prisoner whose petition for review has been granted and who requests counsel.

Appointment by the Supreme Court to represent a poor man is a great honor. For the eminent practitioner who would never, otherwise, dip his fingers into the criminal law it can be an enriching experience, making him think again of the human dimensions of liberty. It may provide the first, sometimes the only, opportunity for a lawyer in some distant corner of the country to appear before the Supreme Court. It may also require great personal sacrifice. There is no monetary compensation of any kind—only the satisfaction of service. The Court pays the cost of the lawyer's transportation to Washington and home, and it prints the briefs, but there is no other provision for expenses, not even secretarial help or a hotel room. The lawyer donates that most valuable commodity, his own time.

A remarkable example of an appointed counsel's conception of his duty, and his dedication in carrying it out, was provided by a Chicago lawyer, Walter T. Fisher. Mr. Fisher was appointed on January 14, 1957, to represent one Alfonse Bartkus, who had been acquitted by a federal jury of robbing a federally-insured bank in Illinois and then had been tried and convicted in the Illinois courts for the same robbery. The Supreme Court had agreed to hear his claim that the successive prosecutions amounted to a kind of double jeopardy barred by the due-process clause of the Fourteenth Amendment. Mr. Fisher wrote a brief, argued the case and lost by a tie vote of four to four, Justice Brennan not sitting. (An equal division results in what is called an affirmance by necessity of the lower-court's decision.) Mr. Fisher petitioned for rehearing, asking Justice Brennan to sit, and the Court granted the petition. The next term Mr. Fisher wrote a new brief, argued the case again— and lost, five to four. He filed a further petition for rehearing, which was denied. But he did not consider his obligation to Bartkus or to the law ended. He asked the Illinois legislature to take action against what he still considered an injustice, and in 1959 the legislature enacted his proposal: a bill barring state prosecution of any person for a criminal act which had previously been the subject of a federal prosecution. That legislation, however, did not affect Bartkus, who remained in prison under a life sentence. Mr.

Fisher filed a clemency petition, wrote letters, pleaded with
the authorities. On January 3, 1961, just short of four years
after Mr. Fisher's appointment by the Supreme Court, Bartkus's sentence was commuted to time served. Mr. Fisher
found Alfonse Bartkus a job and made an arrangement for
him to receive continuing guidance.

As a formality, the poor man whose case is to be heard
by the Supreme Court must ask for a lawyer. The chief
deputy clerk of the Court, Edmund P. Cullinan, sees to it
that he does ask. A distinguished gray-haired gentleman
who joined the Clerk's Office while still a student at Georgetown Law School in 1930, and who has become an authority on how to proceed before the Court, Cullinan has
the recurrent nightmare that some prisoner will want to
argue his own case. (A statute allows anyone—rich or poor,
lawyer or layman—to present his own case in any Federal
court.) To forestall that possibility he writes promptly to
every prisoner whose petition the Court grants. He wrote
Gideon the day the Court granted certiorari in his case,
June 4. (An assistant clerk, Eugene T. Lyddane, on the
same day sent the text of the Court's order to Gideon and
the Attorney General of Florida.) Cullinan's letter to Gideon said: "I assume that you desire the Court to appoint a
competent attorney to represent you in this Court. It will
therefore be necessary for you to forward immediately a
handwritten motion requesting the Court to appoint counsel to represent you."

Gideon was duly consistent in wanting a lawyer. On
June 18th his answer arrived at the Court, again written in
pencil on the lined prison form and stamped "censored."
Gideon said: "I do desire the Court to appoint a competent
attorney to represent me in this Court. Because I do not
know the procedure nor do I have the ability to do so. I
make this formal request to the Supreme Court of the
United States to appoint me a attorney."

Like other matters decided by the Supreme Court, the choice of a lawyer for an indigent petitioner is entirely in the bosom of the justices. They have never laid out any rules for the selection process, doubtless desiring to retain a broad discretion. In the process, Justice Frankfurter once said, "intrinsic professional competence alone matters." The Court naturally tends to pick men known to one or more of the justices personally or by reputation. Mr. Fisher, for example, was an old friend of Justice Frankfurter's, and it is a fair guess that the justice suggested his name. (But friendship is no assurance of a vote; Justice Frankfurter wrote the opinion of the Court rejecting Mr. Fisher's argument on behalf of Alfonse Bartkus.)

Former law clerks to the justices are often appointed. So are law professors and established practitioners; Edward Bennett Williams was appointed for a California prisoner in 1962. The Court frequently names someone from the same area of the country as the prisoner, but that is no rule. In general it can be said that counsel appointed in the paupers' cases are much superior to the average lawyer who appears in the Supreme Court. The average level, unfortunately, is mediocre at best—reflecting the bar generally, since there is no special group of lawyers who argue in the Supreme Court.

The question of counsel for Gideon was ready for discussion at the Court's conference of Friday, June 22, 1962. That was the last conference of the term, as it happened; the following Monday the Court handed down all its remaining opinions, including the controversial decision on the New York Regents' Prayer, and recessed for the summer. Shortly after the conference ended, Chief Justice Warren called in the Clerk of the Court, John F. Davis. The Clerk is the Court's ranking employee, and the job is one of distinction. Davis's predecessor, James R. Browning, is now a judge of the United States Court of Appeals for the

Ninth Circuit; and before he was named Clerk in 1961 Davis had argued more than fifty Supreme Court cases for the Government, including the du Pont-General Motors antitrust case. One of the Clerk's duties is to help with the mechanical arrangements for translating Friday's conference decisions into the printed and mimeographed orders released the following Monday. When a lawyer is being appointed to represent an indigent, Davis also has the job of informally advising him over the weekend so that he may indicate if he has some personal difficulty that would make it impossible for him to accept the assignment. The Court does not want the mutual embarrassment of having a formal appointment turned down. But the Court's appointment of counsel in these circumstances is a little like a Presidential invitation to dine: Few are turned down.

On this Friday evening Chief Justice Warren told Davis that the Court had selected Abe Fortas of Washington to represent Gideon. Davis put in a call for Fortas and found him, eventually, in Dallas. Fortas said he would be happy to serve as counsel for Clarence Earl Gideon. He asked what the issue was in Gideon's case. Briefly, but quite clearly indicating the large stakes, Davis told him: The Court had agreed to reconsider the limits put on the right to counsel by *Betts v. Brady.*

The next Monday the Court entered this order in the case of *Gideon v. Cochran:*

"The motion for appointment of counsel is granted and it is ordered that Abe Fortas, Esquire, of Washington, D.C., a member of the Bar of this Court be, and he is hereby, appointed to serve as counsel for petitioner in this case."

Abe Fortas is a high-powered example of that high-powered species, the Washington lawyer. He is the driving force in the firm of Arnold (Thurman Arnold, who was Franklin Roosevelt's trust-buster and then a judge of the United States Court of Appeals for the District of Columbia, resigning because he found the bench stultifying), Fortas and Porter (Paul A. Porter, former chairman of the Federal Communications Commission). The firm has thirty lawyers, making it substantial in size though nothing like the colossi of Wall Street. It is not what could be called an Establishment law firm; it is too aggressive, or insufficiently stodgy, according to one's point of view. Judge Arnold, as a Yale law professor in the 1930's, was one of the great legal realists, writing books (e.g., *The Folklore of Capitalism*, a classic of law and politics) in which he sought to puncture the myths about judges and portrayed them as men, not priests, with ideas and even prejudices. The realists emphasized what judges did, as opposed to what they said, and recognized that law was not logic alone but that it reflected judges' social, economic and psychological conceptions. Something of this irreverence pervades Arnold, Fortas and Porter. There is a heavy Yale influence, and Yale is popularly supposed to regard law more as a social tool and less as the intellectual exercise attributed to Harvard. Generalizations aside, it is probably true that Yale Law School puts less emphasis on the niceties of arriving at a legal result and more on the social significance of the result. Certainly this "realism" is in the air at Arnold, Fortas and Porter. Arnold actually is a 1914 Harvard Law graduate, for all his later identification with Yale. Porter went to Kentucky and the University of Kentucky Law School and still has the fine political style of the Kentuckian. All three are graduates of the New Deal, and it is not surprising that the firm has a liberal and Democratic flavor. Fortas is an old friend and counselor of Lyndon Johnson and was one of the first men called in to help when Johnson assumed the Presidency. Lawyers from Arnold, Fortas and Porter do drafting and other behind-the-scenes work for liberal legislation in Congress. The firm played an important part in the legal fight against the use of anonymous informers in the Government's loy-

alty and security programs; one victim whose case it took
to the Supreme Court but lost was taken on as an A.F.P.
employee and is still there. But the firm is anything but a
do-good outfit. It is interested in making money, and it
does so in a widely varied practice emphasizing litigation
against the Government—antitrust law, tax law and practice
before the federal regulatory agencies. The premier business-
getter is Abe Fortas.

Fortas had just turned fifty-two when he got the assignment in the Gideon case. He was born to a modest Jewish
family in Memphis on June 19, 1910, went to Southwest-
ern College there and then moved into the great world
through the Yale Law School. He was editor-in-chief of the
Law Journal, the earliest sure sign of intellectual distinction
and will power in a lawyer. After graduation, in 1933, he
went to Washington and worked for such New Deal lumi-
naries as William O. Douglas, who had been his professor
at Yale, Jerome Frank and Harold Ickes. In 1942, at the
age of thirty-two, he became Undersecretary of the Interior. Francis Biddle, who was Attorney General at the
time, tells a wonderfully Rooseveltian story about Fortas—
really about F.D.R. Ickes was out of town, and Fortas sat
in for him at a Cabinet meeting. The President, who was
asking each Cabinet member in turn to report, could not
remember Fortas's name and passed a note down the table
asking for help. Mr. Biddle writes:

> "Fortas," I whispered, and his name was relayed to the
> President, who then wrote on a pad, "Not his last name, his
> first name." And when, going around the table, he came to
> Abe, the President asked, "Well, Abe, what's been going on
> in Interior?"

In 1946 Fortas left the Department of the Interior for
private practice. He is known now as one of the country's
outstanding appellate advocates, skilled in the special tech-

nique of arguing cases to appellate judges that is so largely neglected in this country. In the Supreme Court he has represented, among others, Lever Brothers Company and George Parr (known as the Duke of Duval), the old-fashioned Democratic boss of Duval County, Texas, whose conviction for mail fraud Fortas managed to get reversed.

But Fortas's most important activities as a lawyer take place not in courtrooms but in the offices of corporations. He advises business executives on how to enlarge their market power and their profits while staying within the myriad rules laid down by government. He flies around the country to attend meetings, to handle negotiations, to discuss finances and corporate structure as much as the law. One acquaintance says his business is "corporate wheeling and dealing," adding respectfully: "He is one of our big social engineers." He is unusual in doing so many things well as a lawyer: antitrust litigation, practice at administrative agencies, appellate argument, corporate counselling. His clients include Federated Department Stores, Unilever, Investors Diversified Services, Cyrus Eaton and the Commonwealth of Puerto Rico. (He knows Governor Luis Muñoz Marin intimately.) He also represents the Casals Festival; he is an old friend of Pablo Casals and arranged Casals' performance at the White House.

Unlike most prominent lawyers Fortas has had an interest in criminal law, though more on the philosophical side than in practice. He argued and won the Durham case, in which the Court of Appeals for the District of Columbia laid down a new criminal insanity rule that has had repercussions throughout this country and abroad. (The Court abandoned the old doctrine that a man escaped the responsibility for a criminal act only if he could not tell right from wrong, substituting the broader rule that "an accused is not criminally responsible if his unlawful act was the product of mental disease or defect.") He is a member of a committee appointed by Chief Justice Warren to recommend changes in the rules of procedure for Federal criminal cases, and it could have been his association with the Chief Justice in this work that led to his appointment in the Gideon case. But he is also a friend of Justices Black, Brennan and Douglas, and one of them might have suggested his name.

Fortas is a smallish man with a manner that can be grave or, especially with women, charming; there is a nice touch of Mephistopheles. His speech has a slow, deliberate quality, with tangible intellectual force—the word may be tension—behind it. It is hard to imagine him being entirely spontaneous. Not that he lacks humor, but he always seems controlled. A lawyer who has worked with him says: "Of all the men I have met he most knows why he is doing what he does. I don't like the s.o.b., but if I were in trouble I'd want him on my side. He's the most resourceful, the boldest, the most thorough lawyer I know."

If Fortas has any one hero in the law, it is Justice Brandeis, and that says a good deal about Fortas. Brandeis was the supreme craftsman, probably the ablest lawyer ever to sit on the Court. He was a notably unsentimental man, one who had no qualms about voting against widows or orphans in furtherance of some longer-run interest in the law. But he also had deep social convictions and fought for liberal causes throughout his life. With the Brandeis model in mind, a colleague has said of Fortas: "He values craftsmanship most highly. He is no sentimentalist, and he works for reform of the criminal law because he thinks it is right for society, not because of any illusions about criminals. But under his sobriety and detachment there is passionate conviction. He is an angry man—angry at injustice."

Evidently Fortas enjoys the grand style. He and his wife —Carolyn Agger, an expert tax lawyer—drive a Rolls Royce; he explains that it is really an economical investment.

They have many contemporary works of art in their Georgetown home, but also antique furniture and Chinese scrolls and paintings. The firm is in what was once a Victorian private home, and Fortas's office is dominated by a huge desk made from a Victorian grand piano. There are wing chairs, a soft couch, paintings and mementoes of Casals and other great friends.

A lawyer preparing a case for the Supreme Court has more freedom than might generally be expected. His material has to a large extent been determined by the proceedings in the lower courts, but he can artistically shape that material because he has the choice of facts to emphasize and legal theories to advance for the desired result.

For example, a man may have been convicted of contempt of Congress for refusing to answer a subcommittee's questions about his asserted Communist affiliations. That seems simple enough, but the intellectual ore that lawyers have mined from such contempt records is rich indeed. Was the committee authorized by the House or Senate to conduct this inquiry? Had it passed the authority on to this subcommittee? Did the subcommittee follow its own rules? Were the questions pertinent to the official subject of investigation? Was this pertinence explained to the witness? Was the subject of inquiry adequately stated in the indictment, and proved at the trial? These are some of the questions that appellate counsel have found in the cold records of Congressional contempt proceedings in the last decade, and argued—often successfully—to the Supreme Court. The Court's discretion is as great as the advocate's in selecting the issue for decision, so that it is often difficult to predict on what ground a case will be decided, much less which side will win. The shaping of the facts and the issues into a Supreme Court case is the job of the advocate. The brief and argument that finally appear are only the visible part of the iceberg—the end of a long process of selection and decision and imagination.

It was this process on which Fortas and others in his law firm embarked at the end of June. The first step was to look over the papers that had been filed so far in the Gideon case. A young associate in the firm went up to the Clerk's Office at the Court to read them, and photostats were later made for the Arnold, Fortas and Porter files. These papers were meager: Gideon's petition for review, Florida's response, the rebuttal by Gideon, a copy of his original application for habeas corpus in the Florida Supreme Court and that court's cryptic denial of it. From these, Fortas, or any other interested person, could know only a skeleton of the case: The charge, the conviction, the sentence, Gideon's demand for a lawyer, the rejection of that demand. There were no details about the prisoner or the crime or the trial—nothing, for example, to indicate what a lawyer might have done for Gideon by way of defense that Gideon did not do for himself.

The few facts before Fortas were enough to raise the legal question that the Supreme Court had directed him to argue: Should *Betts v. Brady* be reconsidered and an absolute requirement of counsel be imposed? As the bare record stood, Florida conceded that Gideon was a poor felony defendant whose request for appointed counsel had been denied. Those facts alone as an abstract proposition, Fortas could argue, constituted a denial of due process of law. Moreover, technically speaking, only this skeleton of the Gideon case could serve as the basis for the Supreme Court's adjudication. The Court ordinarily will consider only the record that was before the lower court; counsel may not, as an afterthought, try to introduce new evidence. And in Gideon's case the only document that had been before the Florida Supreme Court was the habeas corpus petition that it rejected; it had no transcript of the trial or other information.

The Florida court regarded Gideon's constitutional claim as so weak—or so obviously foreclosed by *Betts v. Brady*, to put it another way—that factual detail was irrelevant.

But it is against the Anglo-American legal tradition to argue cases in so abstract a setting. A lawyer wants the smell of flesh and blood; he wants a human being for a client, not an abstract principle. And Fortas had been assigned to represent Clarence Earl Gideon, not an abstraction. There was always the chance that a closer examination of the facts in his case would show another reason for setting aside his conviction—a ground easier for the Supreme Court to accept than one that would require overruling of its own precedent. As one example, the trial record might disclose one of the "special circumstances" entitling a man to a free lawyer under the *Betts v. Brady* rule: Gideon might have been insane or hopelessly incompetent, or the judge might have shown prejudice, or the case against him might have been a particularly complicated or legally subtle one. If Gideon could win in the Supreme Court on any such ground, it was Fortas's duty to Gideon to argue that point, even though the result was to eliminate the case as a broad test of the right to counsel. There are few things Supreme Court justices like less than a lawyer who puts his client's interest aside in the zeal to make some great change in the law.

All of these considerations were in Fortas's mind. They presented what he called "a moral problem": Whether he should try to find out more about what had happened to Clarence Earl Gideon—in particular, whether he should get a transcript of his trial. "The real question," Fortas said, "was whether I should urge upon the Court the special-circumstances doctrine. As the record then stood, there was nothing to show that he had suffered from any special circumstances. But if you went behind that bare record, there might be. There was the risk, if it did turn out that Gideon had some special difficulty, that this whole case would turn

out to be an anticlimax—just another case of the Supreme
Court freeing a single prisoner without laying down any
new rule on the right to counsel. But my duty was to Gideon. If I hadn't gotten the record up, I'd never know. If I
lost the case, I'd always worry: 'Is the poor guy in jail because I didn't do my job?' "

Fortas decided to get the trial transcript. He telephoned
Chief Deputy Clerk Cullinan, who arranges such things for
the Supreme Court. Cullinan wrote to the Circuit Court of
Bay County, Florida, and before long a transcript of Gideon's trial was typed by the local court reporter from her
notes, certified by the clerk of the Circuit Court and mailed
to Washington.

5

Gideon was tried on August 4, 1961, by Judge Robert L. McCrary, Jr., and a jury of six men. At the start, after Gideon's unsuccessful attempt to obtain a lawyer, Judge McCrary asked the jurors whether they would "give him the same fair trial, and consideration, since he is not represented by counsel, that you would if he were represented." The transcript shows a joint reply: "Yes, sir."

The Court: Now, Mr. Gideon, look these six gentlemen over and if you don't want them to sit as a jury to try your case, just point out the one, or more, all six of them if you want to, and the court will excuse them and we will call another, or some others, to try your case. You don't have to have a reason, just look them over and if you don't like their looks that's all it takes to get them excused. . . .

The Defendant: They suit me all right, your Honor.

The judge, as Fortas noted when he read the transcript, was obviously trying to protect Gideon but did not inform him of his right to question each juror for possible bias.

Ordinarily, in a criminal case, the prosecutor and the defense counsel make opening statements to the jury, indicating what they expect to prove. The prosecutor, Assistant State·Attorney William E. Harris, made his statement, and then Judge McCrary let Gideon address the jury. "Just walk right around there where you can see them," the judge said, "and tell them what you expect the evidence to show in your favor. Talk loud enough for them to hear you, now." Apparently under Florida practice the court reporter does not take down opening statements. The transcript noted only that Mr. Harris read to the jury the formal charge against Gideon, that on June 3, 1961, he "did unlawfully and feloniously break and enter a building of another, to-wit, the Bay Harbor Poolroom, property of Ira Strickland, Jr., lessee, with intent to commit a misdemeanor within said building, to-wit, petit larceny."

The prosecution's principal witness was one Henry Cook of 108 East Avenue, Panama City, otherwise unidentified. He testified that he was outside the Bay Harbor Poolroom at five-thirty in the morning that June 3rd and saw Gideon inside. He knew Gideon. After a few minutes' watching through the window, Cook testified, he saw Gideon come out with a pint of wine in his hand, make a telephone call at the street corner and get into a taxi that he had apparently called. After following Gideon to the telephone booth he went back to the poolroom and "saw it had been broken into." The front was off the cigarette machine, and its money box was lying on a pool table.

That was the direct testimony, and it was damaging. Then, briefly, Gideon attempted to cross-examine Cook. He asked what Cook was doing outside the poolroom at five-thirty in the morning. Cook said he had "just come from a dance, down in Apalachicola—stayed out all night"; and then this potentially interesting line of inquiry was dropped. Gideon asked whether Cook had ever been arrested, but the prosecutor's objection to that question was sustained by Judge McCrary. Gideon was allowed to ask whether Cook had ever been convicted of a felony; Cook said no. The rest of the cross-examination was a meandering, argumentative affair that got nowhere. (Q: Do you know positively that I was carrying a pint of wine? A: Yes, I know you was. Q: How do you know that? A: Because I seen it in your hand.) Nothing further was brought out about Cook's age, his occupation, his relationship with Gideon, his reputation—all areas that a lawyer would certainly have explored.

There was only one other witness for the prosecution: Ira Strickland, Jr., operator of the Bay Harbor Poolroom. He testified that he had closed the place up at midnight on June 2, 1961, locking all doors and windows. When he returned the next morning at eight o'clock, he found the deputy sheriff; a window had been smashed, he said, and a cigarette machine and juke box broken into. Someone had taken coins from the two machines—Strickland said he did not know how much money was missing—and "a small amount of beer and some wine." On cross-examination Gideon asked a number of questions about what the Bay Harbor Poolroom looked like, and the jury learned that it had a long bar down one side.

Gideon had eight witnesses for the defense. Before they were called at his request, Judge McCrary warned him—without any real legal basis, so far as Fortas could tell—that "the witnesses you call are your witnesses, and it's up to you to vouch for them. You understand that, do you?"

Gideon answered, "Yes, sir, I understand it."

His first witness was the policeman who had discovered the break-in at the Bay Harbor Poolroom, Henry Berryhill, Jr. He said he had not been summoned by anyone—not, for example, by Cook—but had found the front door of the poolroom open on a routine patrol. He "checked with a fellow at the front of the building, a Mr. Cook, and . . . he said he saw you leave the building." Gideon asked nothing further about what Berryhill thought Cook was doing "at the front of the building" at that hour. Berryhill testified that he had called the deputy sheriff, Duell Pitts, to investigate the break-in. After a few questions Berryhill was excused. Just why Gideon had called the policeman as a defense witness remained unclear.

Deputy sheriff Pitts was next, and his status as a defense witness was just as obscure. He said Cook had seen Gideon in the building, and he was satisfied with that evidence of the crime. Then came the cab driver who had picked Gideon up on that morning of June 3rd, Preston Bray. Gideon had little to ask except whether he had seemed drunk that morning; he pressed Bray successfully to say no. (Actually, under Florida law intoxication would have been a defense to this crime; Gideon evidently did not know that, but a lawyer would have.) The prosecutor, on cross-examination, brought out that Bray had known Gideon for some time and asked whether Gideon was unemployed. Bray answered: "I know he was working at the poolroom—now, whether he was getting paid or not, I don't know." That was significant, because Gideon could conceivably have had an excuse for being in the poolroom after closing if he was an employee, but the subject was never explored further.

A Mrs. Irene Rhodes testified that she had been on the front porch of her house, down the street from the poolroom, on the morning of the crime. Gideon asked next whether she had bought him a drink in the poolroom the

night before. "I probably did, if you needed one," Mrs.
Rhodes said, and their relationship was left at that. Gideon
brought out that she had seen him come out of the alley at
the rear of the pool hall that morning—hardly a point for
the defense—but Mrs. Rhodes agreed with him that that
was not unusual because he lived nearby and he often
used the public telephone booth on the street. On cross-
examination Mrs. Rhodes said she had gone down to the telephone booth to ask Gideon whether the poolroom bar was
open because she knew "he helps out in there occasionally."
(Again, nothing more was made of that.) She saw a partly
full wine bottle outside the booth and brought it to her
landlord "because he was sick."

The next three witnesses were the owner of the building
in which the Bay Harbor Poolroom was located and two
poolroom employees. They added nothing. Gideon's last
witness was his landlady, Mrs. Velva Estelle Morris, the
owner of the Bay Harbor Hotel, across the street from
the poolroom. She testified that Gideon usually went out to
the public telephone when he had to make a call during the
night, to avoid disturbing others by using the hotel telephone. Then, again ignoring the possible legal benefit of intoxication, Gideon asked these questions:

Q.: Mrs. Morris, during the time I lived at the hotel did you
ever know of me being out drunk?
A.: No.
Q.: Did you ever see me drunk?
A.: No.
Q.: Did you ever hear of me getting drunk?
A.: No.

That was the case for the defense. Gideon then made a
final argument to the jury, which was not transcribed. The
court reporter noted only that he "talked to them for approximately eleven minutes, emphasizing his innocence."

The prosecutor took only nine minutes for his final argument, which was also not recorded. Then the judge charged the jury, saying in straightforward terms that it could find Gideon guilty if it determined that the crime was committed in Bay County, within the last two years, and by Gideon. (Fortas noted later that the judge had not explained any of the elements of the crime as defined by the Florida Supreme Court, such as the requisite intent to commit petit larceny after breaking and entering. Gideon had not requested such a charge by the judge, as a lawyer might have; but then he was never told that he had the right to make such a request.)

The jury found Gideon guilty. Judge McCrary delayed the sentencing for three weeks, in order to get a report on Gideon's past history. On August 25th, without any argument by Gideon (or, of course, by a lawyer on his behalf), the judge imposed the maximum sentence of five years.

When that transcript was read at Arnold, Fortas and Porter, there was no longer any question about the appropriateness of this case as the vehicle to challenge *Betts v. Brady*. Plainly Gideon was not mentally defective. The charge against him, and the proof, were not particularly complicated. The judge had tried to be fair; at least there was no overt bias in the courtroom. In short, Gideon had not suffered from any of the special circumstances that would have entitled him to a lawyer under the limited rule of *Betts v. Brady*. And yet it was altogether clear that a lawyer would have helped. The trial had been a rudimentary one, with a prosecution case that was fragmentary at best. Gideon had not made a single objection or pressed any of the favorable lines of defense. An Arnold, Fortas and Porter associate said later: "We knew as soon as we read that transcript that here was a perfect case to challenge the assumption of *Betts* that a man could have a fair trial without a lawyer. He did very well for a layman, he acted like a lawyer. But it was a pitiful effort really. He may have committed this crime, but it was never proved by the prosecution. A lawyer—not a great lawyer, just an ordinary, competent lawyer—could have made ashes of the case."

But Abe Fortas's curiosity was not satisfied. There was still mystery about Clarence Earl Gideon, his character, his history. The trial transcript had been singularly uninformative about the human beings involved, except for a general air of shabbiness. Fortas considered going to see his client in the state prison at Raiford, Florida.

"I thought I should find out something about his background, in case a question should come up," Fortas said later. "One question, for example, was whether I should refer to the severity of the sentence—five years for breaking and entering with intent to commit a misdemeanor. He came out of this bar with a bottle of red-eye in his hand; it was a petty crime. It occurred to me that I might make some indignant statement about the severity of that sentence, but then there could be a reason I didn't know. Another thing I specifically wanted to find out was whether he was a Negro. All these things suggested that I see him. On the other hand, there was the chance of involvement, and of going improperly outside the record of this case. I decided against seeing Gideon, but as it turned out I was able to satisfy my doubts by correspondence."

The correspondence was started by Gideon. On August 1st he wrote Fortas that he had had a letter from the Clerk of the Supreme Court "informing me that you were appointed to represent me in my litigation. I have not heard from you," Gideon continued, "and I would like to find out if you are going to represent me. Because I don't know what to do." Fortas replied that he was "indeed going to represent you in the proceedings before the Supreme Court and our office is currently working on the preparation of your brief. There is nothing further for you to do," the letter said reassuringly, adding: "We will, of course, keep you posted as to the course of proceedings in the Supreme Court."

On September 11th Fortas sent Gideon a memorandum filed in the case. Gideon replied on September 16th, expressing his thanks and continuing: "Everthing containing to my case is of the highest interest to me and everone in the prison. And we will certainly welcome all the information about it that is possible. I wish that it was possible to tell you the truth about my case, which I am sure that the record does not show. I did not have the ability to cross-examine the witness nor did I have anyone to investigate things before my trial, so my trial is far from the truth."

A letter from Gideon on October 29th said: "I guess I am impation but it seems to take a long time, but I understand that something like this does. If there is any information that I might be able to give you that will help the case I will give it." Perhaps that suggested an opening to Fortas. On October 31st he replied:

Dear Mr. Gideon:

I acknowledge receipt of your letter of October 29. I can understand your impatience, but I am glad that you realize that a review by the Supreme Court of the United States takes a good deal of time. . . .

As you probably know, the review must be based upon the record in your case. I see no difficulty with the transcript of record because your case will undoubtedly be decided on the very fundamental point as to whether the State of Florida was obliged to furnish you with counsel.

However, as a matter of my own interest, I should be very glad to receive from you a careful and detailed biographical description: when and where you were born, education, employment, family, arrests, and any other information that may come to your mind. I want to emphasize that this is not at all necessary, and that it will serve only to give me a little background. I know that you will be extremely careful to be absolutely accurate in any information that you send along to me. . . .

Sincerely,
Abe Fortas

On November 13th there arrived in Fortas's office a twenty-two-page letter from Gideon, once again printed in pencil on the lined prison forms. It read, in its entirety, as follows.

Mr. Abe Fortas, Esquire
1229 Nineteenth St. N.W.
Washington, D.C.

Dear Sir:

In answer to your letter of October 31. I will try to give you a detailed biographical description of my life. You will understand that due to my limited education and also to the utter folly and hopelessness [of] parts of my life, it will be doubthful if I can put it down on paper with any reasonable comprehension. I will not be proud of this biography, it will be no cause of pride; nor will it be the absolute truth. I can not remember or desire to remember that well. You have emphasize that this is not at all necessary, that you only want it for background. I believe that the state will attempt to use my personal record in their arguments to the Supreme Court and for that reason you can be prepared. Also being only a human being I will try though I know I can not, to justify myself through this outline.

I was born August 30th, 1910 in Hannibal Missouri. My parents where Charles Roscoe Gideon and Virginia Gregory Gideon. My father died a few days after I was three years old. Mother remarried when I was five years old. My stepfather's name was Marion Frances Anderson he died in 1955. Mother is still living. From this union I have a halve sister Mrs. Roy E. Ogden forty-five years old R.F.D #1, Hannibal Mo. A halve brother Sgt. Russell Lee Anderson, U.S.A.F. Mother resides at 2121 Chestnut Street Hannibal Mo. My brother is thirty-two years of age.

My early membery is of my mother's marriage and my step-father. My step-father was a good man all though he was uneducated and worked the largest part of his life in shoe factory. also my mother. We where a family of factory workers class. But allways own their own home, which my mother had first bought with my father's insurance. I went to the public school at Hannibal, Mo. I never had any trouble and made my grades up to the eight grade.

My step-father never could accept me or I could not accept him. My mother was very strict and my life as a child was of the strict discipline. My parents lived by the best moral customs and where members of the Calavary Baptist church Hannibal Mo. which I join when I was about thirteen years of age. My mother still to this day has done nothing that could be class as wrong. Also my sister and brother are of the best kind of character.

I suppose, I am what is called individualist a person who will not conform. Anyway my parents where always quarreling and I would be the scapegoat of those quarrels. My life was miserable. I was never allow to do the things of a ordinory boy.

At the age of fourteen year, I ran away from home, I accepted the life of a hobo and tramp in preference to my home. In a month or so I made it to California. At this time I begin to learn the facts of life. How good people can be and how bad they can be I wandered around over the west for all most a year and came back to Missouri. When to my mother's brother and started living with him until my mother found out where I was at and she came and got me. Had me place in the jail at Hannibal which I excaped from the next day and went back to the country to hide out at this time it was extremely cold weather and a short time later I burglarist a country store for some clothes which I was caught the next day by the store owner with all the clothes on. I was tried in juvnile court in Ralls County Missouri. My mother ask the court to send me to the reformatory which they did for a term of three years. Off all the prisons I have been in that was the worst I still have scar on my body from the whippings I recieved there anyway I was paroled after a year. I was then sixteen years old. Paroles did not mean much in those days. I went to work in the shoe factory at two dollars a day. But was soon put on a piece work job where I made about twenty-five dollars a week I soon married a girl my own age and started a home of my own we done very well together for better than a year until I got without a job and I comitted some crimes in 1928. I was caught and thru a court appointed attorney was sentenced to the Missouri Prison for ten years for robbery with three sentences of Burglary and larcney running concurantly. I was eighteen years of age at this time and prisons where bad in those days. This prison had about five thousand inmates at that time and at the end of three years and four months I was paroled as I said before paroles did not mean much then.

When I was released, around the sixth of January 1932. I was twenty-two years old. This was in the middle of the depression years and jobs just could not be found even for experence labor and trades. I know nothing but shoe factory which I worked at in prison. I lived by my wits and only had one job in a shoe factory up to sometime in later part of 1934. When I was arrested for stealing goverment property to wit a armory. I was tried in Federal Court and on a plea of guilty was sentenced to Ft. Leavenworth Kansas prison for a term of three years with a concurant sentence of three years for conspiracy. I worked in shoe factory again. During this time I saved a little money that I was paid by the prison my parents had lost their home during the depersion. So I sent them my money to make a down payment on another place. I done a little over two years and was released on contional release January 1937. There still where not any jobs all though the goverment was helping the people by this time I was not entitled to any of this because by this time I am a outcast.

During the years of 1937 thru 1940 I done the same as always was arrested in Pike County Mo. some time in Later part of 1939 and escaped from jail was arrested about a year later in Adrain County Mo. for the crime of Burglary and Larcney was tried under the second affender law by a jury and was found guilty, sentenced to state Prison for a term of ten years for Burglary and five years for Larcney to run concurantly admitted to Prison December 31st 1940 escaped from Prison in September of 1943. I falsified a personal record and draft card, went to work in train service as a brakeman. Southern Pacific Railroad in Houston Texas. Work there during the war. Until October of 1944. When I was caught thru the wanted list of the True Detective Magazine, taken back to Mo. state and stayed there until January of 1950 when I was released. Went back to Texas and started gambling was married to Virgil Hoff in 1950 seperated in 1951. Was arrested in Orange County Texas in July of 1951 and on a plea of guilty was sentenced to the State Prison for a term of two years in about thirteen months I was released. Went back to Orange Texas to live. Worked as a cook on tug boat out of Orange Texas and gambled. Taken sick and broke down with Tuberculosis of my right lung in april of 1953. Was hospitalized in the Marine Hospital, U.S. Public Health Service at New Orleans and recieved medical treatment for about eighteen months in october of 1954 received surgery of a section of the upper lobe of my right lung. Left the Hospital for Christmas of 1954. Went back to my mother's at Hannibal

Mo for a visit on New years day of 1955, married Mrs.
Velma Cooper of Hannibal. We went back to Orange
Texas to live. At this time I had quite a lot of money and I
bought a the Orange Domino Club there a Pool hall, domino'es and beer palor. about six months later I left my wife
and sued her for divorce which was granted thirty days
later. In October, 1955, I married my present wife, Ruth
ada Babineaux. Ruth worked for me at this time and I seen
her beat down in a Court Room at Orange for the custody
of her two boys Ralph Babineaux who is now thirteen
years old and Joe Babineaux who is now twelve years old
they where taken by thier father Sofastand Babineaux of
Lake Charles La. Ruth had a daughter Donna Marie who
remained in her custody Donna is now seven years old.
Later I married her and taken Donna out of a Foster Home
I remember it cost me eighty dollars, and a short time after
our marriage I taken back the two boys. In July of 1956 my
first boy was born Ronald Earl Gideon who is now six
years old. At this time I sold the Domino Club for two
thousand dollars to Mr. Roy H. Stokes who now lives at
501 Duval street, Tallahassee Florida. I went back to working tug boats and gambling. On December 31st 1957 my
second boy was born David Wayne Gideon who is now
almost five years old. I started another place of business in
Orange some time in 1957 which was never very successful
I worked most of the time then as a gaurd or watchman for
the Orange protective association. I decided to leave Orange
because my personal record was holding me down so I
came to Panama City, Florida. I went to work as a Auto
Electric mechanic and a month later my wife sold out the
place in Orange Texas which was named Smitty's Bar. The
same being my nick name which I recieved from my Alias
name when I worked on the railroad of Barney Adrian
Smith. She brought the children and came to Panama City
at this time we had five children. I found that the standard

of living and wages in Panama City was much lower than those of Texas and I just barely could get by so I started gambling again. I run afoul of a poker game which was run by Mr. J.C. Tyndall of Springfield Fla. which is ajoining Panama City but has it's own municipality. I believe that the only organize crime in this state is in this form. Which consist of a mayor who is also Judge about three commissioners a chief of Police and a night policeman Anyway J.C. Tyndal had been a commissioner but was not at this time. He was running this Poker game close by my house and I am known as a mechanic in playing cards. I beat this game serval times the last time for about one hundred and fifty dollars. This game was protected by the chief of Police a man by the name of Charlie Kitteral. I was arrested by him and charge with Breaking and Entering to comitt a misdemeanor. This was July of 1959 I was placed in County Jail never given a hearing nor preliminary Trial and on 16th of September I went to trial without counsel, the Court refused to give me counsel. There was only one witness ever to take the stand that was J.C. Tyndal the Trial Judge the late Clay E. Lewis stop the trial and give me a direct virdict of not guilty, with the District attorney asking the court to hold me so he might file further charges. The judge allowed him three days after five days I was released after filing a petition for a writ of Habeas Corpus. J.C. Tyndall a few months later was arrested and convicted of transporting whiskey was sentenced to two years by Federal court to U.S. Prison Tallahassee Florida.

My youngest child and daughter was born April 30th 1959. So this left my wife with six children. During the time I am in jail my wife went to work in a Beer joint in order to feed the children because we where not entitled to welfare. Please bare in mind that this part of the Country is in what is known as the Bible Belt, practically everone is a good Christian, there is lot of churches. During my time in jail

the welfare Dept. decided that my children where not being taken care of proper which they where not. They taken
the children and placed them in Foster Homes My wife
broke over this and started to drink and I don't think she
ever got over it.

When I was released from jail I went back to work that
day as a Auto Electric Mechanic on commission basis I
hunted up my wife and went to the welfare and got my
children. But my wife was to far gone to straiten out and
I could get no help from the social workers Once hearing a
wise old Doctor say that the best thing for a poor person
who did not have the money to hire psychiatry, the best
thing is to send them to church. So I decided to use the
church. I do not like the idea of forcing my children are
enticing them to believe in any certain religion but I have
always wanted them to learn the moral respect that the people of this country has and of all the great religions I have
pick the christian religion because it is based on love. So
in my desperation I pick a Baptist church because that had
been my church when I was a little boy Now I class that
organization in the same class as I do the K.K.K. Because
they hate to many persons and things anyway for the want
of something better I took this way

I started ever Sunday morning of dressing the children
and myself up and going to the Cedar Grove Baptist church
at Cedar Grove Florida another one of those little municipality I mention before I believe it is listed as one of the
worst speed traps not to even be on a major highway by the
A.A.A. The people of the church accepted my children
with all thier heart but me they just tolerated cause they
where mind. My strategy worked my wife decided to go to
church with us so I bought her some new clothes and she
took a big interest in everthing

About this time I took down sick with a terriable pain in
my chest having no money I went to the county clinic for

a X ray and later went to the Welfare the family service of Panama City. They would not help but sent me to the hospital and the Doctor on duty Doctor Webb sent me back to the County Clinic for Sputum Test. At this time the family service paid my rent. The first sputum test that went to the hospital at Tallahassee, Fla. The W.T. Edwards Hospital. Came back positive. The County Nurse was there next day asking me to sign papers to go to the Hospital at Tallahassee which I did. I did not work no more nor did I go to church any more. The welfare or rather the family service gave us ten dollars a week then and until I went to the Hospital which was December 31st 1959.

My wife's interest in the church had matured to the point that when I went to Hospital the church was practicable taking care of my family. But did you ever try to take care of six children on a bill for ten dollars in groceries.

I sent my wife to the Dept. of Public welfare and they said they would investigate which after a time a month or two they said they could not pay my family the American Child Support which in this state is only eighty-one dollars a month they rejected it on account of my record of course my wife's too. Now most of this money comes to the states to be administerated by them, but there is restrictions on not giving it to needy children. I don't know for sure but I can find out and I will. That most of the dollar that comes to this state goes to the cost of administeration and not to needy children.

In the meantime the church is helping to take care of the children and after three months of examinations the staff of Doctors diagnosed my trouble as A-typical tuberculosis. That there was a infection in my lung and I would have to have surgery. Remember, I had surgery before and I hated to take it again but I sign for it.

I am treated the best of kind in this Hospital any thing I want chicken ever day. Can you imagine how I felt ever time I ate my meals of steak and chicken when I would think of my children hoping they had anything at all.

After more examinations I was put to surgery by a master Doctor but I still hardly made it after about two months I begin to get better my wife had quit writing to me and I heard thru different sources that she had quit the church and started back to drinking. I left the hospital and went home and the stories I had heard where true my wife was working in a jute joint and the children where taking care of thier self my wife was living with another man and after the fight and everthing. They had me arrested. But failed to press charges against me so the County hung a drunk charge on me rather than stay in jail I had a friend pay my fine and I went back to Hospital which I left before very long against medical advise. I went to Baton Rouge La. where I had friends and went to work. I sent my wife twenty dollars a week for the children (at this time I was a very unhappy man and I had been hook on drugs during my surgery and recovery which I know now affected me than.) After about a month and a halve I recieved one of my money orders back. I was cooking on a spud barge and we where down in the swamps at Golden Meadows La. then. I called the officer of the Juvnile Court in Panama City and ask him about my children. He told me that the Court had the children but he did not know about my wife. So I made arraingments to go to Panama City the next day.

I went to the Public Welfare and learnt that my wife had given up the children to them and had gotton herself arrested for drunken driving at Blountstown Fla and had been in jail for about thirty days but was out then. also she had recieved three of my money orders and spend them I recovered three which I give to the Welfare Dept. I went and vist the children and contacted my wife so I left her alone

I made a deal with the welfare Dept to pay them one

hundred and eighty dollars a month or forty-five a week I went back to La. and went to work I worked another month and halve and was let go on account of the health Dept. because I left the hospital against medical advice they had turn me in to the La. Health Dept. I came back to Panama City and attempted to make a living by gambling. About then I found out my wife was pregnant. sometime in January I was with a Friend of my Sgt. H. Stickell on Tyndall Air Force Base I had been living at his home for about a month we where building a club for squad service there, when out of the blue sky I was arrested one day he was with me by the F.B.I. office, shrieffs office and the City Detectives of Panama City also they serched St. Stickells home. I was not locked up. There had been a Burglary of the Armory in Panama city. So for no reason except that twenty-five years before I had rob one

I was still sick and could not make any money. My wife had her baby thru one of those professional dealers in little children. also thru the Public Welfare of Panama City, it seems to me that they approve of a woman doing that away, any way they all wanted me to sign the adoption papers for the baby which I did, I was not very happy about the whole thing.

By this time I realized that I would never be able to live with my wife and make a home for my children and I started to make arraignment to have my sister and mother take my children and to get a divorce from my wife.

a short time later I was arrested one night in my bed at the Hotel I lived in, for no reason atall, for investigation and vagrancy. Investigation of a two thousand dollar robbery of the Bay Harbor Bar which was across the street from where I lived. After two weeks in jail they put a charge of vagrancy against me a set bond at two hundred dollars in four more days I was arraigned in County Court and plead not guilty and was turn lose. The Public Welfare seem surprised.

About a month later on June 3rd 1961 I was arrested for the crime I am now doing time on. I was charged with Breaking & Entering to comitt a misdemeanor and was convicted in a trial August 4th 1961 sentenced to State Prison August 27th 1961.

This charge growed out of gambling and was very near simalar to the charge I was tried on before in Panama City I worked in this place and did run a Poker game there. About a month before the Shrieff had been suspended by the Governor Mr. (Doc) Daffin. In the last election he was elected back to the office and will be back in for a four year term begining the first of the year.

I did not break into this building nor did I have to I had the keys to the building and if the building was broke into it was done by one of the parties involed. A short time before Ira Strictland and I had a falling out over a Poker Game he was suppose to fix with the Sheriff in Washington County there is a dog racing tract at Eboe a short ways from Panama City and his sister has a sort of motel there. He failed to do it and with the investagation going on in Panama City. I closed the game there which was not making any money. The State witness Cook who was supposed to identify me. Had a bad police record and the Court would not let me bring that out. Nor that one time I had at the point of a pistal made him stop beating a girl

I always believed that the primarily reason of trial in a court of law was to reach the truth. My trial was far from the truth. One day when I was being arraigned I seen two trials of two different men tried without attorneys. One hour from the time they started they had two juries out and fifteen minutes later they were found guilty and sentenced. Is this a fair trial? This is common praticed thru most of this state. This penitentiary is full of men who are here with five years for Petty Larcney, drunk and minor sex crimes. Of course this is the Bible Belt and the customs here are a lot higher degree of morals. I am a electrician here and one of my fellow workers has two years for drunk and resisting arrest. Most city Police courts would give a citizen a twenty-five dollar fine for the same charge he was tried without a attorney and convicted. This week he is filing a petition to the U.S. Supreme Court for a writ of Certiorari to review a writ of Habeas Corpus. This state still runs there courts on the principal of the common law. And there are actual cases here now of citizens who have sentence with no statues covering the charges. The Supreme Court at Florida handed down a ruling last month involing the rights of man to have charges put against him within a resonable time. This man was held for about three weeks befor being charge. They upheld the lower courts one Justice disenting. They said that it was right that that was the law, but this is different. What it amounted to anyway. The one Justices said "That these laws where not made in Jest." The desenting vote.

There was not a crime comitted in my case and I don't feel like I had a fair trial. If I had a attorney he could brought out all of these things in my trial.

When I was arrested I was put in solitary confinment and I was not allowed the papers not to use the telephone or to write to everone I should. I did get a speedy arraignment and preliminary trial at my arraignment in Circuit Court I was allow more time to try and obtain a attorney which I could not do. You know about the rest of my trial.

I have had no trouble since I have been here. I have work as a electrician ever since I have been here and for the last year I recieved sixty days extra gain time. This prison is all right as for prison. Proable the best in the South Outside of proper medical care I have a lung contion but have never been able to see a doctor, But that is the way prisons are the Doctors are never the best any way. I think I should be receiving medication for my lungs I was when I came in here.

My sister and mother refused to take my children and I have never written to them since I have been here I did write to the Welfare Dept. in Panama City about my children. They thru the Juvnile Court in Panama City did try to do me in for the Custody of the children last may. I recieved a summons by regestered mail to appear in court at the court house Panama City at two-thirty June 4th 1962 or be held in contempt of court. (This is the way these courts operate). I had a complaint from a Ralph V. Barnett out of Pensacola Florida. who I later found out is a professional dealer in children and was the same one who bought my wifes baby I told you about before. He wanted the custody of my three children and my step daughter so he could put them up for adoption. They did not send me a copy of the complaint. I sent in a petition for a injunction against this charging ever thing I could think of. Bill of attainer, due process of law, and slavery. I did not know his address so I sent his copy to the State Attorney General. If you would like to have a copy I will send you one. The court gave me a stay until what ever time it takes the Supreme Court to review my case.

The Welfare Dept. wrote and ask me to sign release papers on my children. I refused, now they will not write me at all

I do not intend to let anyone take my children away from me and I will fight it ever way I know how. I hope to be able to get my children into a home someplace somehow, until I am able to take care of them myself. I believe all though I am a convict and exconvict that I have the rights to have children the same as any one else, also I have the rights to A.D.C. [aid to dependent children] and vocational

training under the social security laws the same as any one
else.

Outside of numerous times of arrest some for investagation, others for compromised convictions, all of the fore-
going statements have been true and can stand the any
kind of investegation. I am not proud of this biography. I
hope that it may help you in preparing this case, I am sorry
I could not write better I have done the best I could.

I have no illusions about law and courts or the people
who are involved in them. I have read the complete history
of law ever since the Romans first started writing them
down and before of the laws of religions. I believe that each
era finds a improvement in law each year brings something
new for the benefit of mankind. Maybe this will be one of
those small steps forward, in the past thirty-five years I have
seen great advancement in Courts in penal servitude. Thank
you for reading all of this. Please try to believe that all I
want now from life is the chance for the love of my children the only real love I have ever had.

Sincerely yours
Clarence Earl Gideon

6

“The question is very simple. I requested the court to appoint me attorney and the court refused.” So Gideon had written to the Supreme Court in support of his claim that the Constitution entitled the poor man charged with crime to have a lawyer at his side. Most Americans would probably have agreed with him. To even the best-informed person unfamiliar with the law it seemed inconceivable, in the year 1962, that the Constitution would allow a man to be tried without a lawyer because he could not afford one.

But the question was really as far from simple as it could imaginably be. Behind it there was a long history—a history that until recently had seemed resolutely opposed to Gideon's claim but now had started to turn and move in his direction. The question that Gideon presented could not be resolved without reference to issues that had been fought over by judges and statesmen and political philosophers—issues going to the nature of our constitutional system and to the role played in it by the Supreme Court.

We have come to take it for granted in this country that courts, especially the Supreme Court, have the power to review the actions of governors, legislators, even Presidents, and set them aside as unconstitutional. But this power of judicial review, as it is called, has been given to judges in few other countries—and nowhere, at any time, to the extent that our history has confided it in the Supreme Court. In the guise of legal questions there come to the Supreme Court many of the most fundamental and divisive issues of every era, issues which judges in other lands would never dream of having to decide.

The consequences are great for Court and country. For the justices power means responsibility, a responsibility the more weighty because the Supreme Court so often has the last word. Deciding cases is never easy, but a judge may sleep more soundly after sentencing a man to death—or invalidating a President's seizure of the nation's steel mills—if he knows there is an appeal to a higher court. Justices of the Supreme Court do not have that luxury.

"We are not final because we are infallible," Justice Jackson wrote, "but we are infallible only because we are final." Men who know their own fallibility may find it hard to bear the burden of final decision. A few months before the Supreme Court agreed to hear Gideon's case, Justice Charles Evans Whittaker retired after only five years on the Court, explaining candidly that he found the strain of its work too great. He told friends that when he wrote an opinion, he felt as if he were carving his words into granite.

Other men may not be bothered by judicial power, may

indeed revel in it. But the existence of power so great inevitably raises questions. Is it consistent with democracy to let nine men, appointed for life and directly answerable to no constituency, make ultimate decisions about the direction of our society? How free should a judge feel to set above the will of the people's elected representatives the principles that he finds in the Constitution? How does he find them, given the Constitution's vague words and the conflicting interpretations of them by judges of the past?

The very legitimacy of judicial review has been questioned repeatedly from the time the Supreme Court first held a federal statute unconstitutional, in *Marbury v. Madison* in 1803. The Jeffersonians accused John Marshall of usurpation. Liberals said the same of the Court in the 1930's, and revisionist historians of that day tried to prove that it really had not been given the power of judicial review. Today the epithets come from extremists of the right, disaffected by the Court's decisions on individual liberty and racial equality.

Scholarly opinion has long since dismissed the charge that judicial review was illicitly imported into our system by John Marshall or anyone else. The Constitution does not explicitly provide for its enforcement by the federal courts, but the text—including the grant of jurisdiction over cases arising under the Constitution—indicates that expectation. The records of the Philadelphia Convention of 1787 point the same way; at least a substantial number of the delegates assumed that the Supreme Court would pass on the constitutionality of state and federal acts that came before it in lawsuits. The delegates, in fact, considered a proposal to go further and have the Court share the President's veto power in a Council of Revision, but that suggestion was rejected on the ground that the Court already had a "sufficient check" by its power to declare laws unconstitutional. The very conception of a written constitution binding on governments as

well as citizens, the great American contribution to political
history, presupposed some institution to enforce the rules.
Theoretically that could have been Congress, but the epi-
sodic and political nature of the legislative process would
have made that choice doubtful. In fact we have lived for
one hundred and seventy-five years with the Supreme Court
as the final interpreter of our fundamental law, and our
whole system of government is now built on that assumption. Justice Jackson, no starry-eyed admirer of judicial review, wrote in 1954: "The real strength of the position of
the Court is probably in its indispensability to government
under a written Constitution. It is difficult to see how the
provisions of a one-hundred-and-fifty-year-old written document can have much vitality if there is not some permanent
institution to translate them into current commands. . . ."

But if the issue of legitimacy is foreclosed, there remain
very live questions of when and how the Supreme Court
should exercise its great power to nullify what other
branches of government have done. These questions have
been the subject of a fierce and unending debate among
commentators and among the justices themselves. The opposing positions can best be summarized in terms of the two
uncommonly able and determined justices who led the debate for a generation, Felix Frankfurter and Hugo L. Black.

Justice Frankfurter's motto was "judicial self-restraint."
He counseled judges to defer to Congress and the states,
even where their actions seemed unwise; to be cautious in
reading prohibitions into the Constitution; to respect history; to balance against the interest of the individual the interest of society. Justice Frankfurter warned that relying
too much on judges to protect our freedoms sapped the
strength of democracy by distracting attention from the political forum where unwise policies should be corrected. He
felt the Court was often less equipped to deal with a problem
than expert administrators or politicians closer to the public

will. He was motivated also by a deep concern for the Supreme Court as an institution, a fear that it might destroy itself if it pressed its power too far. He and others remembered the 1930's, when a self-willed Court tried to stand against history by stopping urgent economic and social measures and thus brought itself to the brink of drastic reform—reform which it avoided only by a political change of course. Not that Justice Frankfurter never found state or federal action unconstitutional. His vote to invalidate school segregation, his concern for the freedom of commerce from state barriers, and his careful scrutiny of police behavior and of state assistance to religion all testify to his acceptance of the Court's role as enforcer of the Constitution. But right up to his retirement in 1962 his opinions preached judicial caution, self-examination and restraint. Since then his restraining role has been carried on by others, especially his friend Justice John Marshall Harlan, who in a notable speech in 1963 criticized what he called the "cosmic" view of the judicial function—the idea "that all deficiencies in our society which have failed of correction by other means should find a cure in the courts."

Justice Black, by contrast, has emphasized the duty of judges to preserve individual liberty, and has argued that excessive deference to other branches of government amounts to abdication of that responsibility. In the Black view, the framers of the Constitution made the decision to protect individuals from governmental repression, so a judge should not feel timid or self-conscious about doing so. Particularly obnoxious to Justice Black is the Frankfurter thesis that the Court must balance individual interests against the needs of government and uphold any reasonable governmental course of action. Justice Black argues that this weighing and balancing of what is reasonable leaves judges too much at large. He looks to history and finds definite rules in the Constitution—"absolutes," as he has called them. His favorite example is the First Amendment: "Congress shall make no law respecting an establishment of religion, or prohibiting the free exercise thereof; or abridging the freedom of speech, or of the press. . . ." To Justice Black, as he has put it, "no law means *no law*." Thus he has gone much farther in finding violations of the First Amendment than almost any other justice, past or present. He has argued, in dissent, that no government has the power to censor obscenity. And he has repeatedly dissented from decisions upholding federal action against the Communist party and its members, decisions in which the majority found the injury to free speech outbalanced by the need of society to protect itself against an international conspiracy.

Sometimes the debate between Justices Black and Frankfurter, or between the schools of thought they represent, has seemed abstract—more words than real ideas. No one, not even a Supreme Court justice, is always perfectly logical in applying his own theories, so it is dangerous to build too many expectations on stated judicial philosophies. Justice Frankfurter, for example, was willing when Justice Black was not to strike down wiretapping as unconstitutional and to forbid the use of state funds for parochial-school buses. But for purposes of the Gideon case the general difference in the Black and Frankfurter approaches was a relevant, inescapable consideration.

As Abe Fortas began to think about the case in the summer of 1962, before Justice Frankfurter's retirement, it was clear to him that overruling *Betts v. Brady* would not come easily to Justice Frankfurter or others of his view. This was true not only because of their judicial philosophy in general, but because of the way they had applied it on specific matters. One of these was the question of precedent.

"In most matters it is more important that the applicable rule of law be settled than that it be settled right." Justice Brandeis thus succinctly stated the basic reason for *stare de-*

cisis, the judicial doctrine of following precedents. In literal translation the Latin words mean "to stand by what has been decided." Anglo-American law is built on the expectation that courts generally will follow what they have said in the past; on that assumption contracts are signed, wills made, lives planned. But *stare decisis* is not an iron rule in the courts of this country, as it is in England. Justice Brandeis went on:

"But in cases involving the Federal Constitution, where correction through legislative action is practically impossible, this Court has often overruled its earlier decisions. The Court bows to the lessons of experience and the force of better reasoning."

While constitutional cases do present the special considerations mentioned by Brandeis, the Court has not in fact restricted to that area its willingness to re-examine past decisions. More than almost any court it looks beneath precedents for the policy they represent. It might be said to be minding the caustic words of Justice Holmes: "It is revolting to have no better reason for a rule of law than that so it was laid down in the time of Henry IV. It is still more revolting if the grounds upon which it was laid down have vanished long since, and the rule simply persists from blind imitation of the past."

Approximately one hundred times in its history the Supreme Court has overruled a prior decision. That is often enough, but overruling has not by any means become a routine step, to be taken casually. Certainty and repose in the law still have their appeal. Changes of mind on the part of the Court have been met by strong dissent—by, among others, Justice Frankfurter.

Justice Frankfurter joined in the most famous of recent overruling cases, the School Segregation decision of 1954, which abandoned the separate-but-equal doctrine laid down in 1896. He was not, therefore, unyieldingly attached to the

doctrine of *stare decisis*. But his instinct was to give great
weight to the demands of continuity with the past in the
law. A 1958 law-review study showed that Justice Frankfurter had dissented thirteen times from decisions overruling
prior cases. Abe Fortas would have to produce compelling
reasons to overcome the respect for precedent felt by Justice
Frankfurter and others sharing his view. Justice Black, by
contrast, felt much freer to turn from past doctrine. In 1958,
for example, he unhesitatingly urged the Court—in dissent
—to abandon one hundred and fifty years of decisions holding that jury trials were not required in prosecutions for contempt of court. He was unlikely to feel bound by what he
considered an erroneous past interpretation of the Constitution.

Another issue between Justices Black and Frankfurter cut
even deeper than *stare decisis*, and closer to Gideon's case.
This was their attitude toward federalism—the independence of the states in our federal system of government.

The relationship of the Federal Government to the states
was a central concern of the men who wrote the Constitution. They created a remarkable political structure which
made Americans subject to two sovereignties, state and nation. To the states was reserved power over the ordinary affairs of men as they appeared in the Eighteenth Century—
birth, marriage, death, business, crime. To the Federal Government went control over interstate commerce, foreign relations, war and other matters necessarily of national scope.
By thus dividing governmental power the framers sought to
lessen the dangers of centralized authority, which they had
seen become tyranny in the hands of English kings. They also
succeeded in giving us what John Quincy Adams called "the
most complicated government on the face of the globe.

Sorting out the complications has been the job of the Supreme Court. From the beginning the Court has been faced
with lawsuits requiring it to draw the boundaries of power

between state and nation. At first the great cases tended to raise questions of the extent of the Federal Government's power. Did the Constitution authorize Congress to charter a bank? That was the question Marshall decided in 1819, in *McCulloch v. Maryland*, and his answer in favor of the Federal Government permanently enlarged its domain.

In the Twentieth Century events have transformed the federal-state issues that come before the Court. The growth of a national economy and the emergence of the United States as a world power have inevitably made us more a nation, and have necessarily increased federal authority. The Supreme Court tried for a time to stand against that current, holding in New Deal days that Congress had no power under the Constitution to deal with the economic crisis in the country's coal mines or farms, but in 1937 it gave up that attempt.

The main arena of controversy today is not the extent of Congressional power but the limitations placed by the Constitution on state governmental action. State officials use the phrase "states' rights." By that they mean the right to handle such matters as race relations and the criminal law as they wish, without restraint by the Federal Constitution. The imposing of restraints on state action has evoked great resentment on the part of many state officials, judges not least. In 1958 the Conference of (State) Chief Justices approved a committee report excoriating the Supreme Court for what was termed an "overall tendency" to "press the extension of federal power and press it rapidly." The report did not deal with the issue of racial segregation, although many thought that was its real inspiration. It put major critical emphasis on Supreme Court decisions laying down minimal guarantees of fairness in criminal proceedings.

The chief justices' report was no scholarly contribution to the debate about the role of the Supreme Court. It passed over significant areas in which the modern Court has signifi-

cantly enlarged state power, notably the power to tax and
regulate the economy. But it did indicate how much emotion
may arise over issues of federalism—and most interestingly,
in relation to Gideon's case, over the right of the states to
run their criminal law without worrying about uniform national standards. For Gideon was asking the Supreme Court
to impose on the fifty states a uniform rule of criminal procedure, the universal requirement that counsel be supplied
to poor criminal defendants. And that claim inevitably
clashed with the belief that diversity among the states was as
important a theme in the Constitution as individual rights—
a belief held by, among others, Felix Frankfurter.

"Whatever inconveniences and embarrassments may be
involved," Justice Frankfurter wrote in 1958, "they are the
price we pay for our federalism, for having our people
amenable to—as well as served and protected by—two governments." As a strong believer in the independence of the
states, Justice Frankfurter was reluctant to impose new restraints on them even in the name of individual liberty. Justice Black was always much readier to cut through the dual-
ity and enlarge protections for the individual against any
government.

The contrast in views was graphically illustrated in the
case of Alfonse Bartkus, the Illinois prisoner who had been
tried by a federal and then an Illinois jury for the same bank
robbery. Justice Frankfurter, writing for the Supreme Court
majority that upheld the second prosecution, said the result
was commanded by our system of dual sovereignties. "The
greatest self-restraint is necessary," he said in the opinion,
"when that federal system yields results with which a court
is in little sympathy." Justice Black viewed the case not as a
problem in governmental structure but as one of fairness to
Alfonse Bartkus. "The Court apparently takes the position,"
he said in dissent, "that a second trial for the same act is
somehow less offensive if one of the trials is conducted by

the Federal Government and the other by a state. Looked at from the standpoint of the individual who is being prosecuted, this notion is too subtle for me to grasp."

Underlying the Bartkus case was one of the great issues of federalism, a subject of conflict in the Supreme Court for nearly a century. This was the question of what provisions of the Constitution's Bill of Rights, if any, applied to the states. The average American would probably have thought that Bartkus's second trial, by the state of Illinois, was barred by the double-jeopardy clause of the Fifth Amendment: "nor shall any person be subject for the same offence to be twice put in jeopardy of life or limb." But that clause had been held to cover only *federal*, not state, criminal proceedings.

The Bill of Rights is the name collectively given to the first ten amendments to the Constitution, all proposed by the First Congress of the United States in 1789 and ratified in 1791. The first eight contain the guarantees of individual liberty with which we are so familiar: freedom of speech, press, religion and assembly; protection for the privacy of the home; assurance against double jeopardy and compulsory self-incrimination; the right to counsel and to trial by jury; freedom from cruel and unusual punishments. At the time of their adoption it was universally agreed that these eight amendments limited only the Federal Government and its processes. Fear of the new central government had been the reason for their adoption, some states even refusing to ratify the Constitution until assured that the Federal Government would be restrained by a Bill of Rights.

James Madison, who as a member of the House was a principal draftsman of the amendments, actually included one to guarantee individual rights against the states. It read: "No State shall infringe the right of trial by Jury in criminal cases, nor the rights of conscience, nor the freedom of speech, or of the press." Madison thought it "the most valuable amendment in the whole list," seeing more danger of abuse "by the State Governments than by the Government of the United States." But the Senate rejected his proposal, and the original Bill of Rights limited only federal action. In 1833, in the case of *Barron v. Baltimore*, Chief Justice Marshall wrote the common understanding into law with a specific decision that the Bill of Rights did not cover the states.

There matters stood until the Fourteenth Amendment became part of the Constitution in 1868. A product of the Civil War, it was specifically designed to prevent abuse of individuals by state governments. Section 1 provided: "No State shall make or enforce any law which shall abridge the privileges or immunities of citizens of the United States; nor shall any State deprive any person of life, liberty, or property, without due process of law; nor deny to any person within its jurisdiction the equal protection of the laws." Soon the claim was advanced that this section had been designed by its framers to *incorporate*, and apply to the states, all the provisions of the first eight amendments.

This theory of wholesale incorporation of the Bill of Rights has been adopted by one or more Supreme Court justices from time to time, but never a majority. The climactic battle came in 1947, in *Adamson v. California*, when four justices read the Fourteenth Amendment as including the entire Bill of Rights—Justices Black, Douglas, Frank Murphy and Wiley B. Rutledge. That five-to-four defeat was the high-water mark of the contention that the first eight amendments were incorporated in toto in the Fourteenth.

But if wholesale incorporation has been rejected, the Supreme Court has used the Fourteenth Amendment to apply provisions of the Bill of Rights to the states *selectively*. The vehicle has been the clause assuring individuals due process of law. The Court has said that state denial of any right deemed "fundamental" by society amounts to a denial of due process and hence violates the Fourteenth Amendment.

For example, freedom of speech is protected by the First Amendment against abridgement by Congress. If a state abridges free speech, the Court regards that freedom as so central to human liberty that it finds a violation of the Fourteenth Amendment's due-process guarantee.

The historical process by which provisions of the original Bill of Rights have thus been applied to state as well as federal action was described by Justice Benjamin N. Cardozo as a "process of absorption" of those rights "implicit in the concept of ordered liberty." It is an ironic note that Justice Black, who had just come on the Court, joined the 1937 Cardozo opinion advancing that formula. As his own philosophy developed, he rejected the "absorption" idea, feeling that it left judges too much at large, and found greater certainty in the thesis of wholesale incorporation. But "absorption" has been and remains the accepted process.

The difficult question has been which provisions of the first eight amendments to absorb. At first the Court was most reluctant to read any into the due-process clause of the Fourteenth. By the year 1900 the justices had refused to apply virtually every guarantee in the Bill of Rights to the states. As late as 1922 the Court said that the protections of the First Amendment—of free speech, press, religion and assembly—did not apply to the states. "But it is one thing to slam the door of the due-process clause and another to keep it shut," Professor Paul A. Freund has written. In 1925 the Court changed its mind and said free speech was so fundamental that a state could not deny it without denying due process of law and violating the Fourteenth Amendment. The other freedoms of the First Amendment followed.

The Court has been much more reluctant to apply to the states the guarantees of fair criminal procedure in the first eight amendments. It evidently felt, over many decades, that the one area in which the states were most clearly entitled to independence was in the application of their criminal law.

Nothing could seem more obvious to us today than that to convict a man in an unfair criminal trial is to deprive him of life, liberty or property without due process of law. Yet it was not until 1923 that the Court specifically said unfair methods in a criminal trial were forbidden by the Fourteenth Amendment. That was an extreme case—five Arkansas Negroes condemned to death after a mob-dominated trial and on testimony said to have been extorted by brutality. Justice Holmes suggested that the entire proceeding was "a mask," with "counsel, jury and judge . . . swept to the fatal end by an irresistible wave of public passion." The decision was only to let the prisoners come into federal court and try to prove their charges of unconstitutional treatment, not to set aside their convictions. Even at that, Justice James C. McReynolds dissented, saying: "The fact that petitioners are poor and ignorant and black naturally arouses sympathy; but that does not release us from enforcing principles which are essential to the orderly operation of our federal system." (The five prisoners eventually had their sentences commuted by state authorities without final legal action.)

Over the years the Supreme Court steadfastly resisted all efforts to apply to the states the specific criminal-law guarantees of the Bill of Rights, such as the Sixth Amendment's provision for trial by jury and assistance of counsel and the Fifth Amendment's ban on double jeopardy and self-incrimination. In 1949 the Fourth Amendment's prohibition on illegal searches and seizures was dealt with in a notable opinion by Justice Frankfurter. He deeply opposed illegal police intrusion on the home—"the knock at the door," he called it—but he could not put aside his firm belief in state independence. In this dilemma he took a curious compromise position. He held that the "core" of the Fourth Amendment was absorbed into the due-process clause of the Fourteenth. But he refused to apply to the states the essential enforcement device that had bound the federal courts since 1914, the rule that illegally seized material must be excluded from evidence at a man's trial.

History, then, showed a special reluctance on the part of the Supreme Court to impose on the states uniform national standards of fair criminal procedure. But there were signs of change in that history. Beginning in 1936, the Court had struck down state criminal convictions based on confessions coerced from the defendant. At first the third degree—physical brutality—was condemned. Over the years the Court gradually raised its standards of decency, condemning psychological as well as physical coercion of prisoners. By the 1950's it was clear that the due-process clause of the Fourteenth Amendment was a pervasive guarantee against convictions based on extorted confessions, whether or not there was external evidence to support the truthfulness of the confession. The aim was not just to rule out suspect confessions but to discourage illegal police practices. That attitude on the part of the Court signaled more vigilance toward state criminal procedure in general.

Another long step was taken in 1956, in the case of *Griffin v. Illinois*. Under the law of Illinois a person desiring to appeal his criminal conviction had to supply to the appellate court a transcript of his trial. A man too poor to buy one could not appeal. The Supreme Court held, five to four, that such a distinction between rich and poor denied the equal protection of the laws guaranteed by the Fourteenth Amendment; a state must provide a free transcript to poor prisoners, or some less elaborate trial record that would furnish a basis for appeal.

The Griffin case marked a significant increase in the Court's willingness to impose minimum standards of fairness on state criminal process. It was met by bitter criticism, from the Conference of Chief Justices among other state sources, but the trend continued.

In 1961, just a year before it granted Clarence Earl Gideon's petition for review, the Court took the step that Justice Frankfurter and a majority had been unwilling to take on illegal searches in 1949. In the case of *Mapp v. Ohio* it overruled the earlier decision and held that the Fourth Amendment was now fully applicable to the states: No illegally seized evidence could be admitted at state criminal trials. Justice Harlan, joined by Justices Frankfurter and Whittaker, dissented.

Mapp v. Ohio certainly had import for the Gideon case. A majority had been willing to overrule a recent decision, and to do so in the face of strongly pressed claims of federalism. The Court had been warned that imposing a uniform national prohibition on illegal evidence would cripple state law enforcement and empty the jails, just as it could expect to be told in the Gideon case about the baleful effects of a uniform counsel requirement.

The ruling in *Mapp*, together with the long series of coerced confession cases and the protection given the poor prisoner in *Griffin v. Illinois*, suggested a broad movement of the Supreme Court away from regard for state independence as a primary value in the constitutional law of criminal procedure. Younger justices, brought up in a United States that had become a nation, were concerned less about federalism and more about national ideals of fairness. Justice Brennan indicated the difference in attitude in a speech a few months before *Mapp v. Ohio* was decided. "Federalism should not be raised to the plane of an absolute," he said, "nor the Bill of Rights be reduced to a precatory trust. . . . Far too many cases come from the states to the Supreme Court presenting dismal pictures of official lawlessness, of illegal searches and seizures, illegal detentions attended by prolonged interrogation and coerced admissions of guilt, of the denial of counsel. . . ."

7

Clarence Earl Gideon probably knew little of the legal history that underlay his case, and nothing of the Supreme Court's great struggles over federalism, *stare decisis* and judicial review. It is doubtful that he could even have defined those phrases. (In that he would not have differed from many more elevated Americans.) But he did have an intuitive sense that his case was larger than himself, that he was part of a movement in history and would affect that movement. Or so it seemed to a stranger, interested in the case, who visited the prison at Raiford, Florida, to talk with him.

"In Betts versus Brady they was trying to allow 'em their states' rights," Gideon said. "They gave the state courts discretion, but they don't use any discretion. They just say no. They talk about states' rights. I think there's only one state —the United States."

Judging from the externals, it would be hard to imagine a figure less likely to be the subject of a great case in the Supreme Court of the United States. Gideon seems a man whose own private hopes and fears have long since been deadened by adversity—a used-up man, looking fifteen years older than his actual age of fifty-two. (He was born on August 30, 1910.) His figure is gaunt, a stooped six feet, one hundred and forty pounds. Behind light-framed glasses are worried eyes, set far back, with deep creases in the skin around them. His features are sharp, his ears prominent, his gray-white hair wavy. His lower lip trembles, and he speaks in a slow, sad, defeated voice.

It would be difficult, too, to create a setting as dejected as the locale of Gideon's alleged crime. Panama City (1960 population 33,275) is a town in the still largely undeveloped northwest panhandle of Florida. Just outside the city limits, twenty minutes from the motels and restaurants and Post Office that make "downtown," is a gigantic International Paper Company plant, its tall chimneys spewing out sulphurous smoke. Huddled near the plant fence, within sight and smell of the chemical fumes, is the community of Bay Harbor. Community is too grandiose a word for it; Bay Harbor is a bitter, decayed parody of a movie set for a frontier town. It is just a few dilapidated buildings separated by dirt roads and alleys and weed-filled empty lots: a bar, a two-story "hotel," a grocery and the Bay Harbor Poolroom. One who happened onto that dark street would be eager to drive back through the dank countryside to the highway and its neon. Gideon had no illusions about Bay Harbor; he called it "Tobacco Road."

Gideon's temporary home, the state prison at Raiford, was cheerful by comparison. At the entrance there was no doubt that it was a prison; there were steel gates and a sign saying, that day, "1986 white males 1303 colored males." (Quarters are completely segregated.) But inside, the scene was unexpectedly unforbidding, with small buildings separated by green lawns and beautifully kept shrubs and flowers. Trusties, wearing uniforms of white fatigues something like a hospital orderly's outfit, wandered around freely; during the lunch hour some sat around outdoors smoking pipes and reading.

Gideon was a trusty. He met his visitor in the prison "courtroom," a bare room with a long table used occasionally by inmates writing to courts. Gideon complained about the facilities.

"Here's the place you have to write your petition," he said, "and you don't have no help. That's what hurts you. The Supreme Court sent me a book of rules, but I still can't understand that. The rules take a pretty educated man to understand them."

He filled a cigarette paper and rolled it in his long, rather artistic fingers, stained with nicotine.

"There's no real lawyers in here now. I guess I know more than most, and I help out. I have one boy in here that can't read or write. I wrote a letter to the Supreme Court of Florida for him asking them to appoint an attorney to write him a petition for habeas corpus. They accepted that letter as a petition and denied it without a hearing, so I wrote the whole thing over and sent it to the Supreme Court of the U.S." (This prisoner was named Allen Baxley, Jr.; the Court was holding the petition until Gideon's case was decided.)

It was clear, in fact, that Gideon enjoyed his role as prison legal expert. And he had some sense of what he was about. He correctly complained, for example, about his trial judge's statement that Florida law did not *permit* appointment of counsel in a non-capital case; Florida law merely did not *re-*

quire such appointment. "That wasn't the law," Gideon said. "He had all the power in the world to appoint a lawyer if he wanted to." Gideon appreciated the quality of the letters he had had from Abe Fortas: "I notice he never makes a statement that isn't well thought out. He never writes you anything that isn't exactly that way."

The prison records concurred with the past that Gideon had described in his long letter to Fortas. The felonies he had listed were all there:

1928, burglary in Missouri, 10-year sentence, paroled after 3.

1934, a federal charge, possession of Government property, 3 years.

1940, another Missouri burglary, 10 years, escaped in 1944, recaptured a year later, released in 1950.

1951, burglary in Texas, 2 years, released Sept. 25, 1952.

After that there was nothing serious until the episode of the Bay Harbor Poolroom in June, 1961. The record did show some arrests for "investigation" in Panama City and a twenty-day sentence for drunkenness there.

A prison report described Gideon as the typical recidivist type—an incurable repeater. Someone had noted in his file: "At present time does not have anyone for the mailing or visiting list."

The prison officials did not mind Gideon's legal activities —indeed they seemed to regard them as therapy. One said: "Usually when they're trying to get out legally, you know they walk on their toes around here." They knew all about his case in the Supreme Court, but even the possible effect of a victory for Gideon on other prisoners who had been tried without counsel did not seem to bother them as it did some prosecutors. An assistant warden said: "Our feeling is: Boys, if you can get out of here legal, we're with you."

Gideon was asked why he had insisted so strenuously on a lawyer, all the way from the circuit court of Bay County to the Supreme Court of the United States.

"I knew that was my only chance," he said. "I don't know if you've ever been in one of these courtrooms, but the prejudice is obvious. In this state—except for Dade County [Miami], in Dade County they go by the books—they just run over people who have nothing. I've never taken the witness stand in this case, nobody knows what I'd say. Without a lawyer, with the criminal record I had, what I'd have said they'd never have paid any attention to."

The idea of prejudice on the part of Florida officials against the poor and unfortunate was a fixation with Gideon. He spoke again and again about the welfare authorities and what he called their attempt to take his children from him. He spoke bitterly of the Florida Supreme Court and its refusal to do anything about counsel for the poor.

"These people are not vicious," he said, and he seemed to be talking about the citizens as well as the officials of Florida. "They just have beliefs they've lived by all their lives. They think it's perfectly all right to take a man into a courtroom and deny him all his rights. I was reading here a while back, I believe it was Milton's essay on liberty, he writes about Socrates and Christ, which was two judicial cases tried by the people. He showed that these people were not any different from what they are now—not mean people or anything, they're just used to things."

As prisoners often do, Gideon complained of so many raw deals that it was hard to separate fact from feelings of persecution. He spoke of harsh sentences some of his fellow inmates had been given and of inequities in Florida law. At times his wanderings into legalism grew incoherent, and he had to be steered back to the point. But he never made any effort to justify his life; he only wanted his rights: "You can't justify a crime, whether it's murder or petty larceny, but they can go by the book in trying you and sentencing you."

He would not say so, but there was every sign that Gideon expected the Supreme Court to rule in his favor. He said all the inmates were thinking about the case, "even though the intelligence of the people in here is not the greatest in the world." A lot of the men, he said, "think they're just going to have to call the buses in here and turn 'em loose."

Afterward, he hoped the American Civil Liberties Union would give him an attorney to help him fight the charge of breaking and entering the Bay Harbor Poolroom at a new trial. He had also thought about what he might do if he were finally free.

"The only reason I never left Panama City was that I couldn't get enough money to leave. That's hard to move, a family. If I get out of here, I'm a good automobile electric mechanic. I wouldn't begin to say I was a journeyman electrician or anything like that, but I'd like to get a maintenance job somewhere, or have a little shop of my own and work on one car at a time, generators and batteries and things like that."

Gideon had thought, too, about the Supreme Court and its part in assuring counsel to every criminal defendant. "Without the Supreme Court it might have happened some time," he said, "but it wouldn't have happened in this state soon."

Had he read any of the recent Supreme Court decisions on the right to counsel? No, "only what you read in the paper, you know you read that some boy was given the right to a lawyer."

If he had read the decisions, and understood them, Gideon could not have been any less confident in victory for himself and his principle. For the Court, in its own sophisticated way, had been groping toward Clarence Earl Gideon's simple feeling about the importance of a lawyer to a poor man charged with crime.

8

"The most innocent man, pressed by the awful solemnities of public accusation and trial, may be incapable of supporting his own cause. He may be utterly unfit to cross-examine the witnesses against him, to point out the contradictions or defects of their testimony, and to counteract it by properly introducing it and applying his own." So wrote William Rawle, a Philadelphia lawyer, in 1825. Probably no one can adequately appreciate the need for a lawyer in a criminal case until he is himself a defendant. The sense of loneliness, the confusion of guilt and outrage, the feeling that one is caught up in machinery he does not understand—all these emotions well up in a person who finds himself arrested for even a moderately serious traffic offense.

And how much greater are the chances today than in 1825 that the average citizen will at some point be caught up in the criminal law. The Jeffersonian dream of a happy rural society of sturdy, independent yeomen has died with industrialization, the growth of cities and the population explosion. The social pressures of urban industrial life are all too familiar, as are the ugly human manifestations they produce. Society has had to respond with a vast proliferation of criminal statutes, covering life with a scope and detail that would have amazed William Rawle. Judge Bernard Botein and Murray A. Gordon, in a recent book, note that more than one million Americans are convicted of crime every year, and they say that many times that number are spared only by inadequate facilities for law enforcement or the "benign discretion of police or prosecutors." With only a little exaggeration, they argue that few citizens are truly "exempt from the coverage of a modern penal code" touching on such matters as gambling, intoxication, sex offenses, tax evasion, traffic violations and business malpractices, not to mention the more traditional crimes of violence. "There is hardly any freedom from technical guilt," they conclude, "only from prosecution."

If the multiplication of offenses has made the lawyer's role more essential, so have the increasing subtlety and complexity of the criminal trial itself. Even the availability of new constitutional protections for the defendant has increased, not lessened, the need for a lawyer. The defendant cannot be expected to effectively assert his right to an impartial jury, his right to keep out illegal evidence, his right to challenge the voluntary nature of a confession; the question of the legality of evidence alone fills volumes of law books. And so, today, few would disagree with the com-

ment of one of the most highly regarded state judges, Walter V. Schaefer of the Supreme Court of Illinois: "Of all the
rights that an accused person has, the right to be represented
by counsel is by far the most pervasive, for it affects his
ability to assert any other rights he may have."

The right to counsel does not, however, go so far back
into history as might be assumed. The common law of
England did not even allow a man accused of treason or
felony to be represented by counsel, except that a lawyer
could argue legal points suggested by the accused. (Full
representation was allowed in misdemeanor cases; apparently
the theory was that the more grave the charge, the less
chance the accused should have to escape conviction.) It
must be remembered that up through the Seventeenth Century, felony defendants were treated in most respects with
what now seems to be unremitting harshness. They were
not allowed to testify, to call sworn witnesses on their behalf or even to see the charges before trial. In 1695 Parlia-
ment mitigated the judge-made rules of the common law
to the extent of allowing treason defendants to be represented by counsel. It was not until 1836, nearly a half-
century after the Sixth Amendment was added to the American Constitution, that another statute extended to all felony
defendants in England the privilege of being represented by
counsel.

The Sixth Amendment provided, among other things,
that "In all criminal prosecutions, the accused shall enjoy
the right . . . to have the Assistance of Counsel for his
defence." As a matter of history, it is clear that the purpose
of the provision was to prevent the adoption in the federal
courts of the old common-law rule barring defense counsel
in felony cases. Most of the thirteen colonies had rejected
that rule and permitted the accused to retain counsel. The
Sixth Amendment was designed to assure that right to all

who might be charged with crime by the new Federal Government.

Historically speaking, the amendment was almost certainly not envisaged by its framers as reaching the problem of the man too poor to hire a lawyer for his defense. But over the years that became the real problem of counsel in American criminal justice. No precise national figures are available, but various states have estimated that between thirty and sixty percent of all those they convict these days cannot afford to retain a lawyer. Certainly the numbers are large, and every justice who was to participate in the Gideon case knew from his experience on the Supreme Court—however brief—that many of the claimed flaws in the criminal convictions brought to that Court resulted from the inability of the prisoner to pay for counsel at his trial.

The treatment of the right-to-counsel issue in the Supreme Court is a fascinating example of how constitutional doctrine develops there, slowly, deliberately, case by case. Understanding does require discussion of a fair number of cases, for few issues have had a more thorough exploration in the Court.

The story begins in 1932, in the Scottsboro Case, *Powell v. Alabama,* one of the few incontestably great cases in the Supreme Court's history. The case started in a freight train "moving slowly across the countryside of northern Alabama," Professor Francis A. Allen of the University of Chicago says in a classic outline of the story. "It was a time of economic distress and social unrest. As if in response to some common impulse, thousands of young people—no one knows how many—left their homes and communities to drift across the land by train and on foot, presumably in search of work, but, in reality, often without any defined or definable objective. In a gondola car of the train rode two groups of youths, one composed of Negroes, the other whites. Among the latter were two white girls. What occurred has ever since been the subject of sharp controversy. It is at least established that a dispute broke out between the Negroes and the whites. There was a fight and all but one of the white boys were thrown off the slow-moving train. Word was sent ahead, and when the freight approached the village of Scottsboro, the Negroes were met by the sheriff and a posse. The charge was rape of the white girls. Fearing the violence of the community, the sheriff moved the defendants to the neighboring town of Gadsden. The militia was called to Scottsboro to maintain order. A few days later the defendants were tried in three separate proceedings. Each of the three trials was completed in the space of a single day. All the defendants were convicted of rape, and the juries imposed the sentence of death on each."

Those were the convictions and sentences before the Supreme Court in *Powell v. Alabama*. The opinion of the Court was written by Justice George Sutherland, one of the four "conservatives" so hateful to New Deal liberals. The question he considered was whether the seven Scottsboro boys, as they were called, had had the effective assistance of counsel. They were tried six days after their indictment. At the trial there was a long, confusing colloquy between the judge and some of the lawyers of Scottsboro in which the judge said he had "appointed all the members of the bar" for the purposes of arraigning the defendants and expected them to carry on at the trial if no one else turned up to represent the accused. "With this dubious understanding," Justice Sutherland said, "the trials immediately proceeded. The defendants, young, ignorant, illiterate, surrounded by hostile sentiment, haled back and forth under guard of soldiers, charged with an atrocious crime regarded with especial horror in the community where they were to be tried, were thus put in peril. . . ."

Justice Sutherland put aside the Sixth Amendment as a guide to decision; the precedents had rejected any claim that it applied to the states or had been incorporated in the Fourteenth Amendment automatically. But the due-process clause of the Fourteenth Amendment, he said, at least required a "hearing," and for a meaningful hearing counsel was "fundamental."

"The right to be heard would be, in many cases, of little avail if it did not comprehend the right to be heard by counsel. Even the intelligent and educated layman has small and sometimes no skill in the science of law. If charged with crime, he is incapable, generally, of determining for himself whether the indictment is good or bad. He is unfamiliar with the rules of evidence. Left without the aid of counsel he may be put on trial without a proper charge, and convicted upon incompetent evidence, or evidence irrelevant to the issue or otherwise inadmissible. He lacks both the skill and knowledge adequately to prepare his defense, even though he have a perfect one. He requires the guiding hand of counsel at every step in the proceedings against him. Without it, though he be not guilty, he faces the danger of conviction because he does not know how to establish his innocence. If that be true of men of intelligence, how much more true is it of the ignorant and illiterate, or those of feeble intellect."

On those premises, the opinion concluded that it would be a denial of due process of law—and a violation, therefore, of the Fourteenth Amendment—for a court "arbitrarily" to deny any party to a case, "civil or criminal," the right to be heard by counsel of his choice. And the facts of this case, Justice Sutherland said, amounted to a denial of "reasonable time and opportunity to secure counsel." But he did not stop there. "Passing that," Justice Sutherland wrote, "and assuming their inability, even if opportunity had been given, to employ counsel, . . . we are of opinion that, under the circumstances just stated, the necessity of counsel was so vital and imperative that the failure of the trial court to make an effective appointment of counsel was likewise a denial of due process within the meaning of the Fourteenth Amendment."

For the first time, the Supreme Court had held that the Constitution could entitle the poor and friendless accused to the lawyer he could not retain himself. But Justice Sutherland carefully limited the holding of the case to its particular facts, "the circumstances just stated," as he had said. "Whether this would be so in other criminal prosecutions, or under other circumstances, we need not determine. All that it is necessary now to decide, as we do decide, is that in a capital case, where the defendant is unable to employ counsel, and is incapable adequately of making his own defense because of ignorance, feeblemindedness, illiteracy, or the like, it is the duty of the court, whether requested or not, to assign counsel for him as a necessary requisite of due process of law."

Powell v. Alabama was an historic advance for liberty. It was the first occasion on which the Supreme Court had actually reversed a state criminal conviction because of unfair procedures at trial. But by any fair reading, Justice Sutherland's opinion meant less than the universal requirement of counsel in every criminal trial that Gideon was asking the Supreme Court to prescribe. Justice Sutherland had taken care to restrict the case to its compelling circumstances—a capital crime, an agitated community, obviously helpless defendants. It was six years before the Court considered the issue of counsel in a less agitated setting.

The next landmark in the history of the right to counsel was *Johnson v. Zerbst*. It was a federal case—a conviction for passing counterfeit money. Justice Black, in his first term on the Court, wrote the majority opinion. He said nothing of any special difficulties under which the defendant labored, and for all that could be told there were none.

The opinion quoted some of what Justice Sutherland had said in *Powell v. Alabama* about the importance of a lawyer, adding only the comment that "the average defendant does not have the professional legal skill to protect himself when brought before a tribunal with power to take his life or liberty, wherein the prosecution is presented by experienced and learned counsel. That which is simple, orderly and necessary to the lawyer, to the untrained layman may appear intricate, complex and mysterious." The opinion did not discuss the history of the Sixth Amendment, with its object of overcoming the English rule against counsel for felony defendants. Justice Black said simply that the language of the amendment now required the appointment of counsel for all who could not afford it in federal criminal cases. The amendment "withholds from federal courts in all criminal proceedings," he said, "the power and authority to deprive an accused of his life or liberty unless he has or waives the assistance of counsel." He had a bare majority for that proposition—Chief Justice Hughes and Justices Brandeis, Harlan F. Stone and Owen J. Roberts in addition to himself.

There matters stood for four years. In the state courts, the Fourteenth Amendment required appointment of counsel in some cases—but just which ones was not certain. In federal courts, the Sixth Amendment required counsel in all criminal cases. Many informed observers thought it was inevitable that the requirement would be extended to the states. But then, in 1942, came *Betts v. Brady*.

Smith Betts was a farm hand in rural Carroll County, Maryland. He was charged with robbery, and he asked the court to appoint a lawyer for him because he was too poor to hire one. The judge refused, explaining—just as a Florida judge was to explain to Clarence Earl Gideon twenty years later—that the practice in Carroll County was to appoint lawyers for the indigent only in prosecutions for

murder and rape. Like Gideon, Betts acted as his own lawyer, cross-examining the prosecution witnesses and calling
his own. The main issues were identification of Betts as
the robber and the validity of an alibi he put forward. The
judge who tried the case believed the prosecution, found
Betts guilty and imposed an eight-year sentence. Eventually Betts filed a petition for habeas corpus with Chief
Judge Carroll T. Bond of Maryland's court of appeals,
claiming that the refusal to give him a lawyer violated
his constitutional rights—again the same procedure that
Gideon was to follow in twenty years. Judge Bond reviewed the record of the trial and rejected Betts's claim in a
detailed opinion. The trial, he said, had been a routine, simple affair, so that "in this case it must be said there was little
for counsel to do on either side." Betts had been able "to
take care of his own interests."

In the Supreme Court, a six to three majority agreed with
Judge Bond. Justice Roberts wrote the opinion for the
majority, rejecting as unworthy of extended discussion any
contention that the Sixth Amendment was applicable as
such to the states. The question was "whether the constraint
laid by the amendment upon the national courts expresses a
rule so fundamental and essential to a fair trial, and so to
due process of law, that it is made obligatory upon the states
by the Fourteenth Amendment." To find the answer the
Court must look to the constitutions, statutes and judicial
decisions of the states originally and at present, "the most
authoritative sources for ascertaining the considered judgment of the citizens of the states upon the question." Justice
Roberts first reviewed the counsel provisions of the thirteen original states at the time of the writing of the Constitution and concluded that they were designed not to assure
lawyers for the poor but to reject the English common-
law rule and let those who could afford it retain counsel.
(In *Johnson v. Zerbst* the majority, including Justice Rob-

erts, had evidently deemed the same history irrelevant to the meaning of the Sixth Amendment today.) In the constitutions and laws of the forty-eight states in 1942 Justice Roberts found a diversity of provisions on counsel, some requiring appointment in all cases, some in capital cases only, some merely permitting appointment in each court's discretion.

"This material demonstrates," he concluded, "that, in the great majority of the states, it has been the considered judgment of the people, their representatives and their courts that appointment of counsel is not a fundamental right, essential to a fair trial. On the contrary, the matter has generally been deemed one of legislative policy. In the light of this evidence we are unable to say that the concept of due process incorporated in the Fourteenth Amendment obligates the states, whatever may be their own views, to furnish counsel in every such case." Justice Roberts added that the logic of the uniform rule sought by Betts would require appointment of counsel in traffic courts, and even in civil cases. "The states should not be straitjacketed" that way, he said. "Want of counsel in a particular case may result in a conviction lacking in . . . fundamental fairness," but that would have to be found from the circumstances.

Turning to the facts of this case, Justice Roberts relied on the findings of Judge Bond. (Altogether, the opinion mentioned Judge Bond by name fifteen times, and Professor Freund has suggested that the esteem in which he was held may have influenced the result.) "The simple issue was the veracity of the testimony for the state and that for the defendant. As Judge Bond says, the accused was not helpless, but was a man forty-three years old, of ordinary intelligence and ability to take care of his interests on the trial of that narrow issue. He had once before been in a criminal court, pleaded guilty to larceny and served a sentence and was not wholly unfamiliar with criminal procedure." Joining the opinion were Chief Justice Stone (as he had become at Hughes's retirement) and Justices Stanley F. Reed, Frankfurter, James F. Byrnes and Jackson.

The dissenting opinion was by Justice Black, and it foretold the philosophy he was to develop as a judge over the next two decades. He said for the first time that he thought the Fourteenth Amendment had been intended to incorporate the Sixth, but he did not press the point. Even "the prevailing view of due process," he said—"a view which gives the Court such vast supervisory powers that I am not prepared to accept it without grave doubts"—required provision of counsel for those too poor to retain their own. Briefly Justice Black, whose opinion was joined by Justices Douglas and Murphy, explained why he thought the right to counsel was "fundamental." He cited the language of some early state cases and of Justice Sutherland in *Powell v. Alabama*. He concluded that no man should be "deprived of counsel merely because of his poverty. Any other practice seems to me to defeat the promise of our democratic society to provide equal justice under the law."

Not long after *Betts v. Brady* was decided, it was severely criticized in a lengthy letter to *The New York Times* by Benjamin V. Cohen, the noted New Deal lawyer, and Erwin N. Griswold, then a professor, later Dean of the Harvard Law School. "The decision in *Betts v. Brady* comes at a singularly inopportune time," they wrote. "Throughout the world men are fighting to be free from the fear of political trials and concentration camps. From this struggle men are hoping that a bill of rights will emerge which will guarantee to all men certain fundamental rights. . . . Most Americans—lawyers and laymen alike—before the decision in *Betts v. Brady* would have thought that the right of the accused to counsel in a serious criminal case was unquestionably a part of our own Bill of Rights. . . ."

That was just a hint of the criticism that began to rain on

Betts v. Brady. Within a few years some students of the Court, perhaps indulging in wishful thinking, suggested that the doctrine was quietly being abandoned. The next two significant right-to-counsel cases, decided in 1945, resulted in seven-to-two reversals of convictions for lack of counsel (Justices Roberts and Frankfurter dissenting). But those were capital cases, and before long it became evident that the Court was drawing a line between trials involving a possible death sentence and all others. In capital cases the Court simply assumed that a fair trial could not be had without counsel; as it said when it finally put the distinction into words, in 1961: "When one pleads to a capital charge without benefit of counsel, we do not stop to determine whether prejudice resulted."

In 1947 the Court made it plain that in non-capital cases it was sticking to the flexible rule of *Betts v. Brady.* Explicitly relying on *Betts*, Justice Frankfurter said the "abrupt innovation" of a universal counsel requirement "would furnish opportunities hitherto uncontemplated for opening wide the prison doors of the land," thus indicating the Court's practical fears. For the next few years, every right-to-counsel case was weighed in terms of its "special circumstances." The approach was best defined in a 1948 opinion by Justice Reed, *Uveges v. Pennsylvania.* "Where the gravity of the crime and other factors—such as the age and education of the defendant, the conduct of the court or prosecuting officials, and the complicated nature of the offense charged, and the possible defenses thereto—render criminal proceedings without counsel so apt to result in injustice as to be fundamentally unfair . . . , the accused must have legal assistance."

Sometimes the differing uses of this formula produced such fine distinctions that virtually no one could understand them. On the same day in 1948 the Court decided two right-to-counsel cases, *Gryger v. Burke* and *Townsend v. Burke*, affirming the conviction in the first and reversing in

the second. Gryger claimed that he had been given a life
sentence because the trial judge—misinterpreting state law
—wrongly thought the statutes required that sentence; a
five-to-four majority found no "fundamental unfairness" in
the absence of counsel to correct such an error. Townsend
said his judge had imposed sentence in the mistaken belief
that he had been convicted on two earlier charges which in
fact resulted in acquittals; a six-to-three majority thought
counsel was constitutionally required in those circumstances.
The only conclusion one could state with certainty about
the two cases was that Justices Jackson and Frankfurter—
who made the difference by voting to affirm Gryger's conviction and reverse Townsend's—saw a distinction. But that
the distinction rose to the level of defining "due process of
law" was beyond most men's belief.

The prevailing scholarly view of the succession of right-
to-counsel decisions in the 1940's was expressed by Professor
Allen: "The cases decided by the Court under the *Betts*
formula are distinguished neither by the consistency of their
results nor by the cogency of their argument. . . . The
rule, therefore, seems vulnerable to fundamental criticism,
and so long as it persists, the law of the subject will remain
in a state of unstable equilibrium."

Sometimes when a constitutional decision comes under
such severe scholarly attack, the Court begins to retreat
from it almost invisibly, paying it lip service but never really
allowing it to stand in the way of desired results. Something
like that seemed to be happening in the 1950's to *Betts v.
Brady*. Opinions still frequently cited the case. But the last
time the Court actually affirmed a state criminal conviction
in the face of a claimed denial of counsel was in 1950. Between that decision and the grant of review in Gideon's case
the Court had held in favor of every state prisoner whose
counsel claim it agreed to hear.

There was an especially significant series of decisions beginning in 1960. In *Hudson v. North Carolina* that year, Justice Potter Stewart found counsel constitutionally required because Hudson's co-defendant had changed his plea to guilty midway in the trial and that might have prejudiced Hudson before the jury. Justice Clark, joined by Justice Whittaker, dissented, remarking acidly that the Court's opinion, "without so much as mentioning *Betts v. Brady*, cuts serious inroads into that holding." That was the last dissent in any right-to-counsel case before Gideon's. The next year, 1961, Justice Whittaker wrote for the Court in *McNeal v. Culver*, reversing a conviction for assault because of the "complex and intricate legal questions" involved under the law of Florida. Justice Douglas, joined by Justice Brennan, wrote a separate concurring opinion of even greater interest. It called flatly for the overruling of *Betts v. Brady*, concluding: "*Betts v. Brady* requires the indigent, when convicted in a trial where he has no counsel, to show that there was fundamental unfairness. . . . This is a heavy burden to carry, especially for an accused who has no lawyer and cannot afford to hire one. It is a burden placed on an accused solely by reason of his poverty. Its only sanction is *Betts v. Brady*, which is so at war with our concept of equal justice under law that it should be overruled. Are we to wait to overrule it until a case arises where the indigent is unable to make a convincing demonstration that the absence of counsel prejudiced him?"

The language of that concurring opinion seemed to look to the equal-protection clause as much as the due-process clause of the Fourteenth Amendment. A few weeks later, in a lecture, Justice Brennan said that he was thinking in terms of equal protection. He cited *Griffin v. Illinois*, holding that a state could not distinguish between rich and poor in allowing appeals from criminal convictions. "The denial of counsel to an indigent accused," Justice Brennan said, "seems almost to be an *a fortiori* case of the violation of the guarantee of equal protection of the laws."

In 1962 the Court said unanimously that the legal issues at a proceeding under a multiple-offender law—committing a man to an extended prison term simply because he had a certain number of felony convictions—were so "complex" as to require counsel. Many authorities would have regarded such proceedings as about as simple and straightforward as any could be in the criminal law. The *Betts* requirement of "special circumstances" to justify counsel had seemingly been stretched to the limit.

Then, on April 30, 1962, the Court decided *Carnley v. Cochran*, the fourth counsel case from Florida in the last four years. Once again it held that in the particular circumstances the defendant should have had a lawyer. The *Betts* approach was still being followed. But in the Carnley case there was a difference. Two justices did not participate in the decision: Justice Whittaker had retired on April 1st, and on April 5th Justice Frankfurter had gone to the hospital; his illness was not then disclosed but was in fact a stroke. Of the seven justices sitting, three—Chief Justice Warren and Justices Black and Douglas—joined in a concurring opinion urging that *Betts v. Brady* be overruled. But everyone knew there was another member of the Court who felt that way, for Justice Brennan had said as much the year before and had certainly not changed his mind. Thus, the day of the Carnley decision, there was at least a four-to-three majority of the justices who favored a flat requirement of counsel in state criminal cases. Justice Brennan simply declined for the moment to invoke that broad ground, voting instead to find counsel required on the particular facts of this case. Why did he do so? Perhaps he felt it inappropriate to overrule a constitutional decision with less than a full bench present, when the result might be said to depend on the accident of vacant seats. Or perhaps he or others thought the grave step of overruling should be taken more deliberately, with counsel in some future case being explicitly directed to focus on the question of the *Betts* doctrine's continuing validity.

It was a little more than two months later when the Supreme Court granted Gideon's petition for review and directed counsel to brief and argue that question.

9

When Abe Fortas started to work on the Gideon case, he recognized that the current of legal history was moving with him. The whole thrust of recent decisions on criminal procedure was at war with the *Betts* philosophy of letting the states manage their trial procedures as they thought best.

But these intimations of mortality for the twenty-year-old doctrine did not mean that Fortas had no significant role to play as counsel assigned to argue for its formal burial. The Court had chosen someone of more than ordinary experience and ability to represent Gideon, and the honor carried with it a special responsibility. If that most basic right, to be represented by counsel, was now to be extended to all those charged with serious crimes in any court, the justices would want all possible intellectual support for taking the step. And each justice would have his own viewpoint. Fortas saw his job as reaching each of the nine. "It's hard for me to describe it without sounding stuffy," he said later, discussing his feelings. "An advocate usually thinks about winning a case and doesn't give a damn whether he wins by five-four or some other vote. But in this case—a constitutional case of fundamental importance, and with political overtones in terms of federal-state relations—it seemed to me the responsibility was not just to try to win the case but to get as many justices as possible to go along with what I considered the right result. If you assume *Betts v. Brady* was going to be overruled, it was right for the institution of the Supreme Court, and for the law, to have as much unanimity as possible."

Fortas thought his chances of winning nine votes were slim. He started with an almost certain four: the Chief Justice and Justices Black, Douglas and Brennan. Justice Stewart, though he had not criticized *Betts*, seemed a hopeful prospect; in his four years on the Supreme Court he had never voted to affirm a criminal conviction where the defendant claimed that he should have had counsel at his trial. Justice Clark was generally regarded as "pro-government" in criminal cases, and he had written the Court's last dissent in a right-to-counsel case, in 1960; on the other hand, he had written the opinion of the Court in the 1961 search-and-seizure case, *Mapp v. Ohio*, reinterpreting the Constitution to outlaw illegal evidence in state criminal trials. The two strongest voices on the Court for federalism and restraint in imposing new restrictions on state criminal procedure were those of Justice Frankfurter, who was ill but expected to return to the bench in the fall, and Justice Harlan; Fortas thought it unlikely that either would vote to overrule *Betts v. Brady*. Finally there was the newest justice, former Deputy

Attorney General Byron R. White, appointed by President Kennedy to replace Justice Whittaker; his views could hardly be known after two months on the bench, although a sharp dissent he had just written from a decision overthrowing a California narcotics law did seem to indicate a hard-boiled attitude in criminal cases.

Since Fortas had been appointed to represent Gideon, his personal belief about the rightness or wrongness of *Betts v. Brady* could not affect his duty, but in fact he strongly believed that representation by a lawyer was an absolute essential of fairness at any criminal trial. His own experience had so persuaded him, and he wished there were some way he could convey to the justices first-hand the atmosphere of the criminal courts. "What I'd like to have said," he remarked later, "was, 'Let's not talk, let's go down and watch one of these fellows try to defend himself.'" But the business of persuading Supreme Court justices is naturally less direct. In his brief Fortas would have to deal with all the themes traced over the last century in the Court's interpretation of the words "due process of law" in the Fourteenth Amendment.

Fortas was not an expert on the Fourteenth Amendment in general or the right to counsel in particular, and so his first need was to educate himself. He began by calling in one of his partners, Abe Krash, a younger man who had worked with him on a number of important cases, and asking him to organize research for *Gideon v. Cochran.* Fortas said he wanted to know everything there was to know about the right to counsel. There immediately got under way the extraordinary process by which a large law firm digests a legal problem. Bright young men break it down into tiny components and write treatises on every conceivable issue—they probe, imagine, cover every exit. Then, from this jumble of material, a skilled lawyer creates a legal work of art, choosing a coherent form for his argument and ruthlessly eliminating all that is extraneous to that form. The end product is a particular understanding of the case, an understanding that informs the brief and the oral argument. A direct question—such as "Should Clarence Earl Gideon have had a lawyer at his trial?"—has become a much more sophisticated constitutional conception, not necessarily more remote from life but richer in its reflection of history and philosophy and judicial attitudes.

The process began at Arnold, Fortas and Porter with a memorandum drafted by an associate, James F. Fitzpatrick, on July 6, 1962, just eleven days after Fortas's appointment by the Supreme Court. It laid out the questions that Fitzpatrick thought the office ought to explore in preparing its brief in *Gideon v. Cochran*. The memorandum, much condensed, went as follows:

Was the historical analysis in *Betts* which buttressed the conclusion that "appointment of counsel is not a fundamental right" correct?

How has state law (on appointment of counsel) changed since 1942?

Has there been a change in the concept of Fourteenth Amendment "absorption" of the Bill of Rights since 1942?

What has been the experience with the *Betts* test?

What is the present status of right to counsel in European countries, in newly emerging countries, in the United Nations Declaration of Human Rights?

What has been the progress of the *Griffin* equal-protection doctrine [that barring a poor man's appeal because he cannot afford a trial transcript denies him the equal protection of the laws]?

In factual terms, can we get an estimate of how many felony defendants go to trial without counsel?

If the Fourteenth Amendment is now held to require counsel in all cases, what would be the additional demands on lawyers?

These issues and research topics raise fundamental policy questions:

1. Should our brief attack the broad, existing rule that the Fourteenth Amendment did not incorporate the Bill of Rights? Should we (alternatively) accept the standard that the Fourteenth Amendment guarantees a fair trial and argue that a fair trial must include the right to counsel?

2. Should we make the twin argument that counsel is required by the equal-protection clause?

3. What should be the shape of a suggested rule? Does it apply to misdemeanors and traffic-court offenses? To pre-trial proceedings? To appeals?

Arnold, Fortas and Porter had taken on for the summer John Hart Ely, a Yale law student who would enter his final year in the fall. Krash decided to have him do the basic *Gideon* research, and for the next two months Ely worked exclusively on this case. A steady stream of type-written memoranda went from him to Krash and Fortas, some in response to requests from them, others his own idea. The first of these was a list of thirty-two relevant law-review articles on *Betts v. Brady*, most of them with titles indicating a critical approach. Another memorandum can-vassed in detail the elaborate history of the Supreme Court's interpretation of the Fourteenth Amendment.

On July 25th Ely submitted his first paper reflecting real thought about the right-to-counsel problem. It was a twenty-five page memorandum headed "Application, Am-biguities and Weaknesses of the Special Circumstances Rule." Ely had examined how the rule of *Betts v. Brady*, calling for counsel only where special circumstances exist, was actually applied in the state courts, especially the Florida courts. He concluded that the state courts used the same language as the Supreme Court of the United States, and mentioned the same factors, but somehow came to different conclusions—almost always rejecting claims to counsel. "The fact that the United States Supreme Court has reversed the Florida Supreme Court in four right-to-counsel cases since 1959," he wrote, "suggests that the two courts have different ideas as to how the factors should be balanced." The real source of confusion, Ely suggested, was the number and variety of factors that the Supreme Court had said were relevant to deciding whether counsel was essential in a particular case. He listed more than twenty such factors that had been mentioned in majority and dissenting Supreme Court opinions, among them these: the complexity of the criminal statute, the defendant's age and education and mental ability and color, inadequacy of the judge's guidance at trial, misbehavior by the prosecutor—and, on the other side, imposition of a lighter than maximum sentence, a helpful attitude on the part of the trial judge, the defendant's prior experience with the criminal law.

"It is difficult to imagine a case," Ely concluded, "in which at least five 'relevant' factors could not be compiled for either side." Nor had the Court been consistent. In 1948 it had rejected a plea for counsel on the ground that the trial judge had misunderstood state law; a mere error of state law was not enough of a special circumstance, the majority said. But in 1961, reversing a conviction, the Court had emphasized the trial judge's "patent violation" of state law in admitting certain testimony.

Then, in the memorandum, Ely explored an idea that had been suggested by Fortas. This was that *Betts v. Brady* might be injurious to the very principles of federalism on which it supposedly rested. "The Court has said," he wrote, "that if it were to discard the *Betts* test, it would be guilty of 'an unwarranted federal intrusion into state control of its criminal procedure.' Perhaps the vagueness of the rule can be used to turn this argument against its proponents." In other words, an absolute requirement of counsel might be less of an intrusion on state criminal processes because it would be clear-cut, in contrast to what Ely called the confusion of the special-circumstances approach. The nature of that approach, Ely said, required state courts to guess in its application—and a wrong guess meant having to try the accused all over again later. Guessing was inevitable, he said, because the *Betts* test was "an amalgam of personal and retrospective factors." The trial judge could weigh such personal elements as the defendant's age, but elements such as the prosecutor's and judge's behavior could only be surveyed later. He said this amalgam "ensures lack of success in application at any level. So long as judges are men, a trial court cannot foresee the progress of the trial; nor can an appellate court cull from a record on appeal a reliable picture of a man's abilities."

Another weakness of the special-circumstances rule, Ely continued in the July 25th memorandum, "is that errors in its application stand little chance of being corrected. For it is unlikely that there are many convicts who, like Gideon, have the knowledge, ability and ambition to institute an appeal. . . . Starting from the questionable assumption that there are on this earth laymen capable of adequately defending themselves against the accusations of the public prosecutor, the special-circumstances rule—if it can be called 'a rule'—is designed to sort out these fortunate and talented individuals. Twenty years of confusion bear witness to its inadequacy."

The next day, July 26th, Ely circulated a note on the distinction made as to the right to counsel in capital and noncapital cases. He said it made no sense in terms of need to

have an automatic counsel requirement only when a possible
death sentence was involved, since many non-capital
charges were more complicated to defend against than
murder. Krash had suggested the relevance of some recent
Supreme Court decisions rejecting the capital–non-capital
distinction in another area of the law. These were the Court
Martial cases, arising from a law providing for military
trial of civilians accompanying the armed forces overseas.
In 1957 the Supreme Court had held this law unconstitutional as applied to wives tried by courts-martial for killing
their soldier husbands; a six-two majority, with Justice Clark
writing a strong dissent, said the wives had been deprived
of their right to trial by jury. Then, in 1960, the court-
martial problem came up in non-capital cases. Justices
Frankfurter and Harlan wanted to draw the line at the
murdering wives and permit civilians to be tried by military
courts for non-capital offenses. But Justice Clark, now
writing for the majority, said he could see no ground for
the distinction and so held unconstitutional all military trials
of civilians overseas. Those cases, Ely said, "should be mentioned in our brief as an example of a realization of the inadequacy of a capital–non-capital distinction." But Ely said
that no strong reliance should be placed on them because a
different provision of the Constitution—the clause on regu-
lating the armed forces—was involved.

In yet another memorandum Ely urged that no attempt
be made to revive the contention that the Fourteenth
Amendment was intended to incorporate the original Bill
of Rights intact. The argument had been decisively rejected,
he said, and so the brief should follow the line that an assured right to counsel was "fundamental" and so implicit
in the guarantee of due process of law. A ten-page memorandum on July 31st discussed the companion clause of the
Fourteenth Amendment, that assuring "the equal protection of the laws." The leading precedent here, as mentioned

by Fitzpatrick, was *Griffin v. Illinois*, holding that a state denied equal protection when it required payment for trial records in order to appeal, thus excluding the poor. Ely noted this sentence from Justice Black's opinion: "There can be no equal justice where the kind of trial a man gets depends on the amount of money he has." He was attracted by the opening that sentence seemed to provide. "The argument from *Griffin* to *Gideon* is a simple one," he wrote, "and in my opinion provides the Court with a convenient method of overruling *Betts* without expressly contradicting its lengthy and explicit declaration that due process does not always demand appointment of counsel."

A memorandum of August 3rd examined the transcript of Gideon's trial to see whether he had been prejudiced by lack of counsel. "At first blush," Ely wrote, "the transcript in *State v. Gideon* seems to present the very model of the myth of *Betts:* a case in which defense counsel is not needed. For the defendant exhibited remarkable skill in cross-examination, and the judge went to great lengths to inform him of his rights." But a closer look convinced Ely that Gideon's ability to defend himself was illusory. He pointed out numerous errors by the judge, examples of prejudice to Gideon, omissions. "An argument could be made along the following lines," he concluded. "Here is a trial in which the defendant was skillful and the judge made every effort to protect his rights. Yet even here close examination of the law and of the facts reveals that defendant was repeatedly hurt by lack of counsel. If such prejudice occurred in this trial, it would seem that there is *no* trial in which counsel is unnecessary. Thus the rule of *Betts* is based upon a false factual assumption."

Here was a perception of Ely's that caught the eye of Abe Fortas, if indeed it had not previously occurred to him. Fortas combined it in his mind with the thesis that the special-circumstances rule might actually result in more, not less, irritation to the states. "I am convinced," Fortas explained later, "that this judge in Panama City, Florida, tried to help Gideon defend himself. He just did a bad job, as any judge would; it's not a judge's role to be a defense counsel. He made mistakes. But how corrosive it is for federal-state relations to have a federal court tell that judge later that he did not do an adequate job!"

It was time now, in August, to see about printing the record of the case. When the Supreme Court agrees to hear a case, an abstract of the lower-court proceedings is printed for the justices' convenience. The Court's print shop does the actual printing, in brown-covered pamphlets that look rather like high-priced paperback books and sometimes run to many fat volumes. Ordinarily the side that eventually loses the decision pays the printing cost, but in a pauper's case such as Gideon's the Federal Government pays if the prisoner loses. The process of compiling the record begins when the lawyer for the petitioner (Fortas in this case) submits to the Clerk's Office a designation of the material he thinks should be printed. The other side may then suggest additions or deletions.

Printing the record in the Gideon case was not a routine matter, because there was a question what "the record" was. At that point the only documents that were officially before the Supreme Court were Gideon's manuscript application for habeas corpus in the Florida Supreme Court and a few other fragmentary items. Since Gideon had begun an independent habeas corpus proceeding rather than appealing his conviction, the transcript of his trial was not technically before the Court. Nevertheless, Fortas wanted to include it in the printed record. "The transcript showed that this was the case in which to reconsider *Betts v. Brady*," he said later. "If we didn't put the transcript in the record, Justice Harlan or someone might say, 'How can we pass on this grave constitutional question without even looking at the transcript?' Hell, if I were on the Supreme Court I wouldn't want to decide a question like this on a bare record."

Fortas submitted a formal designation of record for printing that included the trial transcript. A copy, as required, went to the other side, the Florida attorney general's office. On August 29th Bruce R. Jacob of Florida filed a motion to strike from the printing designation the trial transcript. "Matters which took place at the trial which were not alleged in the petition for habeas corpus," the motion said, "are not involved in the instant case and therefore have no place in the printed record. Inclusion of the trial papers in the printed record herein would be unnecessary and improper. Such inclusion would inject irrelevant matter into the instant case and would prejudice respondent in the presentation of his argument." Fortas replied, on September 13th, that the Supreme Court had ample power to supplement the technical record. "Informed adjudication requires access to all relevant data," he said. "Respondent would blind the Court to information which may be of consequence in resolving the question framed by the Court itself when granting certiorari."

At the Court, Chief Deputy Clerk Cullinan took the conflicting papers in hand and prepared them for submission to the Court when it returned from the summer recess. He personally did not see why Fortas wanted the trial transcript in, since it showed Gideon as a rather shrewd defendant, fully participating in the trial; but then he did not know the approach that was taking shape in Fortas's mind.

The Court opened its new term on October 1st, and two weeks later it handed down a brief and unanimous order settling the dispute about the record in *Gideon v. Cochran:* Florida's motion was denied, the trial transcript was to be included. In about a week the record was printed. Under the rules, the petitioner's—Gideon's—brief was due thirty days later. The party trying to upset the lower court ruling always goes first in briefing and arguing the case; his opponent has the benefit of examining his arguments before making his own. By then Ely had gone back to school. In his place an Arnold, Fortas and Porter associate, Ralph Temple, with some help from another associate, Bruce Montgomery, looked into further questions posed by Krash and Fortas. October 25, Temple to Krash: five pages on the history and contemporary picture of right to counsel in England. October 26, Temple to Krash: a brief note on the large proportion of habeas corpus cases that stem from absence of counsel at trial; if counsel were required, this flood of prisoners' petitions in the federal courts should be reduced. October 26, Temple to Krash: the growth of legal aid in the United States. Up to the year 1950 a total of $3,500,000 had been spent by public and private organizations to defend indigents in the criminal courts. In the next ten years $10,500,000 was spent. October 29, Montgomery to Krash: a description of bills pending in Congress, to provide public defenders and other organized means of representation for the poor in federal courts. October 31, Montgomery to Krash: What is the right to counsel under Russian law? Answer: very little. November 1, Montgomery to Krash: the right to counsel under Florida law. Appointment is specifically required only in capital cases, but judges have discretion to appoint in other cases (contradicting the same erroneous statement by the trial judge that Gideon had mentioned), and some trial judges in populous counties do so in all cases. November 8, Krash to Fortas: "You have asked if it is clear that *Gideon v. Cochran* is properly before the Supreme Court." It must be, because Gideon had followed exactly the same procedure as two other Florida prisoners who had recently won right-to-counsel cases in the Supreme Court.

All along, Krash recognized, Fortas was less interested in abstract conceptual doctrines such as the relation of the

Bill of Rights and the Fourteenth Amendment than he was in practical considerations—which he thought might really worry the justices. In a November memorandum Krash addressed himself to these. Justice Roberts had been concerned in *Betts v. Brady* that an absolute requirement for provision of counsel might logically have to extend all the way down through traffic courts. Supporters of the *Betts* rule still made that argument, saying that the consequence would be an intolerable strain on the American legal system because there simply were not enough lawyers around to provide one for every traffic offender. Fortas did not shy away from that supposed horror. He did not think many persons charged with traffic and other minor offenses would want lawyers, but he was quite prepared to say that a poor traffic offender should be given a lawyer if he asked for one. Krash suggested a more conservative way to argue the Gideon case, which after all did involve a felony and so did not require the more sweeping approach to win the case. The Supreme Court had held that the Sixth Amendment's jury-trial guarantee for federal defendants "in all criminal prosecutions" did not apply to "petty offenses." The same line might be drawn in state cases under the Fourteenth Amendment.

Another practical question was at what stage of the criminal case a lawyer should be supplied. Some authorities felt, and Fortas agreed, that a man needs a lawyer immediately after arrest more acutely than he does later. But the police were strongly against that idea, reasoning that early access to lawyers would discourage prisoners from confessing, and in 1958 the Supreme Court had rejected the claim of a man with adequate funds that he should have been allowed to call in his own lawyer before being questioned by the police. Gideon had sought a lawyer only at trial, and so Fortas need not go back beyond that point; it would be foolhardy to claim any greater right for the poor man than one with funds had been able to establish.

The remaining, and even more important, practical consequence to weigh was the effect of a victory for Gideon on other prisoners who had been tried without counsel. The forecast that an absolute counsel requirement would lead to wholesale emptying of prisons was perhaps the most powerful emotional argument against overruling *Betts v. Brady*— and it was a factor that had been mentioned in opinions since *Betts*. One way to avoid that consequence would be to apply a new, absolute counsel rule only prospectively. For example, the Court could affirm Gideon's conviction, applying to him the established *Betts* doctrine, but warn that all convictions would be set aside in future unless the states provided counsel. Some state courts have done exactly that when they have overruled earlier doctrines, and the Supreme Court has said there is nothing unconstitutional about this procedure of prospective overruling. In *Griffin v. Illinois*, when the Court opened up a new avenue for appeals by saying the states could not deny prisoners the right because of their inability to buy a trial transcript, Justice Frankfurter had been concerned about the effect on cases long since concluded and had suggested applying the new doctrine only to the future. But that proposal was rejected in *Griffin* by the other justices, and the Griffin case was subsequently applied to make the states grant appeals to men who had been in prison twenty years. Krash pointed out that anyone whose conviction was voided as a result of a reinterpretation of the Constitution could be retried. He might even end up with a more severe sentence. One man serving a life sentence in a federal penitentiary had won a new trial when, in 1938, the Supreme Court first imposed an absolute counsel requirement for federal cases; at the new trial he was convicted again and sentenced to death. (The sentence was commuted.)

The consequences of overruling *Betts v. Brady* would also be mitigated by the fact that so many states now provided counsel for the poor in their criminal courts. Exactly what had happened in the states was not clear—no one had done a thorough job of research and compilation—until Professor Yale Kamisar of the University of Minnesota Law School published a definitive article in the Autumn 1962 issue of the University of Chicago Law Review. The article would have been too late for use in Fortas's brief; but Professor Kamisar, knowing about the Gideon case, had telephoned Krash in September and offered to send him a copy of the manuscript. The offer was gladly accepted.

Professor Kamisar showed that at the time of *Betts v. Brady*, thirty states provided counsel as a matter of right in all felony cases. Now thirty-seven did so. That left thirteen with no statewide, formal requirement for provision of counsel except in death cases. But Kamisar had discovered, by corresponding with prosecutors, judges and other authorities in these states, that in eight of the thirteen the practice of appointing counsel had developed without benefit of any statute or rule of court. At least in the larger cities in those eight states, indigent defendants charged with felonies were likely to be given lawyers, although there was no guarantee and the chances were not so good for rural defendants. In Baltimore, for example, counsel was usually provided for any indigent requesting assistance in the criminal courts, although Maryland still held officially to the *Betts* rule that it had spawned, and defendants outside of Baltimore probably had to demonstrate special circumstances to get a lawyer. In Philadelphia, a private defender association made up for the deficiencies of the most populous state still not committed as a matter of policy to provide counsel for all indigent felony defendants. With those eight states added to the thirty-seven, there were left only five that did not assure counsel for the poor except in capital cases: Alabama, Florida, Mississippi, North Carolina and South Carolina. Even in Florida three cities—Miami, Tampa and Fort Lauderdale—had local public defenders. And Professor Kamisar showed that twenty-four states, nearly half, went beyond the line of felonies and provided counsel for misdemeanor defendants.

Ely had written a draft brief before returning to Yale. Krash and Fortas liked it, but they wanted something more finished and more pointed. Krash put the brief through another draft, reshaping it from a scholarly examination of the problems into more of a piece of advocacy, designed to persuade. Fortas soaked himself in the right-to-counsel issue by sitting in the firm library for a week reading cases and commentary—an unusual expenditure of time for a senior partner in a large, busy law firm. Then, one weekend, on his way to join his wife in Westport, Connecticut, Fortas stopped at the Hotel Biltmore in New York and sat in a room for two days blocking out the brief he wanted. From these notes on Biltmore stationery, and after a day's discussion with Fortas, Krash did a fresh draft. Subject to smoothing and tinkering, it was the final product.

But this bare outline of how the brief was completed does not adequately convey the amount of work done. Krash's office diary shows that in the month from the printing of the record to the filing of the brief he spent an average of six hours every working day on the case of Clarence Earl Gideon.

The brief was filed on November 21st. It was fifty-three pages long, packing into that limited space many of the arguments suggested in the memoranda circulated at Arnold, Fortas and Porter in the previous months—but putting them less discursively, more pointedly and as part of a literate whole. The brief did not mention the old controversy about "incorporation" of the Bill of Rights into the Fourteenth Amendment; it assumed the continuing vitality of the Cardozo doctrine that "fundamental" rights were absorbed into the due-process clause. Nor was there any attempt to bring Gideon within the special-circumstances rule by showing that he suffered from any particular disability or prejudice at his trial. The brief was a frontal assault on *Betts v. Brady*.

In an introductory section Fortas said the experience of administering the *Betts* rule over twenty years had "not been a happy one. . . . The quality of criminal justice and the relations between the federal and state courts have suffered." On one side, the doctrine of limiting counsel to those cases where special need could be shown had "not assured and cannot be expected to assure that counsel will be provided where necessary in the interests of fundamental fairness." On the other, the *Betts* rule had turned out not to be "an appropriate adaptation of the Fourteenth Amendment to the demands of federalism. To the contrary, it is a rule which compels continual, unseemly and improper intervention by the federal courts in state criminal proceedings—not on the basis of applying a concrete, fundamental principle but by the corrosive and irritating process of case-by-case review. . . . *Betts v. Brady* has not meant, and will not mean, *less* federal intervention in state criminal proceedings than would be the case if the Fourteenth Amendment were construed to require that counsel be furnished in all state criminal prosecutions. Because of the intensely factual, subjective and post-facto nature of its standards, *Betts v. Brady* means *more* federal intervention on a case-by-case basis, and in a much more exacerbating form." In a separate appendix in the brief Gideon's trial was analyzed to show how a lawyer would have protected Gideon. The analysis vividly demonstrates, Fortas said, "that he did not have a fair trial in the constitutional sense. But it is our opinion that these points [of analysis] are not peculiar to Gideon's case. We believe . . . [they] are present in every criminal prosecution."

That introduction conveyed the essence of what Fortas felt about the case. The brief proper was in five sections, with numerous subsections. These were the five headings and, in briefest summary, the points made under each:

I. The Fourteenth Amendment requires that counsel be appointed to represent an indigent defendant in every criminal case involving a serious offense.

First, "the aid of counsel is indispensable to a fair hearing." Even a trained criminal lawyer will not undertake his own defense. Many constitutional rights, such as the new protection against use of illegally seized evidence, "are meaningless in the absence of counsel." *Second,* the absolute requirement of counsel in federal prosecutions confirms the need. *Third,* reliance on the trial judge to assert the defendant's rights is misplaced because a man cannot be both judge and counsel. *Fourth,* the distinction between capital and non-capital cases is invalid as a basis for determining the constitutional right to counsel. The due-process clause protects one's "liberty" and "property" as well as one's "life." Moreover, the need for counsel is greater in some non-capital crimes. The Court rejected the capital–non-capital distinction in the overseas court-martial cases; because of their importance (Fortas thus rejecting Ely's advice to play them down) they are discussed in a separate appendix. *Fifth,* the equal-protection clause requires provision of counsel, citing *Griffin v. Illinois.*

II. The demands of federalism do not dictate continued adherence to *Betts v. Brady.*

The need for counsel is so obvious that the real argument for *Betts v. Brady* must be federalism. But it is a false argument. *First,* relying on Professor Kamisar's article, the vast

majority of the states now appoint counsel in all felony cases
as a rule or a matter of practice. This removes the factual
premise of Justice Roberts' opinion in *Betts*, that the states'
"considered judgment" was not to regard counsel as "a
fundamental right, essential to a fair trial." In 1961, when
the Court in *Mapp v. Ohio* imposed the exclusionary
search-and-seizure rule on the states, only half of them had
taken that step themselves. *Second*, "*Betts v. Brady* has
created friction between the states and the federal courts"
because "it does not prescribe a clear-cut standard which
the state courts can follow." The rule of special circumstances "involves federal supervision over the state courts
in its most noxious form. In effect, the federal courts are
given a roving commission to scrutinize the proceeding in
the state court to see if it is 'shocking to the universal sense
of justice.'" A flood of habeas corpus petitions has been
spawned, leading to agitation to curtail the great writ of habeas corpus. *Third*, an absolute counsel requirement would
still leave ample room for state experimentation, a benefit
of our federal system. States would try different systems
for providing counsel—public defenders, private voluntary
associations, assigning counsel.

III. The rule of *Betts v. Brady* has not proved to be a satisfactory standard for judicial administration.

First, the Supreme Court's own decisions under the special-
circumstances approach have been confusing and inconsistent, quoting Professor Allen. *Second*, the rule has "only infrequently led the state courts to appoint counsel. Some of
the state decisions are startling." The Pennsylvania Supreme Court, for example, denied relief to a prisoner convicted without counsel at the age of eighteen, although it
recognized that he "was not wholly a normal person. A behavior clinic study of the defendant shortly after his arrest
revealed him to be a high-grade moron with an intelligence

quotient of fifty-nine," equivalent to a "mental age of only nine." *Third*, the special-circumstances rule is inherently unfair in operation because it usually requires an ignorant layman to prepare—without a lawyer's help—the necessarily subtle argument on appeal that the circumstances at his trial required counsel. *Fourth*, the rule is also unfair because many years may elapse between conviction and the finding of special circumstances. *Fifth*, delay is undesirable for the states, too, since witnesses may have died and records been lost so that new trials cannot be held.

IV. The right to counsel minimally includes appointment of an attorney to assist an indigent person at the trial of a serious offense.

It is not necessary now "to delineate all of the metes and bounds of the right to counsel in state criminal proceedings." An accused should have the right to consult a lawyer "at any time immediately after arrest," but this case involves only "the trial stage of the prosecution. Whatever the perimeter of the right, it surely comprehends the assignment of counsel at the trial." As for the kind of crimes reached, it may be noted that the Court has limited the right of trial by jury in federal cases to exclude petty offenses.

V. The practical implications with respect to persons already imprisoned do not militate against overruling *Betts v. Brady*.

A word should be said about the contention that the rule should not be changed because it "may result in releasing indeterminate numbers of prisoners in some states." *First*, anyone whose conviction is reversed is always subject to retrial. *Second*, the Court rejected similar counsels of fear when it decided the Griffin and Mapp cases, changing constitutional doctrine on rights of appeal and excludable evidence. The constitutional claim here is even stronger. And the states have had ample notice of the importance of coun-

sel to a defendant's rights—thirty years since the Scottsboro case, *Powell v. Alabama.*

At the end Fortas quoted from the letter written to *The
New York Times* by Erwin Griswold and Benjamin Cohen after the *Betts* decision: "At a critical period in world
history *Betts v. Brady* tilts the scales against the safeguard-
ing of one of the most precious rights of man. For in a free
world no man should be condemned to penal servitude for
years without having the right to counsel to defend him.
The right of counsel, for the poor as well as the rich, is
an indispensable safeguard of freedom and justice under
law." Then, in the customarily flat, unemotional finale, the
brief concluded: "For the reasons stated, *Betts v. Brady*
should be overruled, and the judgment of the court below should be reversed." It was signed by Fortas, Krash
and Temple, and a footnote acknowledged the "valuable assistance" of one who could not sign because he was not a
member of the bar, "John Hart Ely, a third-year student at
the Yale Law School, New Haven, Connecticut."

Fortas mailed the brief, as required, to the opposing counsel—the Florida attorney general's office. He also sent a
copy to Gideon at the state prison in Raiford, Florida. Gideon replied on November 30th, as follows:

> Dear Sir:
> This is to thank you for sending me a copy of the brief
> you have prepared and presented to the Supreme Court for
> my cause. Everone and myself thinks it is a very wonderful
> and brillant document.
>
> I do not know how you have enticed the general public
> to take such a interest in this cause. But I must say it makes
> me feel very good.
>
> > Sincerely yours
> > *Clarence Earl Gideon*

10

In the ordinary criminal case the advantage is overwhelmingly with the state, which has abundant resources of men and money to bring against the friendless defendant. Certainly that had been true at the trial of Clarence Earl Gideon. But now, in the Supreme Court, the odds were reversed. A large and expert law firm had done many thousands of dollars' worth of legal work on Gideon's behalf, and he had in his favor also the momentum of legal history—the trend of decisions pointing toward the overruling of *Betts v. Brady*.

On the other side, defending that much-criticized decision and seeking to keep Gideon in prison, there was a single young and inexperienced lawyer who before this case had never set foot in the Supreme Court of the United States. He was Bruce Robert Jacob, an assistant attorney general of Florida, twenty-six years old when *Gideon v. Cochran* began its way through the Supreme Court. The attorney general of Florida, Richard W. Ervin, had formal charge of representing the state's interest in the case; but in fact Jacob wrote most of the legal papers, made the argument and bore the responsibility for the case from beginning to end.

Bruce Jacob is a tall, blond, serious-looking young man whose life reached all sorts of turning points during the year of the Gideon case. In addition to the case itself—and not many lawyers make Supreme Court arguments at that age—Jacob went into private practice while he was writing the brief, won a commission as a second lieutenant in the National Guard and was married. It was a busy year.

Jacob was born March 26, 1935, in Chicago, and his family moved to Sarasota, Florida, when he was a junior in high school. They sent him back to Principia College, a Christian Science institution in Elsah, Illinois, but he quit after a year. He finished college at Florida State University in Tallahassee and got his law degree at Stetson Law School in St. Petersburg. After a few months in a law office in Sarasota and six months in the Army, Jacob joined the state attorney general's office and went into the criminal division. When the Gideon case came along, he had been there two years and had argued several criminal cases in the state courts. He was hoping that the assistant attorney general in charge of criminal appeals, Reeves Bowen, would let him argue a case in the Supreme Court of the United States.

The first Jacob heard of the Gideon case was when the Supreme Court, in March, 1962, asked the Florida attorney general's office to respond to Gideon's petition for review. Reeves Bowen gave Jacob the case. He worked alone on the response to Gideon's petition, relying on *Betts* and some of its successor cases not because he was unaware of their shaky status but because he hoped the Court would not choose Gideon's case as the vehicle for overruling. He was courting a girl who worked in the same building, and after hours she typed the response for him. He learned in June that the Court had granted the petition when he read a newspaper story about the case; the formal letter from the Clerk's Office arrived a few days later.

Jacob was due to spend two weeks in June at a National Guard officers' candidate school, but before leaving he talked with one of the more experienced men in the office, George Georgieff, about what might be done. Georgieff suggested writing to the other forty-nine states and asking them to file *amicus curiae* (friend of the court) briefs, with the aim of mustering a demonstration of sentiment in behalf of Florida and *Betts v. Brady*. Jacob thought writing the states was a good idea for another reason—"so that if *Betts v. Brady* was overruled, they couldn't come back and say 'What the heck, why didn't you tell us about it?'" That thought was in his mind because of what he was told by a colleague in the office who had argued, and lost, another recent right-to-counsel case in the Supreme Court. Some time later, this man said, he was with a group of lawyers and was called "a son of a bitch" by some other state official for losing the case. (Jacob was never sure whether this really happened or was made up to tease him.) "Every day in the attorney general's office," Jacob said later, "we'd sit around drinking coffee and they'd kid me and say I'd better be anonymous after this case was decided, I'd better go somewhere and hide. If you get called that for losing a case on special circumstances, think what they'd do to me for losing *Betts v. Brady*. There were a lot of people who didn't want that case overruled."

The night before he left for National Guard camp, Jacob drafted a letter to the attorneys general of the other states. Attorney General Ervin approved it and had the forty-nine copies sent out over his, Ervin's, signature. It read as follows:

Dear General:

Enclosed is a photostatic copy of a letter received by me from the United States Supreme Court stating that certiorari has been granted in the case of *Gideon v. Cochran,* and advising [that] the Court desires briefs on the question of whether the holding of *Betts v. Brady,* 316 U.S. 455, should be reconsidered. Four members of the present Court have expressed the view, at one time or another, that Betts should be overruled and that the concept of the right to counsel under the Sixth Amendment should be embraced within the due-process clause of the Fourteenth Amendment. If the minority can obtain one more vote, Betts will be overruled and the States will, in effect, be mandatorily required to appoint counsel in all felony cases. Such a decision would infringe on the right of the states to determine their own rules of criminal procedure.

Because of the importance of the question, I am hereby inviting the attorneys general of all states to submit *amicus* briefs in the Gideon case. Also, I would appreciate any advice or aid you can offer, including any statistics or information which you believe would be helpful to us in preparing the main brief.

The role of the *amicus curiae* is well established in the Supreme Court, curious as that might seem in a legal system generally devoted to the thesis that only those personally affected may take their complaint to a court. The *amicus* is, by definition, a person or institution not personally involved in the particular lawsuit. The *amicus* may be interested because the Court's resolution of the legal issue in a case may some day have an effect on him or it; that was the case when other southern states came in as friends of the court in the School Segregation Cases, to help those states defending the particular lawsuits. Or an *amicus* may be an organization with a worthy social aim to push; that was the case of the twenty-one racial, religious and civil liberties groups that joined in asking the Court to outlaw restrictive real estate covenants in 1948. The Federal Government very often comes into Supreme Court cases as a friend of the Court; it has done so in virtually every major test of race-relations law in recent years.

There is disagreement about the exact function of the *amicus curiae*. In theory he is supposed to shed some light on a case that the actual parties are not able or willing to provide. One reason for the Supreme Court's frequent invitation to the Federal Government to participate in non-Government cases is that the Solicitor General, the Justice Department lawyer who officially represents the Government before the Court, provides a degree of expertise and responsibility in advocacy that few private counsel can match. One of the deficiencies of the Supreme Court process is that it often depends on the presentations of inadequate counsel, and the *amicus* who (like the Solicitor General) has a continuing awareness of the Court's needs can be helpful. Private groups can perform a service in that respect along with the Solicitor General. The decision in *Mapp v. Ohio*, outlawing the use of illegally seized evidence in state criminal trials, followed an argument in which counsel for Miss Mapp did not raise that constitutional question at all; but a lawyer for the Ohio Civil Liberties Union, appearing as a friend of the court, did make the point, and the Court seized on it.

More often, *amicus curiae* briefs do not really offer anything new or helpful to the Court. They are filed by interested groups or institutions to let the Court know where they stand—a kind of raw tally of public pressures. Most of the twenty-one *amicus* briefs in the Restrictive Covenant cases were in that category: documents designed to register each group's view and make it feel important, not to provide distinct legal theories. The next year the Court, perhaps suffering from the volume of its friends, changed its rules to limit the filing of *amicus* briefs. The general rule now is that one may be filed only with the consent of all the parties to a case, or by order of the Court upon a showing of "facts or questions of law that have not been, or reasons for believing that they will not adequately be, presented by the parties." But the rule does not apply to the Federal Government or to the states, which may enter any case as a friend of the court.

What Florida was setting out to do with the other states was not at all unusual. State attorneys general frequently file *amicus* briefs in the Supreme Court, and almost without exception the purpose of those briefs is to oppose federal restraints on state processes. When the Supreme Court was considering the New York Regents' Prayer the term before the Gideon case, twenty-two states joined as friends of the court asking that New York be allowed to continue the prayer ceremony. Ervin's letter made the traditional appeal to the states as states, asking them to help resist another infringement "on the right of the states to determine their own rules of criminal procedure." Anyone would have expected a substantial show of support for Florida in *amicus curiae* briefs from the states. But the actual result of Jacob's letter was astonishingly different.

Only about half of the attorneys general replied at all, and even those who were sympathetic were not too helpful. Charles J. Adams of Vermont wrote: "My personal views are that individual states should take a position which would be in opposition to the overruling of *Betts v. Brady*, although with cases along the lines of *Mapp v. Ohio*, there seems to be less and less room for a state to establish and maintain its own procedure in criminal matters. . . . As regards our preparing and filing a brief *amicus curiae*, I doubt

very much that we would be able to do so due to the lack of
sufficient staff for that purpose, but I might be interested in
joining with some other state in its brief." Edwin K. Steers
of Indiana wrote that he was "sympathetic with your cause
and agree that the steady trend of the recent decisions in the
Supreme Court of the United States is infringing on state
criminal procedure." But he said Indiana had always provided counsel for the indigent right up through their appeals, so he would have to say no to filing a brief *amicus*.
Similarly, William M. Ferguson of Kansas said a law on
that state's books since 1941 guaranteed counsel in every
criminal case, so that Kansas could not help. "You have,
however, on the basic philosophical issue of states rights my
wholehearted moral support." The deputy attorney general
of Pennsylvania, Frank P. Lawley, Jr., said that state was
"seriously considering the possibility of filing a brief *amicus*. . . . You indicate that in your judgment if *Betts* is
overruled the states would be required to appoint counsel in
all *felony cases*. What worries me most is the possibility that
the Supreme Court, if it did overrule *Betts*, would not limit
such requirement to felony cases."

In mid-August, two months after Jacob's letter went out,
a reply of a quite different kind came in from the attorney
general of Minnesota, Walter F. Mondale. "I believe in
federalism and states' rights too," he wrote. "But I also believe in the Bill of Rights. . . . Nobody knows better than
an attorney general or a prosecuting attorney that in this
day and age furnishing an attorney to those felony defendants who can't afford to hire one is 'fair and feasible.' Nobody knows better than we do that rules of criminal law
and procedure which baffle trained professionals can only
overwhelm the uninitiated. . . . As chief law enforcement
officer of one of the thirty-five states which provide for the
appointment of counsel for indigents in *all* felony cases, I
am convinced that it is cheap—very cheap—at the price. I

can assure you that such a requirement does not disrupt or otherwise adversely affect our work. . . . Since I firmly believe that any person charged with a felony should be accorded a right to be represented by counsel regardless of his financial condition, I would welcome the courts' imposition of a requirement of appointment of counsel in all state felony prosecutions."

The Mondale letter irritated Jacob. "I thought everyone should have a lawyer, we all thought that," he said later. "But I thought the states should do it by themselves, not have it imposed on them by constitutional construction." Jacob felt so strongly that he wrote a reply for Attorney General Ervin. "I am compelled to answer," the letter said, "because I feel that you do not fully understand my position. . . . I have been placed in the position of an advocate, and as I see it, my duty is to present to the Supreme Court the strongest possible argument on why the doctrine of *Betts v. Brady* should be adhered to. My personal feelings on whether *Betts* is a good rule or not are of no consequence." There were two reasons for suggesting participation by the other states, the letter said: Some of them might prefer to make their own decision on providing counsel for all felony defendants; and, absorption of the Sixth Amendment's counsel guarantee into the Fourteenth Amendment might well mean a requirement of lawyers in misdemeanor cases, where fewer than half the states now provided them. Mondale sent a conciliatory reply, saying "I truly understand and respect your position as an advocate," but he reaffirmed his feeling about the issue.

So far as Jacob was concerned, that ended the episode. But unknown to him, Attorney General Mondale's interest in the Gideon case was not over. He sent copies of his correspondence to several persons, among them the attorney general of Massachusetts, Edward J. McCormack, jr. At the time McCormack was known to the public as the man making a race (futile, as it turned out) against Edward M. Kennedy for the Democratic senatorial nomination. Among law officers he was known particularly for the active Division of Civil Rights and Civil Liberties he had set up in his office. He passed the Mondale correspondence on to the chief of that division, Assistant Attorney General Gerald A. Berlin. Shortly before Labor Day, Berlin, who was vacationing on Martha's Vineyard, mentioned the Ervin-Mondale exchange of letters to some friends over cocktails. As they discussed it, Berlin thought of the possibility of writing an *amicus* brief on the other side of the case—in behalf of Gideon. When he got back to the office, he readily got McCormack's approval of the idea. He talked to Professor Clark Byse of the Harvard Law School, faculty adviser to a student organization called the Civil Liberties Research Service, and arranged for it to provide some material. The students were helpful, although the deadline was so close that Berlin had to do more brief-writing than he had expected. Three other members of the Harvard law faculty helped out: Professor Mark DeWolfe Howe, on one section of the brief, and Professors Howe and Roger Fisher and Dean Erwin N. Griswold in checking Berlin's draft.

The Massachusetts brief-writing project was cleared with Mondale, who had wanted to do the same thing but had not got around to it. Mondale helped persuade other attorneys general to sign, and at the last minute McCormack and Berlin got on the telephone and signed up more states. The brief was filed on November 23rd—the Supreme Court Rules require *amici curiae* to file by the same date as the party they are supporting—with the endorsement of twenty-two states, in this listed order: Massachusetts, Minnesota, Colorado, Connecticut, Georgia, Hawaii, Idaho, Illinois, Iowa, Kentucky, Maine, Michigan, Missouri, Nevada, Ohio, North Dakota, Oregon, Rhode Island, South Dakota, Washington, West Virginia, Alaska. It turned out later that

New Jersey had agreed to sign but had inadvertently been omitted; the correction was made just in time to be reflected in the United States Reports, the permanent bound volumes of Supreme Court opinions.

Among the unusual aspects of this brief for twenty-three states was the fact that three of the signers—Hawaii, Maine and Rhode Island—had no general requirement for appointment of counsel in felony cases. The mere fact that twenty-three states would urge the Supreme Court to impose a new standard of fairness on state criminal procedure was the most startling of all. Indeed, when one member of the Supreme Court saw this *amicus* brief, he remarked that he would not have been surprised had the Court instead received one from forty-nine states endorsing Florida's position.

The brief for the twenty-three states called forthrightly for the overruling of *Betts v. Brady*, making many of the same arguments as Fortas. (The two briefs were prepared without consultation or even knowledge of each other's intentions; Fortas was as astounded as the justices when he got a copy of it.) Berlin called the special-circumstances rule a "curious doctrine" and said the Court had "persistently whittled away" at it in cases after *Betts*. Even when the rule had been applied, he said, it was "with reluctance and usually by a closely and sharply divided Court. . . . It is now most unrealistic to expect that the trial judges, looking ahead, can accomplish that which has obviously been so disturbing to this Court from the vantage point of looking back."

The distinctive section of Berlin's brief for the states dealt with the practical results of overruling *Betts v. Brady*. The brief was carefully confined to advocating provision of counsel in felony cases. But it admitted that misdemeanors "might be foreseen as the troublesome next step." It said also that "the question of adequacy of representation will some day present a problem to this Court," and that "representation alone does not solve the problems of the indigent accused, for there may be other vital expenses, such as the traveling expenses, daily fees and subsistence of witnesses." Then the brief faced the problem posed by those already in prison, who might seek their release if *Betts v. Brady* were abandoned. One course, it said, would be to let all these prisoners come under the new decision. That was the practice followed after the Supreme Court in 1938 established an absolute right to counsel in federal criminal trials; however onerous the task of dealing with prisoners' pleas, "the court managed to dispose of them, convinced, evidently, that it was wiser to make the new constitutional guaranty fully effective than to protect themselves from a flood of cases." But there was an alternative, "which in many ways seems more desirable. That is for this Court to determine that, since the standards which it establishes are dependent, not upon the specific intention of the framers of the Constitution but upon the lessons of experience, it is appropriate not to give those standards retroactive effect." Thus, on this point, the states' brief was in direct conflict with Fortas's view that prospective overruling—applying the new right to counsel only in future—was an inappropriate course for the Supreme Court. This section on practical problems ended with the statement that all branches of the legal profession would have to "bestir themselves" to meet the need for counsel if *Betts* were overruled —state and local bar associations, charitable organizations, law schools, individual members of the bar by appointment. Then the brief concluded:

"*Betts v. Brady*, already an anachronism when handed down, has spawned twenty years of bad law. That in the world of today a man may be condemned to penal servitude for lack of means to supply counsel for his defense is unthinkable. We respectfully urge that the conviction below be reversed, that *Betts v. Brady* be reconsidered and that this Court require that all persons tried for a felony in a state court shall have the right to counsel as a matter of due process of law and of equal protection of the laws."

Jacob had no idea that any states were planning an *amicus* brief on the other side. The first he heard of it was just before the brief was filed, in late November. The attorney general of Missouri, Thomas F. Eagleton, mentioned the Massachusetts brief in a letter to Richard Ervin, adding that, "to be abundantly frank," he intended to join it. Jacob was surprised, but he felt he had done the right thing in calling the attention of the other state law officers to the Gideon case. He thought, as he had originally, that they were entitled to know about an issue so important for the state criminal process, even though it had turned out that so many of them were on the other side of the issue.

One more state *amicus* brief came in without notice to Jacob or Fortas. It was from Oregon, and it dealt entirely with Oregon's experience under a 1959 state law allowing prisoners to petition the courts for relief of claimed violations of their federal constitutional rights—including violations long ago at their trials. Since the passage of the act, the Oregon brief said, the courts had ruled in favor of twenty prisoners, finding "substantial defects" in their convictions or sentences. Of those, fifteen had had no lawyers when the defect occurred. Eight prisoners had won their final release from prison under the act; all had lacked counsel "at the crucial point in the original proceeding." The brief was only six pages long, but it made a single point tellingly. This was, as expressed in the conclusion: "The experience of the State of Oregon tends to indicate that it would provide greater protection of constitutional rights, and would be less expensive, to insist upon counsel in each original criminal proceeding than to attempt by a post-conviction proceeding to recover justice lost by defects at the trial."

Florida had also given permission to the American Civil Liberties Union to come in as a friend of the court. Its concern with the case had begun with a telephone call from J. Lee Rankin, the last Solicitor General in the Eisenhower Administration, who had gone to New York to practice. Rankin had a deep interest in civil liberties and was a member of the advisory committee of the Civil Liberties Center at the New York University Law School. When he read about the Supreme Court's grant of certiorari in the Gideon case, and its call for a reappraisal of *Betts v. Brady*, he telephoned the director of the center, Associate Professor Norman Dorsen, and asked whether any civil-liberties group planned to participate. Dorsen carried the idea to Melvin L. Wulf, legal director of the A.C.L.U., who thought an *amicus* brief was desirable. These three men took principal responsibility for the A.C.L.U. presentation, with Rankin as the senior attorney, Dorsen in charge of the brief drafting and Wulf doing particular research.

A distinctive contribution of the Civil Liberties Union brief was an exhaustive survey of the handling of right-to-counsel cases by the state courts under the special-circumstances doctrine of *Betts v. Brady*. The survey, which covered all the reported decisions by appellate courts in states without an automatic counsel rule, showed that those courts very rarely found special circumstances requiring a lawyer. Of forty-four cases in Pennsylvania, only one had been adjudged to present such circumstances; three were remanded for a lower-court hearing. In Maryland three of thirty-eight cases were deemed to show the need for a lawyer, in Florida one of seventeen and one remanded for a hearing. Altogether, of one hundred thirty-nine state appellate court decisions on the special-circumstances issue, only eleven found that the trial judge had erred in failing to appoint counsel.

After losing in the state courts, the A.C.L.U. brief said, the prisoner probably asks the Supreme Court for review, "which is usually denied, often because there was no hearing granted in the state courts that would have revealed the possible validity of a constitutional claim." Then the prisoner can go to a federal district court with a petition for habeas corpus and go through a whole new round—the district court, a court of appeals and then the Supreme Court. All this, said the A.C.L.U. brief, expended large and increasing amounts of judicial energy. The number of habeas corpus petitions filed in the federal district courts had gone up from one hundred twenty-seven in 1941 to eight hundred seventy-one in 1960, and prisoners' petitions in the Supreme Court were increasing even more rapidly. The federal habeas corpus jurisdiction was especially irritating to federal-state relations because the states disliked having constitutional issues retried after a prisoner had gone all through the state appellate process. And many, perhaps most, of these prisoners' cases arose because there had been no counsel at trial. "Overruling *Betts v. Brady* would sharply decrease the volume of cases . . . and reduce the federal-state conflict inherent in the federal habeas corpus remedy."

As late as Thanksgiving, Jacob expected a substantial number of states, perhaps as many as seven, to join in an *amicus* brief on Florida's side of the case. The hope was based on the somewhat vague letters sent by their attorneys general. As it turned out, only two states spoke up for Florida—Alabama and North Carolina. ("I never knew what happened to the others," Jacob said later.) This *amicus* brief was written by George D. Mentz, assistant attorney general of Alabama, who had argued one right-to-counsel

case in the Supreme Court. It made a strong appeal for
federalism and states' rights.

"It is the essence of our federalism," the brief said, "that
states should have the widest latitude in the administration
of their own systems of criminal justice." Some day, "when
finally the millennium is reached," all criminal defendants
will have lawyers and the poor will all be saved "the pangs
of hunger or the discomforts occasioned by a lack of adequate clothing, suitable housing or other creature comforts."
Those are "humanitarian principles," but they are not imposed on the states by the Fourteenth Amendment. "If and
when, in the considered judgment of the people of the individual states, such gratuitous services or aid are warranted
morally or are feasible financially, they will be provided.
Though man's social evolution is slow, history proves that
he does advance in all fields. To be lasting, however, his
progress must result from his own volition rather than come
from judicial fiat."

On the counsel issue more specifically, Mentz's brief went
on, Alabama lawyers at a recent meeting agreed that an
indigent without counsel "stands a better chance of obtaining from a jury either an outright acquittal or less severe
punishment than one represented by an attorney." Only a
few lawyers would, in any case, be "equal matches for
career prosecutors." In this very trial, the record shows
that Gideon "presented the available defense about as ably
as an average lawyer could have done." A universal counsel
requirement might be "an unbearably onerous financial
burden" for poorer counties if they had to pay assigned
counsel. "Furthermore, it is not an uncommon situation in
thinly populated rural counties for there to be more persons
charged with crime than there are lawyers versed in criminal
practice, and some judges may encounter real difficulty in
appointing enough qualified lawyers to serve at their crim-

inal terms of court." (Mentz, had he known, might have told the Supreme Court that there were only seventy-seven practicing lawyers in the six counties of the Florida judicial circuit where Gideon was tried.)

The brief concluded: "Even with its exposure to occasional abuses, the rule of *Betts v. Brady* remains the best one for our American way of life. Any decision to make mandatory the appointment of counsel for all indigents charged with crime in state courts should come not from this Court but from the people of the individual states acting through their elected legislatures or judges."

That left only Florida's brief to be filed. Jacob had worked on it during the summer, but only sporadically, because too many other things were happening. Just after his return from National Guard camp in June, he had been interviewed by a law firm in Bartow, Florida: Holland, Bevis and Smith. (Holland is United States Senator Spessard L. Holland.) Jacob was offered a position in the firm and agreed to take it, beginning in October. He thought the briefs in the Gideon case would all be filed by then, and he got Attorney General Ervin's permission to carry on with the oral argument of the case after leaving the office. But he had not anticipated the conflict with Fortas over what should go into the printed record. The time for filing of briefs does not begin to run until the record is printed, and the delay over that issue pushed everything back about three months. As a result, Jacob wrote Florida's brief after leaving the attorney general's staff.

By the time he began to write it, in the late fall, Jacob had lost the few shreds of hope he had had of winning the case. The episode of the record had not been encouraging. Jacob had not even known that a transcript of Gideon's trial had been prepared and supplied to the Supreme Court until he received Fortas's designation of materials to go into the record. Then he asked around the attorney general's office and was told by old-timers that the same thing had happened—use of a trial transcript in a habeas corpus case where it was not formally at issue—in a Florida case taken to the Supreme Court in 1940. That case was *Chambers v. Florida,* a landmark in the career of Hugo L. Black as a justice because he had been denounced, when appointed, as a racist. Four young Negroes had been convicted of murder on the basis of confessions they claimed had been coerced from them. Justice Black, after what one informed commentator has called "great internal struggles," wrote an opinion for the Court reversing the convictions on the ground that the prisoners had been forced to confess. "Under our constitutional system," he wrote, "courts stand against any winds that blow as havens of refuge for those who might otherwise suffer because they are helpless, weak, outnumbered, or because they are non-conforming victims of prejudice and public excitement."

More discouraging to Jacob than loss of the small struggle over getting the trial transcript into the record was the retirement, on August 28th, of Justice Felix Frankfurter. More than any member of the Supreme Court Justice Frankfurter stood for a belief in federalism, in the right of the states to be free from too limiting national restraints. In the early years after *Betts v. Brady*, Justice Frankfurter had been one of the strongest supporters of its flexible counsel doctrine. In more recent years he had gone along silently with decisions requiring counsel in particular cases, but not with any suggestion of abandoning *Betts.* Not only his vote but his leadership on the Court seemed to Jacob—and to others —essential to any hope of preserving that doctrine. President Kennedy replaced Justice Frankfurter on the bench with Arthur J. Goldberg, the Secretary of Labor, whose training and experience in a different era made it doubtful at best that he would share his predecessor's emphasis on state independence.

"I had been developing some hope that the Court would draw back from this ultimate 'legislating,' " Jacob said later. "When Justice Frankfurter retired, I realized that we had very little chance."

On September 8th Jacob married Ann Wear, the girl he had been courting in the State Capitol. They had a week's honeymoon in Jamaica. Shortly afterward they set up their new household in Bartow, and Jacob began practice at Holland, Bevis and Smith. The firm told him to take all the time he needed on the Gideon case, but he "felt like I shouldn't do that." So he did the work, with clerical help from Ann, on nights and weekends. Research was a problem because there was so little material available in Bartow, which is a prosperous town but has a population of only thirteen thousand and a limited law library. Just about every weekend Jacob and his wife drove the two hundred and fifty miles to Tallahassee. He had a key to the library of the Florida Supreme Court, and there they would work —sometimes all night long. He read cases and other material, underlining things he thought important, and then Ann would copy them. Sometimes, instead of Tallahassee, they went to the Stetson Law School library in St. Petersburg, which was only sixty miles or so from Bartow. When Jacob finally got around to drafting the brief, in late November, he worked at home in the evening; the next day Ann would type up what he had written. The last few days, as the deadline approached, he was forced to take some office time to finish up. Just before Christmas he sent the brief off to the attorney general's office in Tallahassee to be printed. There final printing arrangements were handled by A. G. Spicola, Jr. But no changes were made in the substance of the brief; it remained a one-man product, written under circumstances that could hardly have been in more striking contrast to the time and talent expended on Gideon's side of the case.

The brief, covering seventy-four pages, began with a section arguing that Gideon was not entitled to counsel under existing law—the rule of *Betts v. Brady*. Jacob reviewed the cases that had followed *Betts* in requiring a showing of special circumstances to obtain counsel. Gideon, he said, had "made no affirmative showing of any circumstances of unfairness which would have entitled him to counsel under the Fourteenth Amendment"; he had said nothing about "his age, experience, mental capacity, familiarity or unfamiliarity with court procedure, or the complexity of the legal issues presented by the charge." Jacob held to the position that the transcript of Gideon's trial was not properly before the Supreme Court; but if it were considered, he said, it proved that Gideon had had a fair trial. "He took an active role in his defense and showed that he possessed much skill and facility in questioning witnesses." And beyond the trial transcript, Gideon's prison record showed that he was fifty when arrested, had finished the eighth grade and had been convicted of four felonies—indicating, in the words of Justice Roberts about Betts, that he "was not wholly unfamiliar with criminal procedure."

Jacob had also obtained a letter from the judge who had tried the case, Robert L. McCrary, Jr., saying it was his "opinion that Gideon had both the mental capacity and the experience in the courtroom at previous trials to adequately conduct his defense. This was later borne out at the trial. . . . In my opinion he did as well as most lawyers could have done in handling his case." Jacob did not mention this letter in his brief but sent a copy to the Supreme Court, where it went into the *Gideon* file.

The second and more substantial section of the brief argued that *Betts v. Brady* "should not be overruled or modified." It was under eight subheadings and can be summarized as follows:

First, there is no historical basis "for requiring states to automatically appoint counsel in all cases." Historically, the Sixth Amendment was designed to overcome the English common-law rule forbidding the retention of counsel in felony cases.

Second, our federal system counsels against such a requirement. "The Fourteenth Amendment does not impose upon the states any uniform code of criminal procedure." Holmes had warned against use of the Fourteenth Amendment to "prevent the making of social experiments . . . in the insulated chambers afforded by the several states." If the Court now adopts "an inflexible rule requiring automatic appointment in every case," it would "defeat the very desirable possibility of state experiment in the field of criminal procedure." States would "be prevented from adopting novel forms of procedure, whether fair or unfair."

Third, the flexible test of requiring counsel only to assure a fair trial is consistent with the concept of "due process of law." The due-process clause is "a broad, inexplicit provision, and it is not susceptible of being reduced to a mechanical or fixed formula."

Fourth, "the *Betts v. Brady* rule provides a clear and consistent standard for determination of the right to counsel." The cases indicate ten factors that should be considered, such as the prisoner's illiteracy or youth. The attempt in Fortas's brief (which of course Jacob had studied) to show that there were inconsistencies in the cases decided under the *Betts* rule proves nothing, because the common law is full of inconsistency. "The *Betts* approach is the common-law approach, consisting of the development of a body of law on a case-by-case basis, and lawyers for centuries have thrived in distinguishing one case from another on the basis of factual situations and circumstances."

Fifth, many states require appointment of counsel, but the rules vary, and so the right cannot be called "fundamental." (A separate appendix listed the counsel rules of the fifty states, less comprehensively than Professor Kamisar's survey.)

Sixth, absorption of the Sixth Amendment counsel guarantee into the Fourteenth would have grave consequences. It would be impossible to draw the line at felonies; misdemeanors would have to be included, too. The result would be "an enormous burden on members of the bar. Also, such an imposition would encourage those charged with misdemeanors to plead not guilty and, consequently, more time would be consumed in the trial of minor cases. The entire undertaking would result in unnecessary expense to taxpayers." Moreover, counsel should logically be required in civil as well as criminal cases. It has been argued that overruling *Betts* would cut down "the flood of litigation concerning the right to counsel." But that is unrealistic; the overruling would itself "create myriad and complex new legal questions."

Seventh, appointment of counsel for the poor in all cases should not be required by the equal protection clause of the Fourteenth Amendment. If that clause is read to forbid distinction between rich and poor in the courts, then the states would have to provide counsel for the poor not only at trial but on appeal, and "would logically be required to provide an indigent with bail, with the services of investigators, psychiatrists, etc., since those things are available to the rich man."

Eighth, the practical implications require "adherence to *Betts v. Brady*." A survey of the Florida prisons shows that approximately 5,093 of the 7,836 prisoners in custody were not represented by counsel when tried. "If *Betts* should be overruled by this Court in the instant case, as many as 5,093 hardened criminals may be eligible to be released in one mass exodus in Florida alone, not to mention those in other states."

Jacob ended with a cautionary plea. "If this Court should

decide to overrule *Betts*," he said, "respondent respectfully requests that it be accomplished in such way as to prevent the new rule from operating retrospectively." In other words, the newly defined right to counsel should not apply to persons already in prison—presumably including Clarence Earl Gideon.

Even before he finished the brief, Jacob heard from the Supreme Court about the oral argument of the case. A letter received from Chief Deputy Clerk Cullinan on December 17th said *Gideon v. Cochran* would be "reached for argument on Monday, January 14, 1963."

11

Only a small part of the process of decision in the Supreme Court is exposed to public view, and of that portion by far the most interesting and the most revealing is oral argument. Even the citizen wholly unfamiliar with the Court can gain some sense of the institution by sitting in the back of the chamber and listening to an argument. The exhaustive probing of a single set of facts shows, if it is done well, how our adversary system of justice can make truth emerge from conflict. It shows also how close the questions are that the Supreme Court must answer; characteristically, the listener finds himself persuaded by the last voice he has heard. The comments from the bench—sometimes funny, sometimes quite blunt—bring out the personalities of the justices and remind us that the Court is a collection of strong-minded individuals, much less institutionalized than the typical agency of the Executive Branch.

Oral argument is more important in the Court's decisional process than many lawyers realize. Too often they seem to regard it as a ceremonial affair, serving only to put a gloss on the contentions so carefully made in their briefs. But the Court does not feel that way. The justices who have spoken on the subject—and many have—say that oral argument performs a distinct function, in some ways more influential than that of the briefs. A good argument, Justice Harlan said, "may in many cases make the difference between winning and losing, no matter how good the briefs are."

There are two reasons for this. One is that a brief cannot answer back when a justice reading it expresses doubt about some line of reasoning. Oral argument presents a great opportunity to answer the doubts and questions raised from the bench, to mollify one's critics and arm one's friends. This opportunity is the greater because of the Supreme Court tradition that oral argument is not an exhibition of high school oratory but an exchange between counsel and Court. The rules state that the Court "looks with disfavor on any oral argument that is read from a prepared text"; it is a time for *argument*, not declamation. Justice Frankfurter once said that the Court saw itself not as "a dozing audience for the reading of soliloquies, but as a questioning body, utilizing oral argument as a means for exposing the difficulties of a case with a view to meeting them." And so there are likely to be a great many questions from the bench. Unfortunately, some lawyers—not excluding well-known names of the Wall Street firms—seem to resent them, seeing questions as an intrusion on their well-ordered schemes of argument rather than as invitations to persuade. Justice Jackson, who was one of the great oral advocates of his day before he went on the bench, said in his wonderfully astringent style that he felt "there should be some comfort derived from any question from the bench. It is clear proof that the inquiring justice is not asleep. If the question is relevant, it denotes he is grappling with your contention, even though he has not grasped it. It gives you opportunity to inflate his ego by letting him think he has discovered an idea for himself."

The second reason for the importance of oral argument is the place it has in the timetable of the decisional process. The justices customarily take a tentative vote, at their Friday conference, on all the cases argued that week. The argument is likely to be fresh in their minds. Most members of the Court, Justice Jackson said, "form at least a tentative conclusion from it in a large percentage of the cases." Moreover, a lawyer who at argument succeeds in arousing a strongly favorable interest on the part of even one justice thereby obtains for his cause a spokesman in the privacy of the conference room.

Given the significance of argument, its potential is realized far too infrequently. Many, probably most, arguments in the Supreme Court are dreary affairs. Counsel are often ill-at-ease, ill-prepared or—worse yet—overconfident. One of the worst sins is to brush off questions or answer them less than candidly. (On the other hand, Justice Holmes once complimented a lawyer on his candor and then, as the gentleman was preening himself, remarked: "You know, candor is one of the most effective instruments in deception.") Another mistake is to take the lofty approach, arguing only large abstractions; such tactics inevitably produce glazed expressions on the bench. The justices seem more interested when a lawyer sticks to homely, factual arguments.

Often in their questions the members of the Court try to find out what the case means in human terms, as if in their ivory tower they were lonesome for the real world. Justice

Jackson had a slightly different explanation for the Court's fascination with the facts at arguments. "The purpose of a hearing is that the Court may learn what it does not know," he said, "and it knows least about the facts. It may sound paradoxical, but most contentions of law are won or lost on the facts. They often incline a judge to one side or the other."

It is said, correctly, that no oral presentation, however effective, is likely to be able to change the deep-rooted philosophical positions that a justice inevitably comes to hold after some years on the bench. But there are ways of getting around those entrenchments, of suggesting narrow grounds (which the Court almost always prefers) for a decision in favor of one's client. There are also ways of alienating votes that should be favorable. Probably more cases are lost than won by argument.

The mediocre level of argument in the Supreme Court reflects the lack of a strong tradition of oral advocacy in this country. In England, by contrast, the appellate process is almost entirely an oral presentation. There are no briefs; counsel read out the relevant portions of the lower-court record and then discuss the legal questions, without fixed time limits, until their lordships indicate that they have heard enough. A successful barrister is by definition an effective oral advocate. But in this country many of the most prosperous lawyers never see the inside of a courtroom, and legal training emphasizes written work rather than oral presentation.

Our system was once much more like the British. There was a distinctive Supreme Court bar whose members—such men as Daniel Webster—appeared regularly before the Court. It was not unusual, moreover, for Webster to go on for days. But those spacious times are gone. The only lawyers who appear in the Supreme Court with any regularity are the Solicitor General and the members of his small staff, who argue most of the Federal Government cases. Many arguments are made by lawyers who will appear in the Supreme Court only once in their lives; when they get that chance, few are about to delegate the argument to some modern-day Webster. (Experience is not all; little-known lawyers from far corners of the country occasionally make superior arguments, the better for their freshness of approach.) And time for argument is now rigorously limited. Chief Justice Hughes was said by one of his law clerks to have "called time on a leader of the New York bar in the middle of the word 'if.' " Ordinarily the Court allows either an hour or a half-hour to each side of a case. In the Gideon case each party had an hour, and the Court had taken the unusual step of granting an additional half-hour for oral argument by a friend of the Court on each side: former Solicitor General Rankin, on behalf of the American Civil Liberties Union, for Gideon, and Assistant Attorney General Mentz of Alabama, for Florida.

The argument presented no novel challenge to Abe Fortas, a man of experience and reputation in the Supreme Court. But to Bruce Jacob, who had never even seen the courtroom before, the prospect was unnerving. He flew to Washington on Saturday, January 12th, two days before the Clerk's Office had indicated the case would be reached. The flight was bumpy, doing nothing to improve Jacob's already queasy stomach. He spent the weekend in the hotel trying to anticipate questions he might be asked, worrying over his argument outline, worrying in general. Early on Monday morning he had another minor concern to dispose of: to arrange his admission to the Supreme Court bar. Anyone is eligible after three years in the bar of his state's highest court. Membership qualifies one to file briefs and argue in the Supreme Court. Jacob barely met the three-year requirement, but under the usual practice he would have been admitted *pro hac vice*, for this one occasion only, to make his argument.

About twenty-five hundred lawyers a year pay the twenty-five-dollar fee to become members of the Supreme Court bar, most of them presumably so that they can frame the parchment certificate and hang it in their offices; the Court uses the money to pay the expenses of indigents such as Gideon. Each applicant must be presented for admission, in open court, by a lawyer already a member of the Court's bar, and this rule caused Jacob some unnecessary worry. Senator Holland of Florida had arranged to have former Solicitor General Rankin move Jacob's admission. Jacob was afraid it would be embarrassing to have the favor done by one of his adversaries—an excessive sensitivity on his part—and he got George Mentz of Alabama to present him instead.

As he entered the Supreme Court building that Monday morning and then for the first time watched the justices at work, Bruce Jacob experienced the confusing change of emotions that any sensitive person feels in that curious place. For the Court is a place of contrasts, of paradoxes. It is grandiose and intimate, ritualistic and informal, austere and human—at the same time the most aloof and the most approachable of all the institutions of government.

Grandiose is the word for the physical setting. The W.P.A. Guide to Washington called the Supreme Court building a "great marble temple" which "by its august scale and mighty splendor seems to bear little relation to the functional purposes of government." Shortly before the justices moved into the building in 1935 from their old chamber across the street in the Capitol, Justice Stone wrote his sons: "The place is almost bombastically pretentious, and thus it seems to me wholly inappropriate for a quiet group of old boys such as the Supreme Court." He told his friends that the justices would be "nine black beetles in the Temple of Karnak."

The visitor who climbs the marble steps and passes

through the marble columns of the huge pseudo-classical façade finds himself in a cold, lofty hall, again all marble. Great bronze gates exclude him from the area of the building where the justices work in private—their offices, library and conference room. In the courtroom, which is always open to the public, the atmosphere of austere pomp is continued: there are more columns, an enormously high ceiling, red velvet hangings, friezes carved high on the walls. The ritual opening of each day's session adds to the feeling of awe. The Court Crier to the right of the bench smashes his gavel down sharply on a wooden block, everyone rises and the justices file in through the red draperies behind the bench and stand at their places as the Crier intones the traditional opening: "The honorable, the Chief Justice and the Associate Justices of the Supreme Court of the United States. Oyez, oyez, oyez. All persons having business before the honorable, the Supreme Court of the United States, are admonished to draw near and give their attention, for the Court is now sitting. God save the United States and this honorable Court."

But then, when an argument begins, all the trappings and ceremony seem to fade, and the scene takes on an extraordinary intimacy. In the most informal way, altogether without pomp, Court and counsel converse. It is conversation—as direct, unpretentious and focused discussion as can be found anywhere in Washington.

"It was nothing like I expected," Bruce Jacob said later. "It was so informal—I just couldn't believe it. Usually judges are so sober-looking; they don't laugh. Not that they're inhuman, but they're nothing like Supreme Court justices. I just got the impression that these men had a real good time, talking to each other and asking questions."

The case of *Gideon v. Cochran* was not reached that day. Chief Deputy Clerk Cullinan always has counsel in Court earlier than necessary, so that there is no chance of a case ending early and no other being ready for the justices. There is no exact time for each case to start; the Court simply sits for argument from 10 A.M. to 2:30 P.M. (with 12 to 12:30 out for lunch), Monday through Thursday, and when one case is finished the next is called. Because this was a Monday, arguments were delayed for the reading of opinions. Then, at noon, there was a special interruption because the justices had to be at the Capitol to hear President Kennedy read his State of the Union message. Later that afternoon and the next morning, counsel in the Gideon case sat and listened with at least half an ear to the argument of an important antitrust case by two able advocates, Solicitor General Archibald Cox and Gerhard A. Gesell of Washington. They concluded at 11:06 Tuesday morning.

Chief Justice Warren, as is the custom, called the next case by reading aloud its full title: Number 155, Clarence Earl Gideon, petitioner, versus H. G. Cochran, Jr., director, Division of Corrections, State of Florida. From his desk at the left of the bench the Clerk of the Court, John F. Davis, said, "Counsel are present," and the lawyers in the Gideon case moved forward to two long tables just below the bench.

The justices are seated in an order fixed by tradition. At the far right (as seen by the spectators) was the newest member of the Court, Arthur J. Goldberg of Illinois, fifty-four years old, the gray-haired labor lawyer who had made such a dynamic Secretary of Labor before President Kennedy appointed him to the bench. At the far left was the other Kennedy appointee, Byron R. White of Colorado, forty-five, physically powerful but scholarly in appearance, as befits an All-American football hero who was also a Rhodes Scholar. Next to Justice Goldberg was Potter Stewart of Ohio, forty-seven but still collegiate in his good looks, whom President Eisenhower made a Court of Appeals judge and then raised to the Supreme Court in 1958. Second from the left was the smallish, brisk figure of William J. Brennan, Jr., fifty-six, a New Jersey Supreme Court justice who was a surprise Eisenhower appointee (because he was a Democrat) in 1956; he is the only Roman Catholic on the Court. On the right, again, was John Marshall Harlan, sixty-three, a Wall Street lawyer picked by Eisenhower for the Court of Appeals and advanced to the Supreme Court in 1955, looking perhaps more like a judge than anyone else, appropriately enough for the grandson and namesake of an earlier Supreme Court justice. Third from the left was Tom C. Clark, also sixty-three, a friendly Texan, former Attorney General, the only Truman appointee (1949) still on the Court. To the right of the Chief Justice was William O. Douglas, sixty-four, a ruddy-faced outdoorsman from the state of Washington, a law-school professor and New Deal official appointed by Franklin Roosevelt in 1939. On the other side of the Chief was Hugo L. Black, seventy-six years old but still a tough competitor at tennis, hawk-nosed, with the soft sound of rural Alabama in his voice, a Senator when Roosevelt put him on the Court in 1937. Finally, at the center sat Earl Warren, seventy-one, a county law officer for twenty years, attorney general of California for four, an immensely popular governor for ten, Republican candidate for Vice-President in 1948; a huge, white-haired figure, named Chief Justice by Eisenhower in 1953.

The lawyer arguing a case stands at a small rostrum between the two counsel tables, facing the Chief Justice. The party that lost in the lower court goes first, and so the argument in *Gideon v. Cochran* was begun by Abe Fortas. As he stood, the Chief Justice gave him the customary greeting, "Mr. Fortas," and he made the customary opening: "Mr. Chief Justice, may it please the Court. . . ."

This case presents "a narrow question," Fortas said—the right to counsel—unencumbered by extraneous issues. The charge was a felony, not any lesser offense; Gideon's indigence was conceded; he had unquestionably made a timely request for counsel, and the demand was for a lawyer at his trial, not at any earlier and hence more doubtful point in the criminal proceeding.

Fortas began reciting the facts. In his deep, deliberate, somewhat mournful voice, occasionally removing his horn-rimmed glasses and gesturing with them for emphasis, he told the justices about the morning Clarence Earl Gideon was supposed to have broken into the Bay Harbor Poolroom and stolen "some wine, perhaps some cigarettes and an un-stated amount of money." Fortas described Gideon's active participation in his own trial, his attempts to cross-examine and address the jury. Then, on this brief foundation of the facts, he began to build his legal argument.

"This record does not indicate that Clarence Earl Gideon was a person of low intelligence," Fortas said, "or that the judge was unfair to him. But to me this case shows the basic difficulty with Betts versus Brady. It shows that no man, however intelligent, can conduct his own defense adequately."

At this point Justice Harlan intervened. He was the Court's most convinced believer in the value of state inde-pendence, and Fortas had anticipated the greatest difficulty in persuading him to overrule *Betts*.

"That's not the point, is it, Mr. Fortas?" Justice Harlan asked. "*Betts* didn't go on the assumption that a man can do as well without an attorney as he can with one, did it? Every-one knows that isn't so."

In fact, it could be fairly argued that Justice Roberts, in *Betts*, had gone on exactly that assumption. He certainly had said that that particular trial was so simple that there would have been little for a lawyer to do. But Fortas, instead of challenging Justice Harlan's proposition, accepted it for the implicit concession it was and used it to drive on to his point about federalism.

"I entirely agree, Mr. Justice Harlan, with the point you

are making: Namely, that of course a man cannot have a fair trial without a lawyer, but *Betts* held that this consideration was outweighed by the demands of federalism. . . .

"My purpose was to show that this case is not Tweedledum and Tweedledee with one tried by counsel. I believe this case dramatically illustrates that you cannot have a fair trial without counsel. Under our adversary system of justice, how can our civilized nation pretend that there is a fair trial without the counsel for the prosecution doing all he can within the limits of decency, and the counsel for the defense doing his best within the same limits, and from that clash will emerge the truth? . . . I think there is a tendency to forget what happens to these poor, miserable, indigent people—in these strange and awesome circumstances. Sometimes in this Court there is a tendency to forget what happens downstairs. . . . I was reminded the other night, as I was pondering this case, of Clarence Darrow when he was prosecuted for trying to fix a jury. The first thing he realized was that he needed a lawyer—he, one of the country's great criminal lawyers. . . .

"And so the real basis of Betts against Brady must be the understanding sensitivity of this Court to the pull of federalism."

This last statement of Fortas's seemed, for some not readily understandable reason, to anger Justice Harlan. This usually gentle man visibly reddened, leaned forward and said very sharply, "Really, Mr. Fortas, 'understanding sensitivity' seems to me a most unfortunate term to describe one of the fundamental principles of our constitutional system."

"Mr. Justice Harlan," Fortas replied without a flicker of emotion, "I believe in federalism. It is a fundamental principle for which I personally have the highest regard and concern, and which I feel must be reconciled with the result I advocate. But I believe that Betts against Brady does not incorporate a proper regard for federalism. It requires a case-by-case supervision by this Court of state criminal proceedings, and that cannot be wholesome. . . . Intervention should be in the least abrasive, the least corrosive way possible."

That was the argument that Fortas considered central to his case. He had expected to make it later in his presentation, after more of a build-up, but Justice Harlan's question had given him the opportunity to make the point dramatically; as a skillful advocate he had abandoned his earlier outline and made the thrust at once. Whether the answer satisfied Justice Harlan was a question only the justice could answer, but he did lean back and appear somewhat happier.

Fortas traced the history of the right to counsel in the Supreme Court, beginning with the Scottsboro case, *Powell v. Alabama*, in 1932. He described the *Betts* doctrine and the subsequent cases in which the Court had or had not found the special circumstances requiring counsel.

"I have read all the cases now," he said, "state and federal, and it is a fascinating inquiry. As I read the opinions of this Court, I hope I may be forgiven for saying that my heart was full of compassion for the judges having to review those records and look for 'special circumstances.' "

Justice Stewart: "When was the last time we did not find special circumstances? I think there have been none in my four and one-half terms on the Court."

Fortas: "I think it was Quicksall and Michigan, in 1950. . . . Of course this [the special-circumstances approach] is wrong. How can a judge, when a man is arraigned, look at him and say there are special circumstances? Does the judge say, 'You look stupid,' or 'Your case involves complicated facts'? It is administratively unworkable."

Justice Harlan: "The states are recognizing that."

Fortas took up that point and outlined the situation in the states. He used Professor Kamisar's figures: thirty-seven states now provided counsel for the poor in all felony trials, eight others frequently did so as a matter of practice, five made no regular provision for counsel except in capital cases. But he did not agree with any implication in Justice Harlan's question that the movement by the states to act themselves argued against a step forward now by the Supreme Court. He noted the brief *amicus curiae* for twenty-three states in favor of overruling *Betts* and said he was "proud of this document as an American." Then he argued that the growing acceptance of the right to counsel made a reinterpretation of the Constitution easier.

"I believe we can confidently say that overruling Betts versus Brady at this time would be in accord with the opinion of those entitled to an opinion. That is not always true of great constitutional questions. . . . We may be comforted in this constitutional moment by the fact that what we are doing is a deliberate change after twenty years of experience—a change that has the overwhelming support of the bench, the bar and even of the states."

Justice Goldberg raised the problem of the limits on what Fortas was asking. At what stage of a criminal case must a lawyer be supplied? In what kinds of cases?

"Do we have to pass on that?" Justice Clark interjected.

"No, sir, not at this time," Fortas said. But he went on to give his own opinion anyway: A lawyer should be provided at least from the first arraignment of the prisoner before a magistrate, through his trial and appeal; and the right should apply in all save "petty offenses."

Justice Stewart thought the definition of "petty offenses" might produce difficulties, might be "more of this *ad hoc* judging you're trying to get away from. . . . What about traffic violations?" Fortas said he personally saw no difficulty in providing lawyers even for traffic offenders who wanted them. He knew that sounded strange, but it would work. Only an occasional odd-ball would ask, and it would be easy to say to him: "Yes, sir, go right down the hall to that door, that's the public defender's office, they'll see you."

It was noon by this time, and the Court rose for lunch. Afterwards Fortas hoped to say just a few words more, then reserve about ten minutes of his time for a rebuttal, as the opening counsel is allowed to do. But he was still being questioned when the marshal of the Court, sitting to the right of the bench, threw the switch for the small white light on the lectern that indicates counsel has only five minutes left. And the questions continued.

Justice Stewart asked whether he was right in his impression that Fortas was not arguing the old proposition that the Fourteenth Amendment had incorporated the Sixth Amendment as such. Fortas agreed—he was not. But the answer that pleases one justice may arouse another, and this one aroused the member of the Court who had been arguing for a generation that the Fourteenth Amendment incorporated the entire original Bill of Rights—Justice Black. He asked in a puzzled way why Fortas was laying aside that argument.

"Mr. Justice Black," Fortas replied, "I like that argument that you have made so eloquently. But I cannot as an advocate make that argument because this Court has rejected it so many times. I hope you never cease making it."

Justice Black joined in the general laughter.

"You are saying," Justice Brennan said helpfully to Fortas, "that the right to counsel is assured by the Fourteenth Amendment whether by absorption, incorporation or whatever."

"Mr. Justice," said Fortas, "you seem to know me well."

At that the red light on the lectern went on, meaning that Fortas's hour was up. But as he sat down, the Chief Justice gave him an additional five minutes for rebuttal, adding the same to Jacob's time on the other side.

Next came Rankin's appearance as a friend of the court. As he had when he was Solicitor General, he spoke softly, in homely phrases, and with an air of deep sincerity.

"Judges have a special responsibility here," Rankin began, "and so do lawyers. It just isn't true that laymen know these rules of law (the sophisticated concepts of criminal law). That's what's wrong with *Betts*. It is time—long past time— that our profession stood up and said: 'We know a man cannot get a fair trial when he represents himself.' It is enough of a fiction to claim that an ordinary lawyer can present a case as well as the prosecutor with all his experience in court. But when you take a layman and put him at odds, you can't have a fair trial except by accident."

Thus Rankin, appropriately for his role, was focusing less on Gideon the individual and more on the broad problem from the viewpoint of the legal profession. Justice Harlan accused him of making too "sweeping generalizations" about the impossibility of fair trial without counsel. Rankin agreed that it was not absolutely impossible to be tried fairly without a lawyer's help, but he said *Betts* had the generalization backward—it assumed that only in the special case did a man need a lawyer, while the truth was that it was the rare case where one did not need counsel.

Justice Goldberg: "If it's a generalization (the need for counsel), isn't there substantial support for it in the Constitution? The framers of the Sixth Amendment thought there should always be counsel." [That was, historically, a doubtful proposition.]

Rankin: "That's what I think."

Justice Stewart: "Isn't that generalization the assumption behind the legal profession? Florida wouldn't let Gideon, a non-lawyer, go into court and represent anyone else."

Rankin ended by dismissing as unproved prediction the charge that overruling *Betts* would empty the jails. He said the Court should apply the new doctrine assuring counsel retrospectively, to past as well as future cases. Justice Harlan asked whether the Court could constitutionally limit a decision to future operation. Rankin said he was doubtful.

At 1:10 in the afternoon Bruce Jacob's turn came. Looking extremely young and earnest, he began by giving a little more description of Gideon—his age (fifty-two), color (white) and previous felony convictions (four). Then he complained about the inclusion of the trial transcript in the printed record.

Justice Harlan: "Why do you bother about that?"

Jacob: "Okay, I won't press it."

Justice White: "You are not questioning our jurisdiction in this case?"

Jacob: "No, your Honor."

From then on, Jacob was deluged by questions. There was scarcely a consecutive five-minute period when he could talk without interruption. Considering his unfamiliarity with the process and the unpopularity of his cause, he showed commendable stamina.

Justice Black: "Why isn't it (*Betts*) as much interference with the states as an absolute rule? One of my reactions to *Betts* was the uncertainty in which it leaves the states."

Jacob: "I don't think *Betts* is that unclear."

Justice Black: "How do you know what the 'special circumstances' are?"

Jacob: "Each time this Court decides a case, we know another special circumstance."

Justice Brennan: "In recent years—in four cases I think—we have reversed cases from your state every time."

Jacob: "We prefer case-by-case adjudication. . . . It may not be precise, but we prefer it that way because it gives the state some freedom in devising its own rules of criminal procedure."

. . .

Jacob: "History argues against the drawing of inflexible lines, and this Court has never laid down any fixed rules on the right to counsel."

Justice Brennan: "What about Powell against Alabama? Doesn't that lay down a rule for capital cases?"

Jacob: "That was decided on the circumstances. . . ."

Justice Harlan: "Perhaps so, but subsequent cases have made clear that there is a fixed rule for capital cases. There is no point in your arguing that."

Justice Black: "What historical support have you found for the distinction between capital and non-capital cases?"

Jacob: "Your honor, I can't think of any."

Justice Black: "I can't either. That's why I asked."

Justice Stewart: "There is nothing in the language of the Fourteenth Amendment, certainly, to make the distinction. It speaks of life, liberty or property."

Jacob: "There is a practical distinction between capital and non-capital cases if you want to draw the line somewhere. Everyone is fearful of being put to death. . . ."

Justice Black: "Maybe they're fearful of spending years in the penitentiary, too."

• • •

Jacob: "By imposing an inflexible rule, we feel this Court would be intruding into an area historically reserved to the states. It would stifle state experimentation. For example, a state might eliminate prosecutors as well as defense counsel and leave the whole trial to the judge."

Justice Harlan: "Don't go too far now."

Justice Stewart (repeating a point he had made to Rankin): "Gideon would not be allowed to represent others in court."

Jacob: "If a defendant asked for him, I'm sure the judge wouldn't object."

Justice Black: "The local bar association might!"

Jacob: "I'm sorry, your honor, that was a stupid answer."

Jacob next talked about the consequences of overruling *Betts v. Brady*—grave consequences, as he saw them. The new doctrine would necessarily extend to trivial cases, and the cost of providing counsel would be "a tremendous burden on the taxpayers." The next thing one knew, indigents would also be demanding other free services—psychiatrists, expert witnesses and so forth. "In effect, this court would be requiring the states to adopt socialism, or a welfare program." Finally, Jacob emphasized the 5,093 convicts now in Florida prisons who were tried without counsel and might now be eligible for release if *Betts* were overruled. "If the Court does reverse, we implore it to find some way not to make it retroactive. We have followed *Betts* in good faith. . . ."

Chief Justice Warren wanted to know whether some of those 5,093 Florida convicts were illiterate. His point was plain—and deadly. An illiterate defendant was entitled to counsel even under *Betts v. Brady*, since illiteracy qualified as a special circumstance, so the chances were that any illiterates among those 5,093 tried without counsel had been deprived of their constitutional rights. Because they lacked Clarence Earl Gideon's determination, or luck, they had not won redress in the courts.

"I have no way of knowing," Jacob said to the Chief Justice.

"No, but what do you think?" the Chief Justice pressed. "Do you think most of them are literate or illiterate?"

"I don't know, but I am sure some of them are illiterate."

Jacob concluded without using his extra five minutes, and then George Mentz of Alabama took over. He was an older man, gray-haired, more experienced than Jacob and much more at ease. He was questioned just as frequently, but the questions seemed to give him less pain. He answered in a charming Southern voice, making graceful concessions.

"I candidly admit," he began, "that it would be desirable for the states to furnish counsel in all criminal cases. But we say the states should have the right to make that decision themselves."

Justice Harlan: "Supposing *Betts* is not overruled. How many years is it going to take Alabama to pass a law like New York and the other states?"

Mentz: "I don't know, but there is a growing feeling in the trial courts that something should be done."

• • •

Mentz: "Our judges are conscientious in protecting indigent defendants."

Justice Stewart: "We can assume all of that with you, but a judge's job is to be a judge. This way he would be an advocate for one of the litigants."

Justice Goldberg: "What about the vital matter of the final address to the jury? Surely a judge can't take over that job of advocacy."

Mentz: "That is true. . . . But prosecutors are more lenient with unrepresented defendants . . . ."

Justice Stewart: "Isn't that a matter of trial strategy? It might backfire if the prosecutor were tough and the jury saw the defendant there helpless."

Mentz: "Well, yes, sir."

Justice Stewart: "All you're saying is that the absence of counsel impedes the adversary system of justice."

Mentz: "I didn't mean to go that far."

Justice Stewart: "I'm sure you didn't."

• • •

Mentz: "In actuality, indigents without lawyers probably get off easier. The average Alabama lawyer is not equipped to deal with the career prosecutor. An articulate defendant may get his story across to the jury better."

Justice Black: "That's not very complimentary to our profession."

Mentz (good-humoredly): "No, sir."

Justice Douglas: "Maybe if laymen are as effective as you say, we should get the Sixth Amendment repealed."

Mentz: "Mr. Justice, I didn't mean to go that far. I meant only that laymen are not at so great a disadvantage—"

Justice Douglas: "—as some appellate judges think."

Justice Harlan: "Supposing you had a choice—as you see it, representing the state—of maintaining *Betts* on the books and then having a succession of cases come to this Court every one of which was reversed by finding special circumstances, so that everyone would know we were only paying lip service to *Betts*, or of overruling it."

Mentz: "We'd rather see them decided case by case."

Justice Harlan: "Even though you know how all of them will come out."

Mentz: " 'Hope springs eternal.' " [Laughter in the courtroom.]

Then Fortas got up for his rebuttal. He said a word about *Mapp v. Ohio*, the case in which—two years before—the Supreme Court had reinterpreted the Constitution to bar the use of illegally seized evidence in state trials. "To paraphrase Mr. Justice Clark's opinion there, time has set its face against Betts and Brady." He noted also Justice Clark's opinion in the second overseas court-martial cases, saying they removed any basis for a constitutional distinction between crimes subject to the death penalty and others.

"I think Betts and Brady was wrong when it was decided," Fortas said in his peroration. "I think time has made that clear. And I think time has now made it possible for the correct rule, the civilized rule, the rule of American constitutionalism, the rule of due process to be stated by this Court with limited disturbance to the states."

Justice Harlan had one more question. Had Mr. Fortas, in his research, found any errors in Justice Roberts' exposition of the history of the right to counsel in his opinion in *Betts v. Brady*? Clearly Justice Harlan would find it much easier to overrule *Betts* if that decision could be shown to have been based on erroneous historical premises. But Fortas had no comfort to offer there. He replied: "We would have some differences, perhaps, but I don't say that the historical technique of constitutional interpretation will reach my result."

In order to overrule *Betts*, then, Justice Harlan would have to look at the same problem that had faced Justice Roberts in 1942 and say that a different answer was required in 1963. As a believer in *stare decisis* he would not find that easy to do, and yet he seemed to want to turn away from *Betts v. Brady*. The last word in the argument was Justice Harlan's, and it showed the struggle going on inside him. "What one is left with," he said, "is getting one's hands on something that has happened in the last twenty years . . . ."

12

The justices ordinarily take their first formal vote on the merits of a case at the Friday conference immediately following the oral argument. Within the next few days the Chief Justice, if he is in the majority, sends a formal note assigning the opinion to one member of the Court (or keeps it for himself); if the Chief is in the minority, the senior justice on the side that prevailed at conference assigns the opinion. The minority usually agrees about who will write the dissent. Notwithstanding such assignments, any member of the Court is free to write his own concurring or dissenting opinion if he wishes, and they often do. Jefferson, who feared Chief Justice Marshall's persuasive power over his brethren, thought every member of the Court should have to write his own opinion in every case. A few years ago Justice Harlan, as he began a dissent that was the fourth opinion in the same case, said drily: "We have almost reached Jefferson's ideal."

When draft opinions are completed, they are sent to the print shop in the basement, set in type and proofs run. The proofs are carefully numbered so that no set can stray and opinions thereby leak to the outside world. These drafts are circulated among the Court, and comments come back to the author of the opinion from the other justices.

Occasionally, at this stage, minds change. The justice assigned the opinion may find after research that he cannot support the reasoning he suggested at conference; a new majority may then form behind his revised views, or the opinion may be reassigned. Dissenting drafts may change votes, sometimes enough votes to convert the minority to the majority. Exchanges of view by memoranda, new drafts and personal discussion continue until everyone is as nearly satisfied as is possible in the limited time available. The working papers of Justice Brandeis that were preserved include the thirty-fourth printed draft of one of his opinions. Inevitably, in trying to please eight editors, the author of the majority opinion finds himself removing much of the personal flavor from his product. The dissenter, on the other hand, as Chief Justice Hughes said, can "express his individuality. He is not under the compulsion of speaking for the Court and thus of securing . . . a majority. In dissenting, he is a free lance." Hughes went on —and he might have been speaking of Justice Black's opinion in *Betts v. Brady*—"A dissent in a court of last resort is an appeal to the brooding spirit of the law, to the intelligence of a future day, when a later decision may possibly correct the error into which the dissenting judge believes the court to have been betrayed."

But this whole process of discussion, voting and opinion-writing is entirely concealed from public view. No one but

the justices and their law clerks, and some printers equally
dedicated to secrecy, have any idea how a case is going to
come out until, on some Monday, the opinions are announced.
There are almost no news leaks at the Supreme Court—one
of its many distinctions from all other Washington institutions. Not even the date of decision can be accurately estimated; it may come just a few weeks after argument, or many
months.

For the parties to a case, and their lawyers, the period between argument and decision is a time of frustrating puzzle-
ment, of might-have-beens, of daydreams and nightmares.
Two months after the *Gideon* argument, at the beginning of
March, 1963, Bruce Jacob was still thinking about the strange-
ness of that day.

"It was so different from the Florida Supreme Court," he
told a visitor. "They weren't concerned with precedents.
They didn't ask you about existing law. Instead of asking
about cases the way judges usually do—what did this case
stand for, what did that case—they had all those hypothetical
questions, trying to carry everything to its farthest point. I
wanted to be honest. When they asked me whether there
were some prisoners in Raiford [the state penitentiary] who
should have had counsel, I had to say yes, because I had read
some records and I knew there were. But the more honest I
was, the more they kept putting me on the spot. Some of the
questions were just designed to embarrass our position. I
never had judges make your side look as bad at it could.

"I had been working on this thing for months, but some of
the questions were completely surprising. You could tell that
they knew what they were doing, that they were awfully
smart men, that they had the benefit of the best thinking of
the country."

Jacob had no doubt, now, that the Court would overrule
Betts v. Brady. He wondered who was writing the Court's
opinion. It might have been assigned to some relatively neu-

tral figure, like Justice Stewart, but Jacob thought not. He was sure Chief Justice Warren would give Justice Black the satisfaction of writing into law his dissent of twenty-one years ago. Jacob was still worried about the consequences of establishing an absolute right to counsel. He hoped especially that the Court would limit its decision to future application, so as not to affect all those thousands of current prisoners. "It's easy to think of them as heroes," he said, "but after you've worked in the attorney general's office you know they're not. They're liars, they're terrible." He paused for a moment, thinking, and then added, "It's funny—at law school I was the chairman of legal aid."

Jacob noted that the case would probably have a different name when the Supreme Court decided it. The party against whom Gideon had originally brought his habeas corpus action, H. G. Cochran, Jr., had resigned as director of the Florida Division of Corrections and been replaced by Louie L. Wainwright. The Court had been informed of the change, and Wainwright would, therefore, have the doubtful distinction of sharing Gideon's place in the title of an important legal decision.

It was only a few days later, as it happened, that *Gideon v. Wainwright* was decided. There was no prior notice; there never is. The Court gives out no advance press releases and tells no one what cases will be decided on a particular Monday, much less how they will be decided. Opinion days have a special quality. The Supreme Court is one of the last American appellate courts where decisions are announced orally. The justices, who divide on so many issues, disagree about this practice, too. Some regard it as a waste of time; others value it as an occasion for descending from the ivory tower, however briefly, and communicating with the live audience in the courtroom. Techniques of opinion-reading vary, too. Justice Frankfurter never looked at his text but would expound from memory; once Chief Justice Warren irritatedly accused him of saying things that were not in the opinion. Others stick closely to the text, and some read brief summaries. Justice Black's technique seems to vary with the opinion; he gives fuller—and more emotional—treatment to those he regards as of particular importance.

The reading always begins with the most junior justice who has an opinion that day. On Monday, March 18th, that was the newest member of the Court, Justice Goldberg. For a five-four majority he held that Washington State had not made an adequate trial record available to two indigent prisoners for purposes of their appeal. The next case was unanimous; an opinion by Justice Stewart struck down an Indiana rule allowing the public defender to block a prisoner's appeal as worthless. Then Justice Brennan, for a six-three majority, broke important new ground in federal-state relations by holding that federal courts have the power to release on habeas corpus state prisoners who failed to follow regular state procedures; the result was to free Charles Noia of New York, whose two co-defendants in a murder trial had eventually been freed on a finding that confessions had been coerced from all three, but who had not himself appealed originally and had been turned down by the New York courts when he tried to appeal later.

A fourth state criminal case came from California, and Justice Douglas for a six-three majority said poor prisoners were entitled to free counsel for their appeals. To any informed listener it was obvious that the same rule must apply at trials and that *Betts v. Brady* was about to be overruled. Those who had before them the printed opinions in the California case—page boys bring them around to a few newspaper reporters and the Solicitor General as they are read—knew from the text that they were about to hear the Gideon case decided, because there was a reference to *"Gideon v. Wainwright*, decided today."

The string of criminal cases was interrupted by a Douglas

opinion on the Georgia "county unit" system of tabulating primary election votes to give extra weight to voters in rural areas; an eight-one majority (Justice Harlan dissenting) held this discrimination unconstitutional.

Then, in the ascending order of seniority, it was Justice Black's turn. He looked at his wife, who was sitting in the box reserved for the justices' friends and families, and said: "I have for announcement the opinion and judgment of the Court in Number One fifty-five, Gideon against Wainwright."

Justice Black leaned forward and gave his words the emphasis and the drama of a great occasion. Speaking very directly to the audience in the courtroom, in an almost folksy way, he told about Clarence Earl Gideon's case and how it had reached the Supreme Court of the United States.

"It raised a fundamental question," Justice Black said, "the rightness of a case we decided twenty-one years ago, Betts against Brady. When we granted certiorari in this case, we asked the lawyers on both sides to argue to us whether we should reconsider that case. We do reconsider Betts and Brady, and we reach an opposite conclusion."

By now the page boys were passing out the opinions. There were four—by Justices Douglas, Clark and Harlan, in addition to the opinion of the Court. But none of the other three was a dissent. A quick look at the end of each showed that it concurred in the overruling of *Betts v. Brady*. On that central result, then, the Court was unanimous.

Justice Black began reading sections of his opinion. Since 1942, it said, the problem of the constitutional right to counsel in state criminal trials had been "a continuing source of controversy in both state and federal courts." A footnote cited articles by Professors Allen of Chicago and Kamisar of Minnesota. Justice Black, quoting briefly from the transcript of Gideon's trial, said Gideon had "conducted his defense about as well as could be expected from a layman." The way the whole case had developed, he said, was "strikingly like" what had happened in the Betts case. "Since the facts and circumstances of the two cases are so nearly indistinguishable, we think the *Betts v. Brady* holding, if left standing, would require us to reject Gideon's claim that the Constitution guarantees him the assistance of counsel."

The rest of Justice Black's ten-page opinion was an assault on *Betts*. There was no attempt to show that overruling was required by developments in the two decades since the case was decided. It had been wrong to start with. Justice Black did not press his own theory that the Fourteenth Amendment incorporated the Bill of Rights verbatim. He accepted as the law, for purposes of this case, the Cardozo formulation that particular guarantees of the Bill of Rights "implicit in the concept of ordered liberty" had been "brought within the Fourteenth Amendment by a process of absorption" and thus had been made applicable to state proceedings.

"We accept," he wrote, "*Betts v. Brady*'s assumption, based as it was on our prior cases, that a provision of the Bill of Rights which is 'fundamental and essential to a fair trial' is made obligatory upon the states by the Fourteenth Amendment. We think the Court in *Betts* was wrong, however, in concluding that the Sixth Amendment's guarantee of counsel is not one of these fundamental rights. Ten years before *Betts v. Brady*, this Court, after full consideration of all the historical data examined in *Betts*, had unequivocally declared that 'the right to the aid of counsel is of this fundamental character.' *Powell v. Alabama*, 287 U.S. 45, 68 (1932). While the Court at the close of its *Powell* opinion did by its language, as this Court frequently does, limit its holding to the particular facts and circumstances of that case, its conclusions about the fundamental nature of the right to counsel are unmistakable."

Justice Black mentioned other early cases that had emphasized the importance of counsel, including his own 1938 opinion in *Johnson v. Zerbst*, construing the Sixth Amendment to require counsel in federal criminal trials, and concluded that *Betts* had made "an abrupt break" from these precedents.

"Not only these precedents but also reason and reflection," he wrote, "require us to recognize that in our adversary system of criminal justice, any person haled into court, who is too poor to hire a lawyer, cannot be assured a fair trial unless counsel is provided for him. This seems to us to be an obvious truth. Governments, both state and federal, quite properly spend vast sums of money to establish machinery to try defendants accused of crime. Lawyers to prosecute are everywhere deemed essential to protect the public's interest in an orderly society. Similarly, there are few defendants charged with crime, few indeed, who fail to hire the best lawyers they can get to prepare and present their defenses. That government hires lawyers to prosecute and defendants who have the money hire lawyers to defend are the strongest indications of the widespread belief that lawyers in criminal courts are necessities, not luxuries. The right of one charged with crime to counsel may not be deemed fundamental and essential to fair trials in some countries, but it is in ours."

The opinion came to an end without any mention of the difficult problems of the scope of the decision: what kinds of criminal cases it covered, if any apart from felonies; at what stage of the proceeding counsel was required; whether the decision applied to persons already in prison, so that those who had not had counsel must now be given new trials. All those questions were presumably left to be answered when raised specifically by later cases.

"The Court in *Betts v. Brady*," Justice Black concluded, "departed from the sound wisdom upon which the Court's holding in *Powell v. Alabama* rested. Florida, supported by two other states, has asked that *Betts v. Brady* be left intact. Twenty-three states, as friends of the Court, argue that *Betts* was 'an anachronism when handed down' and that it should now be overruled. We agree.

"The judgment is reversed and the cause is remanded to the Supreme Court of Florida for action not inconsistent with this opinion."

Justice Douglas, while joining Justice Black's opinion, was not content to let the occasion pass without rearguing the old proposition that the Fourteenth Amendment incorporated all the Bill of Rights. "Unfortunately," he wrote in his concurring opinion, "it has never commanded a Court. Yet, happily, all constitutional questions are always open. And what we do today does not foreclose the matter."

Justice Clark did not accept the reasoning of Justice Black and the majority. In his concurring opinion he rested on the fact that the Court had already established an absolute right to counsel in cases involving the death penalty, even under *Betts v. Brady*. He drew the parallel with the overseas court-martial cases. In his own 1960 opinion on that subject, he said, the Court "specifically rejected any constitutional distinction between capital and non-capital offenses as regards Congressional power to provide for court-martial trials of civilian dependents. . . ." He "must conclude" likewise here. "The Fourteenth Amendment requires due process of law for the deprival of 'liberty' just as for deprival of 'life,' and there cannot constitutionally be a difference in the quality of the process based merely upon a supposed difference in the sanction involved."

Justice Harlan also followed a legal path of his own. "I agree that *Betts v. Brady* should be overruled," he said, "but consider it entitled to a more respectful burial than has been accorded, at least"—he added in a respectful gesture to Justice Black's consistency of position for twenty-one years—"on the part of those of us who were not on the Court when that case was decided." Justice Harlan could not agree that

Betts had broken with precedents looking toward an absolute right to counsel. *Powell v. Alabama* had rested on the special circumstances of the Scottsboro trial, and *Betts* had actually enlarged the right to counsel by indicating that it could exist even in a non-capital case where there were special circumstances. But the special-circumstance doctrine, Justice Harlan continued, had had "a troubled journey." It had been abandoned altogether in death cases. In non-capital cases it had "continued to exist in form while its substance has been substantially and steadily eroded." The Court had not found a lack of special circumstances in any case heard and decided since *Quicksall v. Michigan*, in 1950. "The Court has come to recognize, in other words, that the mere existence of a serious criminal charge constituted in itself special circumstances requiring the services of counsel at trial. In truth the *Betts v. Brady* rule is no longer a reality.

"This evolution, however, appears not to have been fully recognized by many state courts, in this instance charged with the front-line responsibility for the enforcement of constitutional rights." Here Justice Harlan cited in a footnote the recent Pennsylvania decision mentioned by both Fortas and the Civil Liberties Union, upholding the trial without counsel of a "high-grade moron." The opinion went on:

"To continue a rule which is honored by this Court only with lip service is not a healthy thing and in the long run will do disservice to the federal system. The special-circumstances rules has been formally abandoned in capital cases, and the time has now come when it should be similarly abandoned in non-capital cases, at least as to offenses which, as the one involved here, carry the possibility of a substantial prison sentence. (Whether the rule should extend to *all* criminal cases need not now be decided.) This indeed does no more than to make explicit something that has long since been foreshadowed in our decisions."

That was the end of Clarence Earl Gideon's case in the Supreme Court of the United States. The opinions delivered that Monday were quickly circulated around the country by special legal services, then issued in pamphlets by the Government Printing Office. Eventually they appeared in the bound volumes of Supreme Court decisions, the United States Reports, to be cited as *Gideon v. Wainwright*, 372 U.S. 335 —meaning that the case could be found beginning on page 335 of the 372nd volume of the reports.

Justice Black, talking to a friend a few weeks after the decision, said quietly: "When *Betts v. Brady* was decided, I never thought I'd live to see it overruled."

13

When a friend telephoned from Washington to give him the news of the decision, Bruce Jacob said: "It's only the beginning." And it was.

"Even if *Betts v. Brady* should be overruled tomorrow," Justice Stewart said in 1960, ". . . there is no way that the Supreme Court could, or indeed that it properly should, see to it that in the day-to-day administration of criminal trials throughout the country truly adequate representation of indigent defendants were provided." That job was up to the bar and the courts and the legislatures of the country. The Supreme Court had sounded a trumpet. The response had to come from society.

Twenty-five years before, in *Johnson v. Zerbst,* the Supreme Court had laid down the rule that federal criminal defendants had an absolute right to counsel, but society had been slow in responding. Despite the urging of every Attorney General in that period, Congress had done nothing whatsoever to provide funds or establish any system of assuring counsel for the poor, except for a District of Columbia legal-aid measure passed in 1960. And so, in 1963, federal judges still used their own random methods to appoint counsel—who had to serve without pay, without even compensation for out-of-pocket expenses.

The result of this non-system, as might be expected, was inadequate representation for many defendants and a wholly unfair burden on a few lawyers.

James V. Bennett, for many years the director of the federal prison system, told Congress on May 20, 1963, that his observations over twenty-five years had convinced him that the use of unpaid assigned counsel for indigents too often resulted in "inept, hasty and perfunctory" representation.

One of many horrible examples cited by Mr. Bennett from his own experience was that of an eighteen-year-old girl who "waived" the right to counsel, pleaded guilty to stealing a letter from the mails and was committed to the penitentiary for five years. "We found that she had an I.Q. of forty-five and that her behavior was that of an impulsive child," Mr. Bennett said. "There was no question but that she was mentally incompetent both at the time of the offense and at the time of trial. . . . In my opinion an experienced public defender or conscientious assigned counsel would have known immediately upon talking to her that she could not intelligently waive her right to counsel. He would have had her examined, and he would have presented to the court the information that she belonged in a state institution for the mentally defective rather than in a court of the United States charged with crime."

Senator Sam J. Ervin of North Carolina, writing in the *American Bar Association Journal* shortly after the *Gideon* decision, cited among other examples a Wyoming lawyer, in practice by himself, who was appointed defense counsel in a major federal criminal prosecution. There were ten days and three nights of actual trial time, plus extended preparation; the Government called one hundred and fourteen witnesses. "For practical purposes," Senator Ervin said, "the lawyer was required to close his office for six weeks. As a result, he was practically bankrupted."

Attorney General Robert F. Kennedy, testifying on May 22, 1963, spelled out the problem: "Federal courts today continue to delegate the defense of the underprivileged to assigned counsel who are not paid for their services. They are not reimbursed for their out-of-pocket costs. They do not receive a shred of investigative or expert help. They are not appointed until long after arrest, when witnesses have disappeared and leads grown stale. They often lack the trial experience essential for a competent defense." On the last point, the competence of assigned counsel, Mr. Kennedy quoted from a national survey undertaken by the Harvard Law Review. It concluded that the responsibility for representation of indigents in the federal courts now necessarily fell mainly on "young, inexperienced lawyers, little versed in the technicalities of the criminal law," and that the quality of representation under these circumstances was "largely fortuitous."

Two years before the *Gideon* decision Attorney General Kennedy appointed a committee of scholars, practicing lawyers and state and federal judges to review the adequacy of provisions for the indigent in federal courts. The chairman was Professor Allen, then at the University of Michigan Law School (he returned to Chicago in September, 1963), whose law-review analyses of *Betts v. Brady* had been so devastating.

The committee proposed comprehensive legislation similar to but more complete than bills that had previously been considered. In summary, the proposal was as follows:

Every federal district court would be authorized and required to choose one of four systems for representation of needy defendants: 1, assigning members of the private bar but, for the first time, compensating them modestly for their time and expenses; 2, hiring a full-time or part-time public defender and staff; 3, using counsel supplied by a local legal-aid society or other legal organization, which would in turn be paid out of federal funds for providing their services; 4, adopting any combination of these first three approaches. Such local option would permit accommodation to the great differences between federal courts in urban areas, with a large volume of criminal cases, and those in the country, where criminal trials are a relative rarity. Those eligible for assistance under the legislation would be persons "financially unable to obtain an adequate defense." Services would deliberately not be limited to the technically "indigent," since the man of modest means may need help in defending against a major criminal charge; defendants would be required to pay whatever they could afford. Counsel would be provided from the moment a defendant is first brought before a judge or commissioner for preliminary hearing, shortly after arrest, and would continue through appeal. There would be funds for investigation, experts and other services.

President Kennedy submitted the Allen Committee measure to Congress, as the proposed Criminal Justice Act of 1963, just ten days before the decision in *Gideon*. It had the important support of the American Bar Association and of the Judicial Conference of the United States, representing all the federal courts. But it faced suspicion and resistance from Republicans and some Southern Democrats in the House of Representatives. The House had always been the sticking point; three times in previous years the Senate had passed measures to provide some kind of compensated system for representation of the needy in federal courts, but no bill had ever even emerged from the House Judiciary Committee.

The Senate again acted promptly in 1963, approving a slightly modified version of the Allen Committee proposal. In the House, a bill emerged from the Judiciary Committee for the first time—but with the option of public defenders struck out and a limit of five hundred dollars put on the compensation to be paid any lawyer in a felony case, three hundred in a misdemeanor. The House passed the bill on January 15th. The necessary conference to reconcile the two versions was delayed by the congressional struggle over civil rights, but only this hurdle stood in the way of a historic first step by Congress to assist in the defense of the indigent.

The Gideon case thus coincided with, and encouraged, an outpouring of concern and activity on the problem of representation in the *federal* courts. The question was whether it would take as long on the *state* level from what Bruce Jacob had called the beginning—the declaration of the right to counsel in *Gideon v. Wainwright*—to an effective, working system of justice for the poor in all fifty states. The problem was both larger and more difficult than in the federal judicial system.

Criminal prosecutions by the Federal Government are only a handful compared to the number brought by state and local governments, which retain the primary responsibility under the Constitution for maintaining domestic peace and security. The typical state or local prosecution, moreover, for such a crime as theft or assault or disorderly conduct, is more likely to involve a deadbeat, down-and-out defendant. The proportion of indigents among state criminal defendants is higher —about sixty percent compared to thirty-three in federal courts.

Even among those intimately concerned with the problem of counsel for the poor there is disagreement over the proper approach, especially as to the proper division of responsibility between the state and the bar. Whitney North Seymour, an eminent New York lawyer who heads the American Bar Association's special committee on counsel for the indigent, said in a 1963 speech that representation was a public responsibility. "Just as doctors are not expected to provide all the facilities for dealing with illness of the poor," he said, "lawyers cannot be expected to bear all the burdens of the decisions of prosecutors to prosecute the indigent. . . . These are not obligations imposed by the Constitution upon the bar alone, they are obligations imposed by the Constitution upon the operation of our system of criminal justice. They are as much a part of the public obligation to support that system as the provision of courthouses, judges, attendants and prosecutors."

One way for society to meet the responsibility is through public defenders paid by the state. First tried in Los Angeles in 1913, defender offices now exist in thirteen states, though only in the largest cities of some; they handle one hundred thousand cases a year. The great advantage of a public defender is that he can match the prosecutor in experience and knowledge of judges, juries and trial tactics. The typical American lawyer has had only the briefest acquaintance with criminal law at law school and none at all in practice; he tends to look down on the "criminal bar" as a collection of grubby characters who cannot make a go of it in the more remunerative corporate practice. Even a dedicated and obviously talented lawyer with criminal practice, such as Edward Bennett Williams of Washington, is regarded with some suspicion. Because the typical lawyer is nurtured in this tradition of distaste for criminal practice and has had little or no experience of it, he cannot be expected to perform with great efficacy when he finds himself appointed defense counsel. This is a strong argument for public defenders.

But the argument can be turned around. If, somehow, the body of American lawyers could be brought actively into the criminal courts, there to participate in the defense of the needy, the practice of criminal law might be elevated, the typical corporate lawyer might be educated in social responsibilities, and the gap in the profession might be narrowed. In England any barrister may find himself appearing in a civil case one day, a criminal case the next. That is not likely here, but some thoughtful lawyers and judges believe a thoroughgoing involvement of the bar in defense of the indigent would be a healthy step for the profession.

Another argument against public defenders is that their position on the public payroll will prevent them from fighting the prosecution as fiercely as private counsel. Communities that have experience with defenders, such as California, deny this; but an understandable feeling remains that a man in trouble will be better served by someone wholly concerned with him in a private relationship. There is also concern about the possibly deadening, conformist, bureaucratic effect of governmental control over any activity. Some of these feelings probably underlay a speech by Justice Clark in July, 1963. He called for an urgent response to the demands posed by the Gideon case but said he did "not support the view that we must create a vast public-defender system. . . . Let us place this function in private hands rather than with the government. The indigent is entitled to private counsel."

On the other hand, it is widely recognized that private counsel cannot do an adequate job if rushed into a case without preparation and given no financial support. And that is the customary situation. Chief Judge J. Edward Lumbard of the Second Circuit Court of Appeals has painted the picture:

"When advised that an indigent needs counsel, the judge usually picks out some lawyer who happens to be in the courtroom. . . . The lawyer then spends a few minutes with his new client at the side of the courtroom, or perhaps in an anteroom under the scrutiny of the bailiff or the marshal. In most of such assignments, after a few minutes of conference, the defendant is advised to plead guilty and he feels he has no choice but to do so. . . . This mock assignment of counsel and the cursory hurry-up job of a busy uncompensated lawyer makes a farce of due process of law and our Bill of Rights. Every one who participates in the farce knows this—the judge, the district attorney, the assigned lawyer, the bailiff, and of course the defendant himself."

In the view of Seymour and other experts, there is no decent alternative in populous urban areas to an office that has a regularly employed staff of lawyers representing indigents in criminal cases. The office could be that of a public defender or, alternatively, a voluntary legal-aid organization. In New York City, for example, the Legal Aid Society provides counsel in sixty thousand criminal cases a year. But the society has had to go outside the organized bar for financial support—to private citizens and business for donations and, finally, to the city treasury for an appropriation. Thus, experienced observers believe that some governmental participation is essential in the big cities that have the real problems of poverty and crime.

Despite their differing emphasis on the proper role of government, Seymour and Justice Clark in their 1963 appraisals agreed that existing informal arrangements for appointment of counsel were inadequate. They were in general agreement on some practical steps to be taken. The young lawyer should be exposed to the criminal law and given experience in it. Justice Clark suggested privately financed internships for just-graduated lawyers to let them learn while helping in the defense of the needy; Seymour proposed appointment of a senior lawyer and a junior assistant in more serious cases. Where there is no regular defender system, counsel should be appointed from rotating lists of all members of the bar, so that the burden is spread. Funds must be provided for investigation, and at least modest compensation for the practitioner who has no large law firm to back him up while he does good works. To that extent at least—minimal provision of public funds for the assigned lawyer—governmental support would seem to be an inescapable element in adequate defense of the indigent. Many states now provide nothing.

Thus the process of converting the ideal of *Gideon v. Wainwright* into reality necessarily involved the participation of legislators, lawyers, judges and citizens across the country. This process got under way with surprising speed immediately after the *Gideon* decision.

Some of the members of the Supreme Court themselves took every opportunity to preach the gospel of *Gideon*. A month after the decision Justice Clark called *Gideon* an "historic case," one that would "possibly have more physical impact on the administration of justice than any decided by the Court." He urged law schools to upgrade the study of criminal law and suggested that state and local bar associations undertake their own programs for criminal representation, with a paid staff and panels of available lawyers. He urged individual lawyers to volunteer more readily for service to the poor; if each lawyer handled only a case or two a year by appointment in the criminal courts, the burden could be carried "for the time being." He said it was "imperative that the bar evidence a more active concern." Other members of the Court sounded similar themes. Chief Justice Warren, talking to a luncheon of the Conference of Judicial Councils in May, said the Gideon case would "amount almost to a revolution in some states." He called representation of the indigent "a public responsibility" that society should bear through orderly systems worked out locally. Whatever expense the states were put to, the Chief Justice said, they would be repaid not only in fairer treatment of the unfortunate but in criminal courts that would work more efficiently and effectively with lawyers' help.

At the time Gideon's case came to decision, several legal organizations launched the broadest attack in this country's history on the problem of legal services for needy criminal defendants. The Ford Foundation made grants totaling $2,-540,000 for a series of projects. The largest part of this sum, $2,300,000, went to the National Legal Aid and Defender Association to establish model defender services in six or eight counties, improve existing services in several major cities and create new law-school techniques of preparation for criminal law work. The American Bar Foundation was given $125,000 for a detailed survey of existing state and local systems of representation, to be carried out in cooperation with state bars and with the special committee, headed by Mr. Seymour, of the Bar Foundation's parent American Bar Association. (At the same time the federal courts undertook their own first study of what the typical appointed counsel actually does in a federal criminal case.) The Institute of Judicial Administration in New York received a grant of $115,000 to continue a noteworthy experiment in the release of impoverished criminal defendants without bail; this study, carried out by the Vera Foundation, had already indicated that men so released were as likely to turn up for trial as those who had posted bond.

The reaction of the states to *Gideon v. Wainwright* was swift and constructive. The most dramatic response came from Florida, whose rural-dominated legislature had so long refused to relieve the problem of the unrepresented indigent such as Gideon. Shortly after the decision Governor Farris Bryant called on the legislature to enact a public-defender law. "In this era of social consciousness," he said, and his words might have given Clarence Earl Gideon wry amusement, "it is unthinkable that an innocent man may be condemned to penal servitude because he is unfamiliar with the intricacies of criminal procedure and unable to provide counsel for his defense." Governor Bryant said the *Gideon* decision had made public defenders essential not only "to protect the innocent" but "in order that valid judgments of guilty may be entered and criminals kept confined for the protection of society." He may have been thinking of all those inmates of the state prisons who had been tried without counsel and now might be entitled to new trials. In May, 1963, barely two months after the Supreme Court had spoken, the Florida legislature approved a statute creating a public defender in each of the state's sixteen judicial circuits.

The four other southern states that had not provided counsel for non-capital defendants acted quickly to adjust to the new constitutional requirement. North Carolina's legislature passed a bill to have the state bar council and state supreme court draft rules for assignment of lawyers in all criminal cases, to authorize compensation of assigned counsel and to appropriate $500,000 for initial expenses of the new system. In Alabama, Mississippi and South Carolina, bar groups prepared rosters of lawyers available for assignment, and plans were drafted for legislation to compensate those appointed. Appraisals of the Gideon case in the South were surprisingly favorable. Howard McDonnell, the chairman of the Mississippi State Bar's criminal law committee, told a meeting that the decision was "far-sighted." He said, "Our penitentiary is loaded with inmates who are there because of no representation or improper representation." The head of the Wake County, North Carolina, Bar Association, R. Mayne Albright, said: "I think few lawyers would disagree with the principle enunciated by the Supreme Court. It was time we recognized the need for the defendant who is indigent to have a lawyer."

Nor did the response to *Gideon v. Wainwright* come only from southern states. The Colorado legislature authorized counties, in a local option statute, to employ public defenders. Oregon created a public defender's office to handle appeals and other post-conviction proceedings by indigent prisoners. (This was a specific response to the California case decided the same day as Gideon's, laying down the rule that indigents are entitled to lawyers on appeal also.) The Minnesota legislature authorized compensation for lawyers representing indigents on appeal. New Hampshire and Vermont moved to strike from their statutes provisions (often ignored in practice) exempting crimes with lighter sentences from the counsel guarantee. Delaware's judges held a meeting to plan extension of the state's appointed counsel system to misdemeanor cases, in the apparent belief that the *Gideon* rule would sooner or later be extended to that level.

"Without the Supreme Court," Gideon had told his visitor in the Florida penitentiary, "it might have happened sometime, but it wouldn't have happened in this state soon." The reaction to his case bore him out. For lawyers and legislators were taking steps that they recognized as requirements of justice—but that they had not taken without the nudge from the Court. For its part, the Court quickly made clear that it would apply continuing pressure to the states on the issue of the right to counsel. In the three months after the *Gideon* decision, during the remainder of the 1962 term, the justices set aside thirty-one lower court judgments and sent them back for reconsideration of prisoners' claims to counsel in light of the new rule. The cases came from ten states: Alabama, Florida, Illinois, Louisiana, Maryland, Missouri, North Carolina, Ohio, Oklahoma and Pennsylvania. Among them was the case of Allen Baxley, Jr., the illiterate Florida prisoner for whom Gideon had drafted a petition. In April the Court unanimously reversed a Maryland conviction because the defendant had not had a lawyer at his preliminary hearing, at which he pleaded guilty. That decision made clear that counsel was constitutionally guaranteed not only at trial but at any earlier proceeding, however brief or informal, at which the prisoner enters a plea. In response, the Baltimore Municipal Court, which holds preliminary hearings on criminal charges to be tried later in the higher courts, called an emergency meeting and obtained a pledge from the local bar associations to supply the needed lawyers.

On the first business day of its next term, October 14, 1963, the Supreme Court began dealing with one of the difficult issues it had left undecided in *Gideon*—whether to apply the new counsel rule retrospectively, to prisoners tried when *Betts v. Brady* was the law. Ten Florida prisoners convicted without the aid of counsel before March 18, 1963, petitioned for review of the Florida courts' refusal to grant them writs of habeas corpus. In a brief order the Court granted the petitions, set aside the Florida judgments and sent all the cases back to the Florida Supreme Court "for further consideration in light of *Gideon v. Wainwright*." The justices had not themselves made the decision to apply the new rule retrospectively, but they seemed to be inviting the Florida court to do so. Justice Harlan dissented, saying the Supreme Court should have decided the issue itself.

Florida went ahead and applied the *Gideon* rule retrospectively, to all who had been convicted of felonies without counsel. The results were spectacular. By January 1, 1964, nine hundred seventy-six prisoners had been released outright from Florida penitentiaries, the authorities feeling that they could not be successfully retried. Another five hundred were back in the courts, and petitions from hundreds more were awaiting consideration.

It will be an enormous social task to bring to life the dream of *Gideon v. Wainwright*—the dream of a vast, diverse country in which every man charged with crime will be capably defended, no matter what his economic circumstances, and in which the lawyer representing him will do so proudly, without resentment at an unfair burden, sure of the support needed to make an adequate defense. England already approaches that ideal. No poor man there is tried for at least a serious crime without the offer of counsel; assign-

ment in such cases is an expected part of a barrister's life, and
he receives a fee from the state comparable to what a private
client would pay in that kind of case. But England is, by comparison, a small and homogeneous society, with a simpler legal system and a much less serious crime problem. There is a
long road to travel before every criminal court in the United
States reaches the goal that appears on the façade of the Supreme Court building: *Equal Justice Under Law.*

The new responsibilities imposed by the Gideon case on
the bar and the courts will be heavy, but there is no sign that
the American legal community regards them as unjustified.
The president of the American Bar Association, Sylvester C.
Smith, Jr., hailed *Gideon* and the Supreme Court's other
criminal-law decisions on March 18, 1963, as "great advances
in the administration of criminal justice in our country."
Chief Justice Carleton Harris of Arkansas, speaking to the
Conference of Chief Justices in 1963, said he had "no fault
to find with *Gideon.* The law as to the right of an indigent
prisoner to counsel is now, for the first time, positively
stated." In the Record of the Association of the Bar of the
City of New York, Ernest Angell wrote: "In retrospect the
Gideon decision seems to have been long overdue."

The St. Petersburg Times, a highly regarded newspaper
in the state where Clarence Earl Gideon was tried and imprisoned without the help of a lawyer, rejoiced in his victory.
"There will be those," the *Times* said, "who will decry the
Supreme Court's 'softness' toward persons accused of crimes.
Ironically, many uttering such criticisms are the same ones
who decry the ever-increasing size and centralization of government. Most persons, we are sure, will be thankful that the
Supreme Court clings to the ancient democratic tradition of
protecting the individual against the tyranny of any governmental agency."

The Washington Post said: "Like the Gideon of old who
was summoned by an angel of the Lord to lead Israel and

overcome the Midianites, Clarence Earl Gideon of Panama City, Florida, championed the cause of justice for all indigent defendants. . . . It is intolerable in a nation which proclaims equal justice under law as one of its ideals that anyone should be handicapped in defending himself simply because he happens to be poor."

The case of *Gideon v. Wainwright* is in part a testament to a single human being. Against all the odds of inertia and ignorance and fear of state power, Clarence Earl Gideon insisted that he had a right to a lawyer and kept on insisting all the way to the Supreme Court of the United States. His triumph there shows that the poorest and least powerful of men—a convict with not even a friend to visit him in prison—can take his cause to the highest court in the land and bring about a fundamental change in the law. But of course Gideon was not really alone; there were working for him forces in law and society larger than he could understand. His case was part of a current of history, and it will be read in that light by thousands of persons who will know no more about Clarence Earl Gideon than that he stood up in a Florida court and said: "The United States Supreme Court says I am entitled to be represented by counsel."

That is the wonder of the law: that it moves case by case, seeking justice for each individual, but that any single case may be part of some larger movement. These great currents may not at first be perceived, even by those who set them flowing. When Justice Sutherland wrote about the right to counsel in 1932, in *Powell v. Alabama*, he must have had a sense of participation in a great event. He must have known that in holding unconstitutional the trial of the Scottsboro boys without adequate counsel, the Supreme Court was doing something it had never done before—setting aside a state criminal conviction because the procedure used to obtain it was unfair. But Justice Sutherland could hardly have imagined the scope of the constitutional revolution that was to follow *Powell v. Alabama*.

The constitutional law of criminal procedure has been wholly transformed in the three decades since *Powell v. Alabama*. When the process started, a state law-enforcement officer could say with confidence that there were virtually no limits in the federal Constitution on how he went about his job, and virtually no chance that any conviction he won would be reversed by a federal court. Today a pervasive system of constitutional restraints covers almost every aspect of state criminal law enforcement, from arrest through trial and sentence to appeal. All of these limits have been developed by the Supreme Court, case by case, from the vague words of the Fourteenth Amendment: due process of law and equal protection of the laws.

Just as the Gideon case was part of a movement of the law on the right to counsel, and that in turn was but one aspect of the fundamental change taking place in the constitutional doctrine of fair criminal procedure, so the criminal law trend was part of a larger picture. In many other areas the Supreme

Court in the last generation has enlarged the dimensions of individual liberty. It was just six years after *Powell v. Alabama* when the Court began to enforce the "equal" aspect of the doctrine allowing provision of "separate but equal" facilities for Negroes. Missouri must provide a legal education for Negroes within the state, the Court held, not send them elsewhere. A dissent warned that the Court's reasoning would eventually threaten the very institution of segregation—as it did. The decisions since have expunged the legal basis for racial discrimination in the United States, if not yet the actuality.

Outside the racial area the Supreme Court has developed in the last decades a whole panoply of new freedoms for the individual—to read what he wishes, speak what he will, join organizations without fear of governmental reprisal. Some, including Justice Black, have wished the Court to go further in these directions, especially in protection against penalties for Communist associations; but the overall movement remains libertarian in its direction. Most recently, in the Reapportionment case, there has come the first promise of fair representation for the individual in his legislature.

The unmistakable thrust of the Court toward exaltation of the individual, and restraint on governmental power over him, has been met by the severest criticism, not least for the criminal-law decisions. So much of this criticism is hyperbolic and uninformed that any serious observer is tempted to dismiss it out of hand. But there is good reason not to. Professor Louis L. Jaffe of the Harvard Law School wrote:

"There will be and there should be popular response to the Supreme Court's decisions; not just the 'informed' criticism of law professors but the deep-felt, emotion-laden, unsophisticated reaction of the laity. This is so because more than any court in the modern world the Supreme Court 'makes policy,' and it is at the same time so little subject to formal democratic control. . . . It is in politics, and that in a democracy means that it must be prepared to withstand the angry howls of outraged citizens."

Professor Jaffe's comment is a reminder of an easily forgotten truth: That the Court must justify itself to every generation as one of the three great centers of power in the Federal Government. Why should nine appointed lawyers play so large a role in a country that calls itself a democracy? Is it appropriate that the Supreme Court, rather than elected legislators, should reform the country's criminal procedure or its race relations? Those are the questions raised by *Gideon v. Wainwright*—or any other decision invoking the extraordinary power of the Supreme Court to measure the acts of other governmental agencies against the law of the Constitution and declare them void.

In examining the wisdom of judicial review, it is important first to observe that democracy does not exist as a pure commodity anywhere in this country's governmental processes. State legislatures have long been notoriously unrepresentative of the voters, because of distorted districts. In Congress a handful of senior members from one-party districts hold vastly disproportionate power, and the Senate's rules allow a minority to block action. The point is not that pure democracy would be desirable; it is that the American system of government includes other elements—and one of them is the balancing power of the judiciary to intervene on behalf of individual freedom.

The Supreme Court indeed often provides a forum for those—the despised and rejected—who have no effective voice in the legislative chamber. One example is Clarence Earl Gideon. "The poor man charged with crime has no lobby," Attorney General Kennedy has said. Enlightened opinion holds, without sentimentality, that treating criminal defendants in a decent way serves the interest of a civilized society. Yet legislatures, feeling no demand from the voters, will rarely do anything about unfairness in the administration

of the criminal law except under pressure from the courts—
or until the courts, especially the Supreme Court, generate
a broad moral concern. The criminal-law decisions of the
Supreme Court have awakened significant forces in society
to the moral considerations, and the result has been a fruitful
interplay between court and legislatures. Certainly the concern shown for the right to counsel in 1963 by the Kennedy
Administration, Congress, the Ford Foundation and the
many bar groups grew in large part out of the Supreme
Court's decisions on the issue over three decades.

The racial situation is an even more telling example of the
Court's function as a forum for those without a political
voice. In some southern states Negroes are virtually excluded
from the political process; they carry no weight—less than
no weight—in the legislatures. In that circumstance is it un-
democratic for the Supreme Court to intervene? Similarly
with the issue of legislative apportionment. The Florida legislature, which had long refused to provide counsel for the
poor, was so inequitably districted that at the beginning of
1963 some 12 percent of the state's citizens could elect a
majority of the members in both houses. In Florida, as in
other states, a small rural minority had power and simply
refused to give it up. Again it must be asked whether there
was not justification—democratic justification—for opening
up avenues of judicial relief, as the Supreme Court did, so
that the disenfranchised majority would have some way to
break out of the cage.

The Court can in fact serve as a safety valve, relieving intolerable social pressures that build up when legislatures are
unresponsive to urgent needs. Explosive as the racial situation
is today, it might have been much worse if the Supreme
Court over the last half-century had joined Congress and the
southern state legislatures in doing almost nothing to end
racial discrimination—nothing about the right to vote, to

serve on juries, to use public facilities, to obtain an adequate
—not to mention integrated—education.

But the failings of our legislatures, state and national, are at
best a negative justification for judicial power. The great
role of the Supreme Court can only be justified, in the end,
by the *process* it brings to bear on public problems—by the
distinctive characteristics of the judicial process.

The Gideon case demonstrated those characteristics. One
is the tendency of courts to focus their attention on individual human beings—in this case Gideon. Legislatures necessarily deal in abstractions, usually large abstractions, which
is very different from consideration in terms of the impact on
an individual. As a general proposition it may seem desirable
to enact a statute requiring the deportation of aliens who
once belonged to the Communist party. But when that law
is applied to a particular person who is fifty-two years old,
who came to this country as an infant of six months and
joined the party briefly during the Depression, the moral considerations seem very different.

The Court is forbidden by the Constitution to consider
anything but concrete cases, involving the real interests of
particular litigants. In a civilization growing less human all
the time, with budgets beyond the grasp of men and weapons
that can wipe out continents, surely there is special value in
an institution that focuses on the individual.

In comparison with the other agencies of government, the
Court also retains an intimate and non-institutionalized character. It does its own work, in Brandeis's phrase, and every
justice bears personal responsibility for what is done. Why
this characteristic of the judicial process is important is hard
to explain, but anyone who has ever tried to grope his way
through the faceless bureaucracy of government and pin
down responsibility for a mistake will understand. The obstacles to bringing about a change in governmental policy are

symbolized in the traditional defeatist question: "Why fight City Hall?" But in the Supreme Court even Clarence Earl Gideon can freely seek re-examination of past positions, and counsel arguing a case has the most direct and personal opportunity conceivable to reach the minds and hearts of those who decide.

Argument itself reflects the distinctions of the judicial process. It is so much more concentrated and intellectually focused than, for example, a legislative debate. At its best, a Supreme Court argument can be as searching and uninhibited an examination of an intellectual problem as is found in Washington. In Congressional hearings or debates the real issue often seems—to the listeners' frustration—to be around the corner. In the Supreme Court justices and counsel can deal directly, in the curiously intimate way that so surprised Bruce Jacob, with the heart of a problem. This is not to say that the Court's way of doing things is better than the legislators'—only that it is different. The diffused, discursive methods of the legislature reflect the fact that its decisions must be political, reflecting compromises and accommodations of interests that may be concerned with issues entirely apart from the one under consideration. But of Supreme Court justices we demand a process of reason. They must not be legislators, engaged in political bargaining, but lawyers, reasoning by analogy from limited materials, creating the new from the old, shaping experience and ideals into workable principle.

The search for principle is the essence of the judicial process. It can never be enough for a court to say, as a legislature properly can, "X wins the case because he has more votes behind him." Especially in the Supreme Court, which must find in the vague words of our fundamental law the guideposts for a nation, every decision should be supported by reasons that appeal to the intellect and to the ethical sense of Americans. The requirement that a court give reasons for its judgments is a basic safeguard, as the country began to realize belatedly during that shameful era when men were labeled "security risks" by boards of quasi-judges who gave no reasons at all and thus avoided responsibility for their conclusions.

Professor Arthur L. Goodhart, an American who became an English lawyer, master of University College, Oxford, and a great interpreter of the Anglo-American legal tradition, sees in that tradition three great protections against arbitrariness: "The judges sit in open court; there is no secret evidence and no secret arguments to which they can listen. . . . The judges give reasons publicly for their judgments. . . . The judges act not as a body, but as individuals. Each one is free to dissent. They are thus each other's severest critics." Professor Goodhart's three points might be restated as one aspect of what distinguishes the Supreme Court's process from a legislature's: Each justice is personally responsible for decisions that must be based on principle openly argued to the Court and persuasively reasoned in an opinion.

Supreme Court justices are enabled to search for principle, free from the political passions of the moment, by one of the wise borrowings in our Constitution from English practice. They "shall hold their Offices," the Constitution says, "during good Behaviour"—which as a practical matter means as long as they can and wish to, since impeachment is so remote a prospect. The freedom to decide as one's conscience and intellect demand, without fear of political retribution, is a rare luxury for any office-holder, and it certainly helps to explain what happens to men when they don the robes of a Supreme Court justice. The southern Senator required to go through the motions of defending segregation—and many in the Senate today are only going through the motions—can shed that dispiriting burden if he goes on the bench. The state judge who has to look to political bosses for re-election—as many do—cuts that tie upon appointment to the Supreme Court. The independence given to the justices enables them

to do things that others know are right but have never had the
courage or the determination to do by themselves.

Shortly before the Gideon case was decided, Abe Fortas
was having lunch in the Supreme Court cafeteria with an
eminent lawyer from Pennsylvania, the largest state without
a requirement for appointment of counsel in all felony cases.
"I've told the lawyers of my state and the officials again and
again that they should make the appointment of counsel compulsory," the Pennsylvania lawyer said. "They all know it
in their hearts. But regardless of their personal or professional
convictions, they won't move until this great institution tells
them to."

Just as life tenure protects the justices from political pressures, so are they cut loose from regional influences. No man
can escape, or should, his background and experience, but a
Supreme Court justice is more likely than most to outgrow
parochial prejudices. And it is increasingly important to have
a national voice speaking out on questions such as that posed
by the Gideon case. We live under a federal system, with the
states retaining a large degree of independence, but we have
become a nation. Most of us think of ourselves first as Americans, not as, say, Floridians. And we are a nation with a world
responsibility.

Justice Schaefer of Illinois has advanced "the relation of
the United States to the rest of the world" today as one argument for national standards of criminal procedure. "The
quality of a nation's civilization," he wrote, "can be largely
measured by the methods it uses in the enforcement of its
criminal law. That measurement is . . . taken from day to
day by the peoples of the world, and to them the criminal
procedure sanctioned by any of our states is the procedure
sanctioned by the United States."

Apart from what other countries may think, more and
more Americans have a national conscience that is troubled

by unfairness in law enforcement in any state—or by any state's racial discrimination. It is no longer possible for Mississippi to go her own way without disturbing not only the image the United States projects to the outside world, but the one it projects to itself. And the Supreme Court is in a strategic position to give voice to national ideals.

Even the Congress of the United States is deeply affected by regional allegiances. Of all this country's governmental instruments, only the Presidency and the Supreme Court are wholly free of sectional ties, and only the Court is given the function of regularly measuring state and local policy against the national standards of the Constitution. It is no exaggeration to say, as Holmes did, that the United States might not survive as a nation without the unifying power of the Supreme Court. Nor is the job finished. At almost every term of the Supreme Court some community claims the right to put a restriction on interstate commerce, or outlaw some book or movie accepted by the rest of the country. It is the Court's duty to preserve a union, one without tariff walls or ideological walls between the states.

Professor Goodhart has said that the Supreme Court confronts problems "more important and more difficult than any other court in the history of the world has had to face." A justice brings to the task only his character, his intellect, his education, his experience, his human understanding, his imagination. There are really no mysteries; no one teaches a course on how to be a Supreme Court justice. The Court is not a place for experts or for specialists. Indeed, it stands for the proposition that it is wise to have the final decisions made by generalists, not specialists. Rather than let tax experts have the last word on tax law, and criminal law specialists the last in their field—with all the ferocious quibbles that experts can produce—we deliberately arrange for an infusion of common sense. Perhaps that is the ultimate curiosity of the Supreme Court: That it must have a sense of our society's common understandings, that it cannot cut itself off from the people.

Discussing the due-process clause of the fourteenth Amendment, Justice Frankfurter wrote once that it was the Supreme Court's duty to ascertain "the conscience of society." That could not properly be a suggestion that the Court find some minimum level of acceptability by an intuitive public opinion poll. The Court's function is not to reflect mass ideas but to lead enlightened opinion, to educate. At its best the Court is a great teacher, illuminating issues and then drawing support for further steps from the more sensitive public attitudes it has helped to create. When the School Segregation case was decided in 1954, the largest part of public opinion in this country was at best inert on the racial question; the man in the street did not feel its ethical imperative. It was only when the ugly face of racism showed itself at Little Rock and elsewhere that Americans saw the moral issue in racial segregation—and began to give the Court's decision the support it needed to become effective.

Yet when it made the choice in 1954, the Court surely chose correctly. In the long run Americans could not have accepted the principle that separation of human beings on account of the color of their skins satisfied the demand for "equal protection of the laws." After Adolf Hitler the world knew that racial separation was an expression not of equality but of hatred.

The relationship between the Court and society is just as significant in the area of the Gideon case, criminal law. In its steady march toward higher standards of fairness in criminal procedure, the Court was not reflecting popular ideas; the public was probably uninformed and unconcerned about the issues in particular cases. But taken as a whole, the movement was followed and supported by enlightened opinion. Between *Powell v. Alabama* in 1932 and *Gideon v. Wain-*

wright in 1963 there surely developed an overwhelming acceptance of the proposition that "states' rights" should not include the right to ignore civilized decencies in the enforcement of the criminal law. Court and country were both part of a larger phenomenon. The experiences of totalitarian brutality through which the world had passed since 1932 had made the citizens of many lands more sensitive to the danger of unrestrained official authority. Justice Black took note of this in his opinion in *Chambers v. Florida* in 1940. "Today as in ages past," he said, "we are not without tragic proof that the exalted power of some governments to punish manufactured crime dictatorially is the handmaid of tyranny."

Professor Allen, looking back at the course of the Supreme Court's criminal law decisions, wrote: "Perhaps it may be worth observing that the decision of the Powell case and the rise of Hitler to power in Germany occurred within the period of a single year. It would, of course, be facile and specious to suggest that these two events are related by any direct causal connection. Yet . . . in some larger sense the two occurrences may be located in the same current of history. Both events are encompassed in the crisis of individual liberty which has confronted the western world since the First World War. The Court has been sensitive to the crisis and has responded emphatically to it. It is not only in the state criminal cases that constitutional doctrine has expanded at a remarkable rate. Virtually all of the law of free speech, assembly and press, for example, has been articulated in the last forty years. When viewed against a background of such momentous events a little criminal case involving the misbehavior of local police officers may take on a peculiar significance."

A century ago, De Tocqueville said of the justices of the Supreme Court: "Their power is enormous, but it is the power of public opinion." What is given to the justices is the opportunity not to command but to persuade. The eloquence

of a Brandeis—the ability to perceive great moral truths and
to articulate them in a way that excites the imagination of the
citizen—is as important to the Supreme Court as the power
of sword or purse to the other branches of government.
When the Court in history has lost touch with the true current of American life, it has only damaged itself. A Court
that thought it knew best said in the Dred Scott case that
Congress had no constitutional power to forbid slavery in
new territories. Another said that a state could not limit
bakers' work to ten hours a day. Those decisions turned to
dust because they sought to enshrine as eternal principles the
prejudices and limited economic understandings of mere
men. That is the risk the Supreme Court takes—the risk of
failure.

When *Betts v. Brady* was decided in 1942, the majority
of the Court thought it was expressing a meaningful principle. But trial and error—the case-by-case process of the
courts—showed that the *Betts* rule did not work, that it expressed no principle. When the Court in *Gideon* laid down
the universal requirement of counsel, it was only articulating
a principle that most of those with an opinion—lawyers,
judges, state officials themselves—had already recognized.

Gideon v. Wainwright was a triumph for Hugo Black,
but in a way the case suggests that there was not always so
deep a gulf between his view of the law and Felix Frankfurter's as the occasional ferocity of their well-known debate
suggested. Although he speaks of absolutes, Justice Black has
actually dealt with the Constitution as a living document,
changing his views as conditions have changed. One of his
able disciples, Professor Charles A. Reich of the Yale Law
School, a former law clerk to him, has written that Justice
Black's opinions during a quarter-century on the Court reflect an unstated assumption that the Constitution's protections of individual liberty must grow just as the powers of
government have been allowed to expand to meet new prob-

lems. The issue of the right to counsel in fact does not fit Justice Black's public position that history provides satisfactory guides to the meaning of the Constitution. The Sixth Amendment was designed by its framers to assure the right to be represented by counsel to those who could afford to retain their own. But that history rightly presented no obstacle to Justice Black when he wrote *Johnson v. Zerbst* for the Court in 1938, holding that the Sixth Amendment required the Federal Government to provide in its courts a lawyer for any defendant who was too poor to hire one himself and who did not waive the right. And in *Gideon* Justice Black's opinion rested not on absolutes but on the single proposition that the right to counsel provided by the Sixth Amendment was fundamental and was therefore embraced in the fourteenth Amendment.

Justice Frankfurter was just as dedicated to fair criminal procedure as Justice Black. It was Justice Frankfurter who wrote, in a Federal criminal case, "The history of liberty has largely been the history of observance of procedural safeguards." His deep belief in federalism made him draw back from imposing identical requirements on the states, but even there his difference with Justice Black—for all the talk—may often have come down to a question of timing. In 1942, Justice Frankfurter might have said, the country was not ready for a universal requirement of counsel in serious criminal cases; the bar was not prepared for such a burden; the states would have resisted, and the decision would have been widely ignored. But that would not have ended the matter for Justice Frankfurter. "It is of the very nature of a free society to advance in its standards of what is deemed reasonable and right," he once wrote. "Representing as it does a living principle, due process is not confined within a permanent catalogue of what may at a given time be deemed the limits or essentials of fundamental rights."

Shortly after the Gideon case was decided, Justice Black

visited Justice Frankfurter at home and told his ailing colleague about the conference at which the case had been discussed. He had told the other members of the Court, Justice Black said, that if Felix had been there he would have voted —faithful to his own view of due process—to reverse the conviction of Clarence Earl Gideon and overrule *Betts v. Brady*.

Justice Frankfurter said: "Of course I would."

EPILOGUE

Resolution of the great constitutional question in *Gideon v. Wainwright* did not decide the fate of Clarence Earl Gideon. He was now entitled to a new trial, with a lawyer. Was he guilty of breaking into the Bay Harbor Poolroom? The verdict would not set any legal precedents, but there is significance in the human beings who make constitutional-law cases as well as in the law. And in this case there was the interesting question whether the legal assistance for which Gideon had fought so hard would make any difference to him.

Soon after the decision Abe Fortas wrote Gideon suggesting that in the future a local Florida lawyer should represent him. Fortas said he had written to a Florida Civil Liberties

Union attorney about the case. This lawyer was Tobias Simon of Miami, who had signed the *amicus* brief presented to the Supreme Court by the American Civil Liberties Union. Gideon, who before the decision had expressed the hope that the A.C.L.U. would give him a lawyer, wrote Simon on April 9, 1963.

"I humbly am asking you for any help that you can give me in the present situation," Gideon said. "Because no one knows any better than me of what I am up against. I have no reason to believe now that I would receive a fair trial in the same court than I did before even with a court appointed attorney. I have my plea already to make but it probably will be denied me."

Simon replied on April 15th that someone from the Civil Liberties Union would represent him at his new trial. Gideon acknowledged that letter with thanks on April 29th, adding that he wondered how long the Supreme Court of Florida could take to act on his case now "without becoming contemptible of the United States Supreme Court."

A few days later Simon went to Raiford and interviewed Gideon for an hour and a half. He found Gideon to be "an irascible but spunky white male." Gideon spoke even more forcefully than in his letters. He was under the illusion that a new trial would constitute double jeopardy and that the Florida Supreme Court should already have released him outright. (A new trial won by a prisoner as a result of his own appeal is not double jeopardy under American law.) He said he could never get a fair trial in Panama City, and when Simon tried to reassure him Gideon "became exceedingly bitter and refused to discuss his case any further." But he "did agree that we would be able to represent him in the forthcoming new trial," Simon reported to the A.C.L.U.

The Florida Supreme Court had received the official notice of the United States Supreme Court decision—the mandate—in April; and on May 15th it issued an order entitling Gideon to a new trial. The circuit court of Bay County set July 5th as the trial date.

On July 4th Simon went to Panama City with Irwin J. Block, an experienced criminal lawyer, until recently the chief assistant prosecutor in Miami, who had agreed to help him. They interviewed some witnesses and former neighbors of Gideon who seemed to have "admiration for a man who fought so hard against odds so great." Then they went to see Gideon, who had been brought from Raiford to the local jail. Mr. Simon described the meeting.

"Gideon refused to be represented by either of us; he refused to be tried; he stated that the court had no power to try him, and that his trial in Panama City would only mean his return to the penitentiary. All efforts to calm him and to have him place some trust in us failed."

The next morning, the time set for trial, Simon and Block met with the prosecutors in the chambers of Robert L. McCrary, Jr., the judge who had presided over Gideon's first trial and was to handle the second. Gideon was also present. Judge McCrary began by noting that Simon had signed some papers and was appearing as defense counsel.

"I didn't authorize Mr. Simon to sign anything for me," Gideon said. "I'll do my own signing. I do not want him to represent me."

Judge McCrary asked warily, "Do you want another lawyer to represent you?"

"No," said Gideon. After a pause he added: "And I'm not ready for trial."

There must have been a touch of bewilderment in the judge's next question. "What do you want, then?"

"I want to file for an order to move my case from this court," Gideon replied. "I can't get a fair trial in this court; it's the same court, the same judge, everything, and every-

body connected with the court is the same as it was before
and I can't get a fair trial here. . . . You're not even going
to let me plead my case."

At this point Simon explained his position in the case, reading to the judge, among other documents, Gideon's letter
"humbly asking" for help. But Simon said that of course he
and Block did not want to represent Gideon if he did not
want them.

Gideon repeated his wish: "I want to plead my own case.
I want to make my own plea. I do not want them to make
any plea for me."

"You don't want Mr. Simon and Mr. Block to represent
you?" Judge McCrary asked, making absolutely certain that
all this was really happening.

"No," said Gideon, "I don't want them to represent me.
I DO NOT WANT THEM.". (The court reporter used
capitals.)

The judge excused Simon and Block, but he also made
clear that under no circumstances did he want Gideon to try
his own case again. After ascertaining that Gideon had no
money to hire a lawyer of his own choice, Judge McCrary
asked whether there was a local lawyer whom Gideon would
like to represent him. There was: W. Fred Turner.

"For the record," Judge McCrary said quickly, "I am going to appoint Mr. Fred Turner to represent this defendant,
Clarence Earl Gideon."

A member of the prosecuting staff suggested that the
public defender just appointed for that judicial circuit under
the new Florida public-defender law assist Fred Turner.

"I don't want him in it," Gideon said, evidently preferring
a private attorney with no touch of welfare.

The judge said, "We will just let Mr. Turner handle this
case." Then he advised Gideon to get in touch with his new
lawyer to file any motions he desired.

"I want to file my own motions," Gideon said. "If this

is to be a matter of just sending me back to the penitentiary I want to do it my own way. It has been more than two years now since this crime is alleged to have been committed, and if I'm going back to the penitentiary for the same crime I want to do it my way. I want to file my own motions."

He pulled from his hip pocket two crumpled pages, type-written single-spaced, that were the motions he had pre-pared. Judge McCrary asked Gideon to read them to the court reporter. The motions were full of legalistic language, and Gideon seemed to have some trouble reading them; fi-nally the judge called a short recess to let Gideon look them over before reading them to the stenographer. These long documents made two main points: That a new trial was barred by the rule against double jeopardy and by Florida's two-year statute of limitations on his alleged crime. (The statute of limitations does not, in fact, apply when an appeal results in a new trial.)

Judge McCrary listened attentively during the reading of the motions and said he would rule on them later. Then he set a new trial date, August 5th, exactly one month later. The judge offered to free the prisoner on $1,000 bail, but Gideon could not raise it and was returned to the peniten-tiary.

Simon later wrote a report on the episode for the Florida Civil Liberties Union, which he subtitled, "How the Florida Civil Liberties Union Wasted $300, and How Two Attor-neys Each Traveled over 1200 Miles and Killed an Other-wise Perfectly Enjoyable July Fourth Weekend." But by the end of the report his anger seems to have softened. He wrote:

"It has become almost axiomatic that the great rights which are secured for all of us by the Bill of Rights are con-stantly tested and retested in the courts by the people who live in the bottom of society's barrel. Thus, many of our freedom-of-religion cases developed out of efforts by mem-

bers of small sects to force religious tracts upon people who
did not want them; our freedom-of-speech cases have developed from the efforts of the police to jail persons who ranted
and raved against others, including Catholics, Jews and Negroes. . . .

"In the future the name 'Gideon' will stand for the great
principle that the poor are entitled to the same type of justice as are those who are able to afford counsel. It is probably
a good thing that it is immaterial and unimportant that Gideon is something of a 'nut,' that his maniacal distrust and
suspicion lead him to the very borders of insanity. Upon the
shoulders of such persons are our great rights carried."

Gideon's new lawyer, Fred Turner, wrote to Judge
McCrary on July 12th asking that the trial be postponed
three weeks. He said there were "many, many legal problems" in this case—a case once considered so simple that the
defendant could be required to try it himself on a few minutes' notice. Judge McCrary refused the postponement.

On August 1st the judge denied a series of motions including Gideon's own, presented by Turner, to dismiss the
charges. Courtroom observers thought Gideon looked pleased
at the denial and was looking forward to the new trial. Judge
McCrary warned him not to interfere with Turner or try
to take over his own defense.

The courthouse in Panama City is a large brick building,
painted yellow, with peeling white columns. It stands on a
rather seedy square set with palms. The courtroom is a
simple, good-looking room with pale green walls and seats
for about one hundred and fifty. It is air conditioned, a
necessity in Panama City in August.

The trial began promptly at nine A.M. on August 5th.
After the sheriff's traditional opening (" . . . God save the
United States of America, the State of Florida and this hon-
orable court"), Judge McCrary read a prayer ending "and

help us to do impartial justice, for Christ's sake. Amen."
Forty-eight years old, with black hair, informal and gracious
in his dealings with the lawyers but decisive when necessary,
McCrary was not an awesome figure in his robes. To his left
and below him was the court reporter, Mrs. Nelle P. Heath,
a motherly figure with firmly upswept hair and pearl ear-
rings. ("I reported this case originally, and I thought it was
just another run-of-the-mill case. I never thought that Gideon was different from anyone else—that he would just
keep on goin' and goin' and goin'.") The prosecution table
was just in front of the bench. The original prosecutor,
Assistant State Attorney William E. Harris, a tanned, bulky
man, again sat there. But this time, indicating the importance
the case had acquired, his boss was there, too—the state attorney for the circuit, J. Frank Adams, a foxy-looking figure
in a bow tie—and also another assistant, J. Paul Griffith. The
prosecutors seemed confident. Adams said, "If he'd had a
lawyer in the first place, he'd have been advised to plead
guilty."

Judge McCrary announced "the case of State of Florida
versus Clarence Earl Gideon. Is the state ready for trial?"
Harris said it was. Turner, who was sitting with Gideon at
a table back near the rail that separated the spectators from
the trial area, got up without waiting to be asked. "We're
ready, your Honor," he said, enthusiastically rolling a pencil
between his two flattened hands. Turner was thin and dap-
per, reminiscent of Fred Astaire, "forty-one summers" old,
he said when asked.

Ordinarily a jury of six is used in Florida. There was a
panel of twenty-eight white men in the courtroom. (Why
no Negroes? "They just don't call any," a local newspaper
man explained.) The first six men were called forward and
questioned first by Harris for possible prejudice. Harris was
satisfied with all of them. Then Turner questioned the same
six; they said they had no prejudices in the case, and they

agreed that they would give the defendant the benefit of any reasonable doubt. Without explanation, Turner excused two of the six. Later he said, privately, that he had gone over the whole jury list in advance—"you've got to know who they are, what they think"—and dropped the two men because he knew that one didn't like alcohol and that the other was "a convicter."

The jury was sworn just before ten A.M. Harris made a two-minute opening statement to the effect that the state expected to prove Gideon had broken into the Bay Harbor Poolroom through a rear window; a witness had seen him inside and in an alley after leaving. Turner waived his right to make an opening statement.

Henry Cook, the eyewitness, was the first to take the stand. He turned out to be a sallow-faced youth of twenty-two, with greasy black hair cut in a pompadour and long sideburns. Under Harris's questioning he told the same story he had at the first trial. He had come back to Bay Harbor from a dance in Apalachicola, sixty miles away, at five-thirty that morning and had spotted Gideon inside the poolroom; he had followed Gideon down the alley to a telephone booth, then back to the poolroom; Gideon's pockets bulged.

Turner began his cross-examination by asking who had driven Cook back from Apalachicola that night. When Cook had trouble remembering, Turner suggested some names. (Turner had driven to Apalachicola a few days earlier to try, without success, to find the other young men who had been in the car.) Cook said the car was "an old model Chevrolet."

"Why did they put you off two blocks from your home when they'd driven you sixty miles?" Turner asked.

Cook mumbled inaudibly, then said, "I was going to hang around there till the poolroom opened up—seven o'clock."

Turner began addressing the witness with irritating familiarity, "Well now, Henry . . . ," and took him back over the events of that night. Cook said he had had a beer or two, but then the stores had closed in Apalachicola at midnight. This brought Turner back to the question of why Cook and his friends had stopped outside the Bay Harbor Poolroom. Turner had a suggestion—an accusation.

"Mr. Cook," he said, "did you go into the Bay Harbor Poolroom?"

"No, sir."

"Did you all get a six-pack of beer out of there?"

"No, sir."

Turner led Cook over a detailed discussion of the geography of Bay Harbor and the poolroom, indicating an intimate acquaintance with it himself. (He had spent a day nosing around Bay Harbor and talking with people, to prepare for the trial.) Weren't there some advertising boards in the front window? How could Cook have seen past them and spotted Gideon, as he claimed? Weren't the windows on the alley too high to see through?

"You did not call the police then or later," Turner asked. It was as much a comment as a question.

"That's right."

After more questions, Turner asked, "Ever been convicted of a felony?"

"No, sir, not convicted. I stole a car and was put on probation."

That answer set off a long wrangle between the lawyers. At the first trial, when Gideon asked whether he had ever been convicted of a felony, Cook had answered: "No, sir, never have." Turner said that was a false answer that reflected on Cook's character and credibility as a witness. State Attorney Adams popped up and said it was not necessarily false because Cook had evidently pleaded guilty; that was not the same as being "convicted." Turner said it was the same. There was a suggestion that the plea might have been in a juvenile court, where there are no formal convictions.

Finally the judge allowed this exchange, which closed the cross-examination:

Turner: "Have you ever denied being convicted of a felony?"

Cook: "Yes, sir."

Turner: "When and where did you deny your criminal record?"

Cook: "Right here—at his last trial."

On redirect examination Harris got Cook to say he had not understood the question about a felony at the first trial. Turner moved to strike this testimony, saying "I don't think this should go to the jury with any excuses or any embellishments. . . . I don't care if he's ignorant of the law or I am, that still doesn't change the spots on the leopard. He's a convicted felon." Judge McCrary let Cook's explanation stand, but Turner had made the score he wanted—impressing the jury with Cook's record.

The prosecution's second witness was the man who had operated the Bay Harbor Poolroom, Ira Strickland, Jr., twenty-nine years old, growing bald. He was no longer in the poolroom business; now he was a stock clerk. Questioning him, State Attorney Adams went into much greater detail about the poolroom and Gideon's relationship to it than at the first trial. Had Gideon worked for Strickland? "Never on the payroll," but he had helped out sometimes.

"Was he authorized to be in the poolroom on the morning of the third day of June, 1961?"

"No."

On cross-examination Turner asked whether others had not operated the poolroom for Strickland.

"Occasionally."

"Even this defendant, Gideon, operated it sometimes, didn't he?"

"Well, occasionally." There was no further explanation. Turner pressed Strickland to say exactly what he missed

from the poolroom when he arrived that morning, but Strickland said he could not be precise.

"Are you sure there was money in that cigarette machine
[the night before]?"

"Yes."

"How can you be sure?"

"I bought a pack myself."

Shortly before noon Judge McCrary recessed the trial for
lunch. Afterward the state called the detective who had arrested Gideon in 1961. Duell Pitts was a square-faced, hand-
some man, thirty-seven years old, wearing a sports jacket and
salmon-colored tie. Like the other prosecution witnesses, he
seemed to have no animus toward Gideon; indeed he spoke
rather gently of him. On direct examination he testified that
he had been called by the policeman who discovered the
break-in, was given Gideon's name at the scene by Cook, and
arrested Gideon in a downtown Panama City bar the same
morning.

Under cross-examination Pitts produced his notes of what
Strickland had told him was missing from the poolroom that
morning: four fifths of wine, twelve bottles of Coca Cola,
twelve cans of beer, about five dollars from the cigarette
machine and sixty dollars from the juke box. Then Turner
asked a question that boomeranged: "When you arrested
Clarence Earl Gideon that morning, how much money did
he have on him?"

Pitts answered, "Twenty-five dollars and twenty-eight
cents in quarters, nickels, dimes and a few pennies."

On redirect, that damning point was re-emphasized: "This
twenty-five dollars and twenty-eight cents—he had no bills?"

"Not that I remember."

Preston Bray, the cab driver who was called by Gideon
the morning of the crime and drove him downtown, testified
that Gideon had paid him six quarters. He said that Gideon
had told him: "If anyone asks you where you left me off,

you don't know; you haven't seen me." But on cross-examination he said Gideon had told him the same thing on other occasions.

"Do you know why?"

"I understand it was his wife—he had trouble with his wife." There were these further exchanges between Turner and Bray:

Q: "What was his condition as to sobriety?"

A: "What's that?"

Q: "Was he drunk or sober?"

A: "He was sober."

Q: "Did he have any wine on him?"

A: "No, sir."

Q: "Any beer?"

A: "No, sir."

Q: "Any Coca Cola?"

A: "No, sir."

Q: "Did his pockets bulge?"

A: "No, sir."

That was the prosecution's case. The jury was sent out; and then Turner moved for a directed verdict of acquittal, arguing that the evidence went only to show Gideon in the poolroom, not breaking into it. Judge McCrary listened politely and then said without hesitation: "The motion will be denied. Call the jury back."

Turner produced a surprise defense witness who had never appeared in the case before. He was J.D. Henderson, owner of the grocery in Bay Harbor. Between eight and nine on the morning of June 3, 1961, Henderson said, Henry Cook had come into his store and told the grocer that "the law had picked him up for questioning" about the break-in.

"Picked who up?" Turner asked with an air of mock disbelief.

"Henry Cook."

Henderson said Cook had told him about seeing someone in the poolroom but was "not sure who it was. He said, 'It looked like Mr. Gideon.'" If such a statement had been made by Cook, it was much less positive than his subsequent testimony.

On cross-examination Harris asked whether Henderson had ever had "any trouble with Henry Cook."

"No."

"Does he owe you any money?"

"He owes a grocery bill, forty-one dollars, for almost a year."

The second and last witness for the defense was Clarence Earl Gideon.

Q: "On the morning of June 3, 1961, did you break and enter the Bay Harbor Poolroom?"

A: "No, sir."

Q: "What was the purpose of your going into town?"

A: "To get me another drink."

Q: "Where'd you get the money?"

A: "I gambled."

Q: "What kind of games?"

A: "Mostly rummy."

Q: "Did you ever gamble with Henry Cook?"

A: "Sure, I gambled with all those boys."

Q: "Did you have any wine with you?"

A: "I don't drink wine."

Q: "Any beer? Any Coke?"

A: "No."

Q: "What did you purchase in town?"

A: "I didn't purchase nothin' except somethin' to drink."

Q: "That's what I mean. What did you purchase to drink?"

A: "Four or five beers, and I bought a half-pint of vodka."

Q: "What do you say to this charge that you broke and entered the pool hall?"

A: "I'm not guilty of it—I know nothing about it."

On cross-examination, Harris asked where Gideon was employed at the time. "I wasn't employed. I was gambling."

There was a long exploration of when Gideon had last held a regular job. He had painted some rooms at the Bay Harbor Hotel and was given free rent (a $6-a-week room) in exchange. He had run poker games for Strickland in the poolroom. There followed some questions about gambling that Gideon answered with a puzzled air, as if bewildered at Harris's failure to understand.

Q: "Why did you have all that money in coins?"

A: "I've had as much as one hundred dollars in my pockets in coins."

Q: "Why?"

A: "Have you ever run a poker game?"

Q: "You would carry one hundred dollars in coins around for a couple of days at a time?"

A: "Yes sir, I sure wouldn't leave it in a room in the Bay Harbor Hotel."

Q: "Did you play rummy that night?"

A: "No—I was too busy drinking."

Q: "Have you ever been convicted or pled guilty to a felony?"

A: "Yes, five times, including this one."

At two-forty P.M. the testimony was all in. Judge McCrary recessed the trial and called the lawyers and Gideon into his chambers to discuss how he should charge the jury. The lawyers wrangled for half an hour, ending with a squabble over how much time they would have for closing arguments. Judge McCrary settled this by allowing each side forty-five minutes; as it turned out, neither used that much.

In his address to the jury Turner was the model of the practiced criminal lawyer—dramatic but not too dramatic. His whole argument focused on Henry Cook.

"This probationer," he said scornfully, "has been out at a dance drinking beer. . . . He does a peculiar thing [when he supposedly sees Gideon inside the poolroom]. He doesn't call the police, he doesn't notify the owner, he just walks

to the corner and walks back [as Cook had testified]. . . .
What happened to the beer and the wine and the Cokes? I'll
tell you—it left there in that old model Chevrolet. The beer
ran out at midnight in Apalachicola. . . . Why was Cook
walking back and forth? I'll give you the explanation: He
was the lookout."

Having accused Cook and his friends of actually committing the crime, Turner turned to the defendant.

"Gideon's a gambler," he said, "and he'd been drinking
whiskey. I submit to you that he did just what he said that
morning—he walked out of his hotel and went to that telephone booth [to call the cab]. . . . Cook saw him, and here
was a perfect answer for Cook. He names Gideon."

For the state, Assistant Prosecutor Griffith had made a
straightforward closing argument, summarizing the testimony without dramatics. Now, in rebuttal to Turner, Harris
got a little more folksy.

"Twenty-five dollars' worth of change," he said, "that's
a lot to carry in your pocket. But Mr. Gideon carried one
hundred dollars' worth of change in his pocket." He paused
and raised his eyebrows. "Do you believe that? . . . There's
been no evidence here of any animosity by Cook toward
Gideon. There's no evidence here that Cook and his friends
took this beer and wine."

The jury went out at four-twenty P.M., after a colorless
charge by the judge including the instruction—requested by
Turner—that the jury must believe Gideon guilty "beyond
a reasonable doubt" in order to convict him. When a half-
hour had passed with no verdict, the prosecutors were less
confident. At five twenty-five there was a knock on the door
between the courtroom and the jury room. The jurors filed
in, and the court clerk read their verdict, written on a form.
It was *Not Guilty*.

"So say you all?" asked Judge McCrary, without a flicker
of emotion. The jurors nodded.

Judge McCrary had written of Gideon's first trial: "In my opinion he did as well as most lawyers could have done in handling his case." But Gideon had not done as well as Fred Turner. He had none of Fred Turner's training, or his talent, or his knowledge of the community. Nor could he prepare the case as Turner had, because he had been in prison before his trial.

Turner had spent three full days before trial interviewing witnesses and exploring the case. He went out in the backyard and picked pears with Cook's mother to see what he could find out about the prosecution's star witness. Actually, Turner already knew a good deal about Cook because he had twice been Cook's lawyer—a coincidence that was not a great surprise in a small town like Panama City, where part of a lawyer's job is to know everyone. He had represented Cook in a divorce action and defended him successfully against a charge of leading a drunk out of the Bay Harbor Poolroom, beating him up and robbing him of $1.98. Gideon's insistence on having a local lawyer—Fred Turner—may well have won the case for him. It is doubtful that the Civil Liberties Union lawyers from Miami could have been so effective with a Panama City jury.

After nearly two years in the state penitentiary Gideon was a free man. There were tears in his eyes, and he trembled even more than usual as he stood in a circle of well-wishers and discussed his plans. His half-brother, the Air Force sergeant, was coming home from Japan and would adopt Gideon's children. Gideon would see the children the next day, then go off to stay with a friend in Tallahassee. That night he would pay a last, triumphant visit to the Bay Harbor Poolroom. Could someone let him have a few dollars? Someone did.

"Do you feel like you accomplished something?" a newspaper reporter asked.

"Well I did."

NOTES

The following are mainly source notes. They generally follow legal methods of citation, which may need a word of explanation. *Betts v. Brady*, 316 U.S. 455, 462 (1942), means that the Supreme Court decided the case in 1942 and that the opinions begin at page 455 of volume 316 of the *United States Reports*, the official volumes of the Court's decisions; the particular passage quoted or mentioned is at page 462. In the early years the reports bore the name of the editor, such as Cranch or Wheaton or Howard: *Martin v. Hunter's Lessee*, 1 Wheaton 304 (1816). Federal statutes are cited by title and section in the United States Code, the compendium of federal laws; 28 U.S.C. 1915(a) means Title 28 of the code, section 1915(a). Articles in law reviews are cited by author, title, the volume and name of the review, page and date: Schaefer, *Federalism and State Criminal Procedure*, 70 Harv. L. Rev. 1, 25 (1956). Books are cited by author, title, page and year of publication: Freund, *The Supreme Court of the United States* 47 (1961). The author's full name and further details of publication are given in the list of suggested readings.

Chapter 1

Page
4   The *in forma pauperis* statute is 28 U.S.C. 1915(a).
8   *Betts v. Brady*, 316 U.S. 455 (1942).
     The quoted passage from *Betts* is on p. 462.

Chapter 2

12   Jackson, *The Supreme Court in the American System of Government* 12 (1955).

13   The 1938 decision requiring federal judges to follow state-court decisions in diversity cases was *Erie RR. v. Tompkins*, 304 U.S. 64.

15   *Martin v. Hunter's Lessee*, 1 Wheaton 304 (1816).

18   Supreme Court review of state-court decisions is controlled by 28 U.S.C. 1257.
     Thompson v. Louisville, 362 U.S. 199 (1960).

19   *N.A.A.C.P. v. Alabama*, 357 U.S. 449 (1958). Holmes spoke of "springes" in *Davis v. Wechsler*, 263 U.S. 22 (1924).

20   The Dred Scott case is *Scott v. Sandford*, 19 Howard 393 (1857).
     Justice Brandeis's great statement of the barriers to constitutional decisions is in *Ashwander v. Tennessee Valley Auhority*, 297 U.S. 288, 346 (1936). Quotations from Brandeis later in this chapter are from the same opinion.
     "The most important thing we do is not doing" was often said by Brandeis to his law clerks and has been recalled especially by one of them, Professor Paul A. Freund.
     The birth-control cases: *Tileston v. Ullman*, 318 U.S. 44 (1943), and *Poe v. Ullman*, 367 U.S. 497 (1961).

21   The security case: *Peters v. Hobby*, 349 U.S. 331 (1955).

22   The Hughes letter can be found at 81 Congressional
      Record 2814 (1937).

23   Story's remark about the size of the Court is quoted in
      Hughes, *The Supreme Court of the United States* 238
      (1928).

      In the early years of the Court, Congress fixed the
      number of justices at varying levels, from six to ten. Since
      1869 there have been nine.

24   Taft's testimony is in House Judiciary Committee Hear-
      ings on H.R. 10479, 67th Congress, 2d Session, p. 2. It is
      quoted in Justice Frankfurter's dissenting opinion in
      Dick v. N.Y. Life, 359 U.S. 437, 447, 452 (1959).

25   The Vinson address is printed at 69 Sup. Ct. Reporter
      VI (1949). (The citation is to a privately published set
      of reports of Supreme Court decisions.)

27   Justice Brennan's statement is in Brennan, *Supreme Court
      Review of State Court Decisions*, 38 Michigan State Bar
      Journal, No. 11, pp. 14, 18 (November, 1959).

      The School Segregation case: *Brown v. Board of Edu-
      cation*, 347 U.S. 483 (1954).

28   The Frankfurter warning: *Foster v. Illinois*, 332 U.S.
      134, 139 (1947).

      ## Chapter 3

29   The Brandeis phrase was recalled by a former law clerk,
      James M. Landis.

30   Jackson, *The Supreme Court in the American System of
      Government* 16 (1955).

      Hughes' remarks are in 11 Proceedings of the Ameri-
      can Law Institute 313, 314 (1934).

31   Jackson on law clerks: op. cit. at p. 20. Clark, *The Su-
      preme Court Conference*, 19 Federal Rules Decisions
      303, 304 (1956). (The last citation is to a reporter that

covers decisions of all courts interpreting the federal
rules of legal procedure.)

32   Justice Frankfurter in *Brown v. Allen*, 344 U.S. 443, 493
      (1953).

33   The decision construing the paupers' statute was *Adkins
      v. du Pont Co.*, 335 U.S. 331, 339 (1948).

34   Douglas, *The Supreme Court and Its Case Load*, 45 Cor-
      nell Law Quarterly 401, 407 (1960).
          Schaefer, *Federalism and State Criminal Procedure*, 70
      Harv. L. Rev. 1, 25 (1956). The Douglas quotation is
      from his Cornell article, op. cit., p. 408.

35   Justice Douglas uses only one law clerk. With three for
      the Chief Justice and two for each of the others, the total
      for the Court is eighteen.

40   Frankfurter, *Chief Justices I Have Known*, in *Of Law
      and Men* (Elman editor) 111, 133 (1956). The Jackson
      quotation, op. cit., p. 15.

41   Justice Frankfurter's view on dismissing writs of certio-
      rari was in his dissenting opinion in *Rogers v. Missouri
      Pacific RR.*, 352 U.S. 500, 524 (1957).

Chapter 4

45   Rule 53(7) of the Supreme Court Rules provides for the
      appointment of counsel and the payment of transporta-
      tion expenses.
          Bartkus v. Illinois, 359 U.S. 121 (1959).
          The new Illinois statute barring double prosecutions
      can be found in the compendium of Illinois laws at 38 Ill.
      Smith-Hurd Ann. Stat. 3-4.

46   The right to present one's own case is granted by 28
      U.S.C. 1654.

47   Justice Frankfurter in *Dennis v. United States*, 340 U.S.
      887 (1950).
          The New York prayer case: *Engel v. Vitale*, 370 U.S.
      421 (1962).

50   Biddle, *In Brief Authority* 176 (1962).

51   *Durham v. United States*, 214 F.2d 862, 874 (1954). (The citation is to the Federal Reporter, 2d series, reporting decisions of the United States Courts of Appeals.)

52   For a comment on the unsentimental Brandeis and widows and orphans, see Freund, *Mr. Justice Brandeis: A Centennial Memoir*, 70 Harv. L. Rev. 769, 787 (1957).

Chapter 6

80   Jackson in *Brown v. Allen*, 344 U.S. 443, 540 (1953).

81   *Marbury v. Madison*, 1 Cranch 137 (1803).

82   Jackson, op. cit., p. 26.

     A notable expression of Justice Frankfurter's belief in judicial restraint was his dissent in the second Flag Salute case, *West Virginia Board of Education v. Barnette*, 319 U.S. 624, 646 (1943).

83   Justice Harlan's address at the American Bar Center, August 13, 1963.

     The outstanding statement of Justice Black's view on constitutional absolutes is in his lecture, *The Bill of Rights*, reprinted in *The Great Rights* (Cahn, editor) 43 (1963) and also reprinted in a collection of Black's writings, *One Man's Stand for Freedom* (Dilliard, editor) 33 (1963).

84   The wiretapping case: *Goldman v. United States*, 316 U.S. 129 (1942). The school-bus case: *Everson v. Board of Education*, 330 U.S. 1 (1947).

     Brandeis on precedent: *Burnett v. Coronado Oil and Gas Co.*, 285 U.S. 393, 405, 406 (1932).

85   Holmes on Henry IV: *The Path of the Law*, an 1897 address reprinted in *Collected Legal Papers* 167, 187 (1920).

     The separate-but-equal doctrine was laid down in *Plessy v. Ferguson*, 163 U.S. 537 (1896).

86   The law-review study of overruling is Blaustein and

Field, *"Overruling" Opinions in the Supreme Court,* 57
Michigan L. Rev. 151, 162 (1958).

Justice Black's criminal contempt dissent was in *Green
v. United States,* 356 U.S. 165, 193 (1958).

87   *McCulloch v. Maryland,* 4 Wheaton 316 (1819).

The Supreme Court invalidated major New Deal measures for coal mines in *Carter v. Carter Coal Co.,* 298 U.S.
238 (1936), and for farms in *United States v. Butler,* 297
U.S. 1 (1936). The Court's symbolic turning point was
N.L.R.B. v. Jones & Laughlin Co., 301 U.S. 1 (1937),
sustaining the Wagner Act.

The report of the Chief Justices is printed at 104 Congressional Record A7782 (1958).

88   Frankfurter on federalism: *Knapp v. Schweitzer,* 357
U.S. 371, 380 (1958), and *Bartkus v. Illinois,* 359 U.S.
121, 138 (1959).

The quotation from Justice Black in *Bartkus* is at p.
155.

89   The Madison material can be found in Brennan, *The Bill
of Rights and the States,* reprinted in *The Great Rights*
(Cahn, editor) 69-70 (1963).

90   *Barron v. Baltimore,* 7 Peters 243 (1833).
      Adamson v. California, 332 U.S. 46 (1947).

91   The Cardozo formulation was in *Palko v. Connecticut,*
302 U.S. 319 (1937).

The Court held First Amendment restraints inapplica-
ble to the states in *Prudential Insurance Co. v. Cheek,* 259
U.S. 530 (1922).

Professor Freund's wry observation is in Freund, *The
Supreme Court of the United States* 47 (1961).

The free-speech guarantee was read into the Fourteenth Amendment in *Gitlow v. New York,* 268 U.S.
652 (1925).

92   The Arkansas case: *Moore v. Dempsey,* 261 U.S. 86
(1923).

The search-and-seizure case: *Wolf v. Colorado,* 338 U.S.
25 (1949).

93   The first coerced-confession case was *Brown v. Missis-*

sippi, 297 U.S. 278 (1936). An example of a later case depending on psychological rather than physical coercion is *Watts v. Indiana,* 338 U.S. 49, 52 (1949), where Justice Frankfurter wrote: "There is torture of mind as well as body; the will is as much affected by fear as by force." In *Spano v. New York,* 360 U.S. 315, 320 (1959), Chief Justice Warren said: "The abhorrence of society to the use of involuntary confessions does not turn alone on their inherent untrustworthiness. It also turns on the deep-rooted feeling that the police must obey the law while enforcing the law; that in the end life and liberty can be as much endangered from illegal methods used to convict those thought to be criminals as from the actual criminals themselves."

94 *Griffin v. Illinois,* 351 U.S. 12 (1956).
Mapp v. Ohio, 367 U.S. 643 (1961).
Brennan, *The Bill of Rights and the States,* in *The Great Rights* (Cahn, editor) 67, 82, 85-6 (1963).

Chapter 8

102 Rawle, *A View of the Constitution* 127-8 (1825).
103 Botein and Gordon, *The Trial of the Future* 51-52 (1963).
104 Schaefer, *Federalism and State Criminal Procedure,* 70 Harv. L. Rev. 1, 8 (1956).
105 *Powell v. Alabama,* 287 U.S. 45 (1932).
Professor Allen's account: Allen, *The Supreme Court and State Criminal Justice,* 4 Wayne L. Rev. 191 (1958).
106 There were originally nine of the Scottsboro boys, but the Northern liberal groups that interested themselves in their fate did not take to the Supreme Court the cases of two juveniles who fared better in the Alabama courts. After the Supreme Court reversed the convictions of the seven, the alleged ringleader, Haywood Patterson, was retried alone, convicted and again sentenced to death.

The trial judge set the verdict aside. At a third trial Patterson and Clarence Norris were convicted and sentenced to death. In 1935 the Supreme Court reversed these convictions on the ground that Negroes had been systematically excluded from the jury. *Norris v. Alabama,* 294 U.S. 587; *Patterson v. Alabama,* 294 U.S. 600. In the next two years Alabama authorities quashed the indictments against five of the nine; the other four were again convicted, but only Norris drew a death sentence. That sentence was commuted, and by 1946 all had been released on parole save Patterson. He escaped in 1948 and reached Michigan, whose authorities rejected an Alabama request for extradition. The whole Scottsboro Case was a national cause celebre during the 1930's, including among other elements conflict between Communist and non-Communist forces involved in the defense of the boys. There is an account by Patterson, *Scottsboro Boy*, Doubleday & Co., Garden City, N.Y. (1950).

108   *Johnson v. Zerbst*, 304 U.S. 458 (1938).

112   The Cohen-Griswold letter is in the *New York Times* of August 2, 1942, section 4, p. 6.

113   The 1945 decisions were *Williams v. Kaiser*, 323 U.S. 471, and *Tomkins v. Missouri*, 323 U.S. 485.

      The 1961 capital case: *Hamilton v. Alabama*, 368 U.S. 52, 55.

      The 1947 case: *Foster v. Illinois*, 332 U.S. 134, 139.

      Uveges v. Pennsylvania, 335 U.S. 437, 441.

      Gryger v. Burke, 334 U.S. 728 (1948). *Townsend v. Burke*, 334 U.S. 736 (1948).

114   Allen, *The Supreme Court, Federalism and State Systems of Criminal Justice*, 8 De Paul L. Rev. 213, 230-31 (1959).

      The last decision rejecting a claim for counsel was *Quicksall v. Michigan*, 339 U.S. 660 (1950).

115   *Hudson v. North Carolina*, 363 U.S. 697, 704 (1960).

      McNeal v. Culver, 365 U.S. 109, 119 (1961).

      The Brennan lecture was *The Bill of Rights and the States*, in *The Great Rights* (Cahn, editor) 67, 81 (1963).

116   The 1962 case involving the multiple-offender law was
       Chewning v. Cunningham, 368 U.S. 443 (1962).
           Carnley v. Cochran, 369 U.S. 506 (1962).

Chapter 9

123   The 1948 decision rejecting a judge's error of state law as
       a special circumstance requiring counsel was *Gryger v.
       Burke*, 334 U.S. 728. The 1961 case looking the other
       way: *McNeal v. Culver*, 365 U.S. 109.

125   The court-martial cases: *Reid v. Covert*, 354 U.S. 1
       (1957); *Kinsella v. Singleton*, 361 U.S. 234 (1960).

130   The 1958 decision: *Crooker v. California*, 357 U.S. 433.

132   The case of the death sentence after a new trial with
       counsel: *Robinson v. United States*, 324 U.S. 282 (1945).
           Kamisar, *The Right to Counsel and the Fourteenth
       Amendment*, 30 U. Chicago L. Rev. 1 (1962).

136   The Pennsylvania case was *Commonwealth ex rel. Simon
       v. Maroney*, 405 Pa. 562, 565-7, 176 A.2d. 94, 96-7 (1961).
       (Citations are to the Pennsylvania reports and to the At-
       lantic Reporter, covering decisions in Pennsylvania and
       nearby states.)

Chapter 10

143   The restrictive covenant cases: *Shelley v. Kraemer*, 334
       U.S. 1 (1948).

144   Supreme Court Rule 42 covers *amicus* briefs.

147   Omission of New York from the list of states on the
       amicus brief may seem surprising. New York law has
       long required representation of the indigent in criminal
       cases. Nevertheless, Attorney General Louis J. Lefko-
       witz decided not to join the *amicus* brief attacking *Betts
       v. Brady*. He explained that in New York criminal cases

defendants frequently challenged the validity of prior convictions without counsel in other states—convictions that could be relevant, for example, to the severity of the New York sentence to be imposed—and prosecutors relied on *Betts* to uphold the prior convictions. Mr. Lefkowitz and his staff thought it inappropriate to challenge a rule on which they had so often relied. The same problem did not trouble other states.

155   *Chambers v. Florida,* 309 U.S. 227, 241 (1940). The comment on Justice Black's "great internal struggles" is in Reich, *Mr. Justice Black and the Living Constitution,* 76 Harv. L. Rev. 673, 679 (1963). Before going on the bench Justice Black had criticized the old Court for upsetting state action on economic matters. The question for him was whether it had any greater warrant to invoke the Constitution on matters of personal liberty. This case marked an early stage in the development of his answer: Yes.

158   The Holmes phrase is from *Truax v. Corrigan,* 257 U.S. 312, 344 (1921) (dissenting opinion).

Chapter 11

162   Supreme Court Rule 44(1) deals with oral argument. Frankfurter on oral argument: *Memorial for Stanley M. Silverberg,* in *Of Law and Men* (Elman, editor) 320, 321 (1956).

      Jackson, *Advocacy Before the Supreme Court,* 37 Amer. Bar. Assn. Journal 801, 862 (1951).

163   The Holmes remark is quoted in Freund, *The Supreme Court of the United States* 169 (1961).

164   Jackson on advocacy, op. cit., p. 803.

165   The Hughes story is in McElwain, *The Business of the Supreme Court as Conducted by Chief Justice Hughes,* 63 Harv. L. Rev. 5, 17 (1949).

166   The Stone letter about the Court building is in Mason,

       Harlan Fiske Stone, Pillar of the Law 405-6 note (1956)

172   The Supreme Court had decided twelve right-to-counsel cases since *Quicksall v. Michigan.*

Chapter 12

183   Hughes, *The Supreme Court of the United States* 68 (1928).

186   The cases decided March 18, in order, before *Gideon v. Wainwright: Draper v. Washington,* 372 U.S. 487; *Lane v. Brown,* 372 U.S. 477; *Fay v. Noia,* 372 U.S. 391; *Douglas v. California,* 372 U.S. 353; *Gray v. Sanders,* 372 U.S. 368.

191   The Pennsylvania case: *Commonwealth ex rel. Simon v. Maroney,* 405 Pa. 562, 176 A.2d 94 (1961).

Chapter 13

193   Stewart, *Right to Counsel,* 18 Legal Aid Brief Case 91, 93 (1960).

194   The Bennett testimony was before the Senate Judiciary Committee.

195   Ervin, *Uncompensated Counsel: They Do Not Meet the Constitutional Mandate,* 49 Am. Bar Assn. Journal 435, 436 (1963).

       Attorney General Kennedy's testimony was before House Judiciary Subcommittee No. 5, May 22, 1963.

198   Whitney Seymour spoke to the National Conference of Bar Presidents in Chicago, August 10, 1963.

199   The Clark speech was to the Virginia State Bar Association, July 13, 1963.

       Judge Lumbard's comment was in an address to the New England Conference on the Defense of Indigent Persons Accused of Crime, Cambridge, October 31, 1963.

201   Clark, Law Day address at St. Louis University, April 20, 1963.

        Warren, remarks at the luncheon of the Conference of Judicial Councils, May 23, 1963.

202   The first reaction in the states to *Gideon v. Wainwright* was summarized in the *New York Times,* June 30, 1963, p. 39.

204   The Maryland case was *White v. Maryland,* 373 U.S. 59 (1963).

205   The cases on restrospective application: *Pickelsimer v. Wainwright,* 375 U.S. 2 (1963).

206   The Smith statement is in 8 American Bar News No. 4, p. 8. Chief Justice Harris of Arkansas addressed the Conference of Chief Justices in Chicago Aug. 9, 1963.

        Angell, *The Burial of Betts v. Brady,* 18 Record of the Assn. of the Bar 265, 271 (1963).

        The *St. Petersburg Times,* March 20, 1963, p. 14-A.

        The *Washington Post,* Aug. 11, 1963, p. E4.

Chapter 14

209   In the development of the constitutional law of criminal procedure the line of coerced-confession cases begins with the revolting physical brutality of *Brown v. Mississippi,* 297 U.S. 278 (1936). (Three Negroes were charged with murder; one was hanged from a tree until he confessed, and the other two had their "backs cut to pieces with a leather strap with buckles on it," in Chief Justice Hughes' words.) Now psychological pressure is enough to void a confession. A week after the Gideon case the Court barred the use of a statement that the police had obtained from a woman by threatening to take her children from her if she did not confess. *Lynumn v. Illinois,* 372 U.S. 528 (1963). The Court has also begun to move in on the ugly American phenomenon of pre-trial publicity prejudicial to the defendant. In *Irvin v. Dowd,* 366

U.S. 717 (1961) it set aside the conviction of an accused murderer because a majority of his jurors admitted that they had been prejudiced against him by stories describing him as a "mad-dog killer." In *Rideau v. Louisiana,* 373 U.S. 723 (1963), a defendant's oral confession to the sheriff was filmed in jail and broadcast to the community on television three times. Justice Stewart, writing for the Court, said these "kangaroo-court proceedings" were "a more subtle but no less real deprivation of due process of law" than the torture in *Brown v. Mississippi.* In one generation the meaning of due process had been enlarged by the Supreme Court to prohibit not only physical cruelty but the latest electronic methods of degrading the human personality.

210 The Missouri law-school segregation case was *Missouri ex rel. Gaines v. Canada,* 305 U.S. 337 (1938).

The Reapportionment Case: *Baker v. Carr,* 369 U.S. 186 (1962).

Jaffe, *Impromptu Remarks,* 76 Harv. L. Rev. 1111 (1963).

211 The remark of Attorney General Kennedy was in testimony before House Judiciary Subcommittee No. 5, May 22, 1963.

213 For an illustrative deportation case see *Niukkanen v. McAlexander,* 362 U.S. 390 (1960).

215 Goodhart, *Legal Procedure and Democracy,* 47 Journal of the American Judicature Society 58, 61 (1963).

Appointment of judges to serve during good behavior was established in England by the Act of Settlement of 1700.

216 Schaefer, *Federalism and State Criminal Procedure,* 70 Harv. L. Rev. 1, 26 (1956).

217 Holmes on the unifying national role of the Supreme Court: in *Law and the Court,* a 1913 address reprinted in *An Autobiography of the Supreme Court* (Westin, editor) 134, 137 (1963).

218 Justice Frankfurter used the phrase "conscience of society" in *Bartkus v. Illinois,* 359 U.S. 121, 128 (1959).

The interplay of the Court and public opinion on school segregation is brilliantly traced in Bickel, *The Least Dangerous Branch* 266-7 (1962).

219   *Chambers v. Florida*, 309 U.S. 227, 241 (1940).

The quotation from Professor Allen is at p. 219 of his De Paul article, op. cit.

De Tocqueville, I *Democracy in America* 151 (Knopf edition 1951).

220   The case of the bakers' ten-hour day was *Lochner v. New York*, 198 U.S. 45 (1905).

Reich, *Mr. Justice Black and the Living Constitution*, 76 Harv. L. Rev. 673 (1963).

221   Frankfurter on procedural safeguards: *McNabb v. United States*, 318 U.S. 332, 347 (1943). And on the advancing standards of due process: *Wolf v. Colorado*, 338 U.S. 25, 27 (1949).

SUGGESTED READINGS

The Supreme Court.

Freund, Paul A., *The Supreme Court of the United States*, Meridian, Cleveland (1961). A paperback that gives an intimate and sensitive view of the Court and its function.

Curtis, Charles P., Jr., *Lions Under the Throne*, Houghton Mifflin, Boston (1947). The argument is that, ultimately, the Court must be subordinate to the political arms of Government.

Bickel, Alexander M., *The Unpublished Opinions of Mr. Justice Brandeis: the Supreme Court at Work*, Harvard University Press, Cambridge (1957). A revealing, scholarly portrayal of a justice at work.

Cahn, Edmond (editor), *Supreme Court and Supreme Law*, Indiana University Press, Bloomington (1954). Essays and dialogue on the Court's direction at the beginning of the contemporary period.

Frank, John P., *Marble Palace: the Supreme Court in American Life*, Alfred A. Knopf, New York (1958). A layman's view of the Court, lively but one-sided.

Warren, Charles, *The Supreme Court in United States History*, revised edition in two volumes, Little, Brown, Boston (1960). The history of the Court in fascinating if uncritical detail, from the beginning to 1918.

By and About the Justices.

Jackson, Robert H., *The Supreme Court in the American System of Government*, Harvard University Press, Cambridge (1955). The final views of the most articulate recent justice, published posthumously.

Westin, Alan F. (editor), *An Autobiography of the Supreme Court*, Macmillan, New York (1963). A collection of extra-Court articles and comments by the justices, from early days to the present, including most of the Jackson book cited above.

Henson, Ray D. (editor), *Landmarks of Law*, Harper and Brothers, New York (1960). A broader collection, including famous legal articles not by Supreme Court justices as well as comments.

Jackson, Robert H., *The Struggle for Judicial Supremacy*, Vintage, New York (1941). His views after the Roosevelt Court-packing struggle and before he went on the bench himself.

Frankfurter, Felix, *Of Law and Men* (Elman, Philip, editor), Harcourt, Brace and Co., New York (1956). A collection of essays expressing Justice Frankfurter's influential views.

Black, Hugo L., *One Man's Stand for Freedom* (Dilliard, Irving, editor), Alfred A. Knopf, New York (1963). The other side: Justice Black's opinions and out-of-Court comments collected.

Hughes, Charles Evans, *The Supreme Court of the United States*, Columbia University Press, New York (1928). Written just before Hughes went back on the bench as Chief Justice, and still a classic comment on the Court.

Howe, Mark DeWolfe, *Justice Oliver Wendell Holmes: I The*

Shaping Years, Belknap Press of Harvard University Press, Cambridge (1957). *Justice Oliver Wendell Holmes: II The Proving Years*, Belknap, Cambridge (1963). The outstanding judicial biography of our day has not yet brought Justice Holmes to the Supreme Court but has already exposed the sources of his ideas.

Mason, Alpheus Thomas, *Harlan Fiske Stone: Pillar of the Law*, Viking, New York (1956). A rambling, occasionally obtuse biography whose use of the Stone papers has been criticized as improper but which is not the less interesting for them.

Dunham, Allison (editor), *Mr. Justice*, University of Chicago Press, Chicago (1956). Sketches of nine justices.

Judicial Power.

Hand, Learned, *The Bill of Rights*, Harvard University Press, Cambridge (1958). Judge Learned Hand's Holmes Lectures at Harvard, the leading recent expression of skepticism about the benefits of judicial review.

Wechsler, Herbert, *Principles, Politics and Fundamental Law*, Harvard University Press, Cambridge (1961). Among the collection: a follow-up to Judge Hand, less skeptical but still troubled by judicial performance.

Bickel, Alexander M., *The Least Dangerous Branch: the Supreme Court at the Bar of Politics*, Bobbs-Merrill, Indianapolis (1962). Comments on Professor Wechsler and the role of the Court generally, still on the skeptical side.

Black, Charles L., *The People and the Court: Judicial Review in a Democracy*, Macmillan, New York (1960). An enthusiastic endorsement of judicial power.

The Right to Counsel.

Equal Justice for the Accused: Report of a Special Committee of the Association of the Bar of the City of New York and of the National Legal Aid and Defender Association (1959). What is now done for indigent defendants across the country.

Assistance to the Indigent Accused: A Problem Pamphlet by the Joint Committee on Continuing Legal Education, of the American Law Institute and the American Bar Association (1961). A handy collection of legal and political materials on the problem and what to do about it.

Beaney, William M., *The Right to Counsel in American Courts,* University of Michigan Press, Ann Arbor (1955). Especially valuable for its history of the issue.

Brownell, Emery A., *Legal Aid in the United States,* Lawyers Cooperative Publishing Co., Rochester (1951). Supplement (1961). A survey of prevailing systems.

Fellman, David, *The Defendant's Rights,* Holt, Rinehart and Winston, New York (1958). A concise and accurate statement, before more recent Supreme Court decisions, of all the rights available to criminal defendants—going beyond counsel.

McKay, Robert B., *An American Constitutional Law Reader,* Oceana Publications, New York (1958). A paperback tracing in concise and readable form the major trends in constitutional decision from the beginning until now. Criminal law fitted into the larger picture.

TABLE OF CASES

NOTE: The cases of *Betts v. Brady* and *Gideon v. Wainwright* (*Gideon v. Cochran*) appear so frequently that they are not indexed.

INDEX

About the Author

ANTHONY LEWIS, who has been with the *New York Times* since 1955, is now Chief London Correspondent for the *New York Times;* for nine years before that he was their Washington correspondent, covering the Supreme Court and the Justice Department.

Mr. Lewis was born in 1927 in New York City. After graduating from Harvard in 1948, he spent four years with the Sunday department of the *New York Times* and then became a general assignment reporter for the *Washington Daily News*. While working for the *News* he won a Pulitzer Prize for national correspondence and the Heywood Broun Award in 1955 for a series of stories on the Federal loyalty-security program. He was a Nieman Fellow in 1956-1957. In 1963 he won a second Pulitzer Prize for his reporting on the Supreme Court. He is the co-author, with the *New York Times*, of *Portrait of a Decade: The Second American Revolution*.

Mr. Lewis is married and has three children.